YOU DON'T HAVE TO BE A Mixologist
To party and have a good time!

A Fusion of Creative "Kick Azz" Drink Masterpieces and a "Crazy-Insane" Epic Traveling Adventure in the Dominican Republic

Elson Clinton Williams III (Tré)

You Don't Have To Be A Mixologist To Party And Have A Good Time!

Copyright © 2016 and Copyright © 2019 by Elson Clinton Williams III.

"Dominican Rum Fiesta Punch" photo by Elson Clinton Williams III.

All rights reserved. All materials contained in this book are copyrighted.

ISBN: 978-0-692-07099-4

Editor, Charles Wartts, Jr. – Email: charleswarrts@sbcglobal.net
Graphic Designer, Elaine A. Young – www.HopscotchCommunications.com

The Copyright Law prohibits that no unauthorized portion of this book can be reproduced, scanned, photocopied, stored in a retrieval system, reprinted or transmitted by any means of distribution ---- (electronic, digital, mechanical, audio, visual, etc.) without the prior written permission of the author.

Elson Clinton Williams III (Tré)

PART I

Fun & Exciting Homemade Drink Recipes

Create Your Own "Kick Azz" Creative Masterpieces & Celebrate With the People You Love

PART II

Santo Domingo Euforia

Una Loca Aventura Épica En La República Dominicana

(A Crazy Epic Adventure in the Dominican Republic)

BY

ELSON CLINTON WILLIAMS III (Tré)

The recipes contained in this book are meant to be enjoyed in safe moderation. The publisher & author of this book are not responsible for any outcomes stemming from the usage of information contained in this book in regards to your precise health & allergy obligations that could require medical treatment and supervision.

IV

You Don't Have to Be a Mixologist to Party and have a Good Time!   v

CONTENTS

INTRODUCTION 1

PART I: FUN & EXCITING HOMEMADE DRINK RECIPES
Create Your Own "Kick Azz" Creative Masterpieces and
Celebrate with the People You Love 5
The China Doll Iced Tea 6
Strawberry Passionate Kiss Euphoria 8
Le Cognac de Pêche 11
Tré's Magical Love Potion for Passionate Closet Freaks 14
A Sensual Heart's Wet Dream 16
ÄÑ Å-P-P-Ł-É-Ľ-Ï-Ć-Ì-Ö-Ú-Ş M Ę Ļ Ó Ď Í Ç M. Ī. Ń. Đ. F Û Û Č K 17
Angelic Lust (An Angel's Sexual Craving for the Human Body) 19
Dominican Rum Fiesta Punch 21
The Iron Man (Mr. Stark's Drink of Choice) vs The Kryptonite
(Not Even Superman Can Handle This) 22
Tropical Brazilian Breeze 24
Delicious Vanilia Cinnamon Godiva Kisses 26
Effervescent Glow (Kool Times in a Kool Klub-Like Atmosphere) 28
CRAZY...ZANY...CoCo-LoCo CHILLED...CARIBBEAN-POP-SHOTS
(THE FRIDAY NITE SPECIAL) 31

PART II: A CRAZY EPIC ADVENTURE IN THE DOMINICAN REPUBLIC
Getting Ready 33
Day One 47
Day Two 62
Day Four 159
Day Five 194
Fun Facts about the Author 224
Acknowledgements 225

VI You Don't Have to Be a Mixologist to Party and have a Good Time!

INTRODUCTION

Hello everyone! My name is Elson Clinton Williams III, but my friends and family all call me Tré. For five years, I had the wonderful blessing of working with one of the biggest and best liquor distributors in the U.S.A. This special company gave me the opportunity to create and execute fresh, "out of the box" High-Themed Special Events for top tier liquor suppliers based here in the United States and around the globe. It was during this period in my career that I discovered a special gift for designing illusionary worlds of fantasy and making them come alive for my clients, professional sales personnel, and fans in the liquor industry.

Probably the next most important thing I should tell you about myself is that I am a Mixologist, one who specializes in creating unique drink concoctions. This is how it happened. Whenever I executed one of my High-Themed Special Events, just for fun I would always push the limits with regard to creating my own drink recipes. These exotic cocktails proved to be a big hit and always succeeded in creating a strong buzz among frequent partygoers who always came out to my events. The buzz was real, a fact that quickly got the attention of many large liquor suppliers. These companies frequently bestowed enthusiastic praise as well as requested that my unique drink recipes be sent to their national headquarters for review by upper management.

Growing up in the liquor industry, I somehow always had my finger on the pulse of the drinking public in terms what people were craving to experience in a cocktail. So I listened attentively to what my clientele was thinking out loud. By diligently following where their "pulse" led me, I began experimenting with and creating my own fun and interactive cocktail recipes. Over the years I have engaged in constant experimentations, using the hottest and most exciting new brands of liquor on the market. My objective was always the same: to create exciting drinks that were universal in that they possessed a titillating taste that everyone could enjoy.

After years of hard work, during which I managed to make a name for myself, people would often ask for my advice because they wanted me to help them to turn up the energy at their own personal events. My way of going about this was to introduce their guests to some of my crazy "off the chain" interactive drink recipes. The results were like magic in enhancing their parties and celebrations.

A few years ago my family and friends began insisting that I needed to write a drink recipe book in order to share my knowledge with others. In this regard, my two favorite cousins from Detroit—Tammy and Fred—have always been the most vocal and eager in urging me to actually take on the project. For too long I ignored their requests until four years ago when I heard the message loud and clear while I was walking the beaches of Copacabana, Ipanema, and Leblon in Rio De Janeiro, Brazil during the 2014 World Cup Finals.

I was having a horrible day. I was feeling mentally toxic and needed to defuse by talking to God so I could vent my agitated emotions. As I was walking along these beautiful and tranquil beaches, venting and talking to God, I was told to write a drink recipe book. I was also instructed to add a short story to accompany these recipes. During our conversation, God explained to me very vividly that my drink recipe book needed to be uplifting, that it should make people smile or even laugh out loud while taking them on an unforgettable journey. In short, it is my desire that this book will inspire hope and provide some mental relief to millions of people by making them forget about their current problems for a brief time.

It has been four years since my fateful conversation with God, and I have since put together fifteen mind-blowing drink recipes accompanied by an epic adventure in Santo Domingo, Dominican Republic to share with my readers!

Ironically, when I returned home to the States after World Cup Brazil, I immediately discovered that my mother had been diagnosed with a life-threatening illness that was going to require all of her physical, mental, and spiritual strength to overcome. During this time my mother's full recovery became the main concern of our family and close friends. So I decided to use my book manuscript as a kind of balm to help her with the healing process. I became ferociously inspired and motivated to make my mother smile or laugh everyday along with the millions of readers around the world that I imagined would one day read and be affected by the positive and hopeful message of my book.

I decided to call my drink recipe book, *You Don't Have to be a Mixologist to Party and Have a Good Time* because it is my Intention to make it "pressure free" when it comes to creating "kick azz kool drinks" for the people you love. My mantra is, "Have fun and don't worry about making mistakes!" The more you practice, the better you will become!

Perfected over the past five years, my creative drink concoctions are awesome tasting, easy to make, and are ideal for adult outings, high-energy parties, after work social engagements, business functions, special events, as gifts of affection, and as the ultimate elixir for naughty minds!

My hope is that, with my recipe book in hand, you will get together with a group of fantastic people who all just want to party and have a good time!

ENJOY & GOOD LUCK!

PART I
Fun & Exciting Homemade Drink Recipes

Create Your Own "Kick Azz" Creative Masterpieces and Celebrate with the People You Love!

THE CHINA DOLL ICED TEA
(Main Liquor Ingredient: 1-2 Bottles-(Liter) of Glenlivet 12 Single Malt Scotch Whiskey)

Pour ½ of a 1-liter bottle of Glenlivet 12 Year Single Malt Scotch Whiskey in a large glass fusion drink jar. Add ½ carton of (pre-chilled) high quality lemon flavored iced tea. Stir, and add 5-7 fresh yellow lemons (sliced in circular cuts); then add 1.5 to 2 fresh mint leaf trays. Make sure you rinse the mint leaves in cool water & allow to dry in a strainer before using!

1. Add ¼ bottle of Trader Joe's Blue Organic Raw Agave Sweetener (11.77 oz) to your mixture & continue stirring slowly. Then pour the remaining ½ liter bottle of the Glenlivet 12 Year Single Malt Scotch Whiskey & the remaining ½ carton of lemon flavored iced tea to the mix. Continue stirring.

2. For a slightly sweeter taste, add another ¼ bottle of Blue Agave Sweetener to your creative masterpiece & continue stirring.

3. Add five Luzianne Green iced tea bags to your drink mixture and continue to stir.

4. Throughout the process, PLEASE TASTE. Everything should blend perfectly. Neither the Glenlivet nor the lemon flavored ice tea SHOULD BE OVERPOWERING. There should be a harmonious balance between them with just a hint of fresh lemons and mint. Trust me, there is a perfect balance!!! Your "China Doll Iced Tea" should be smooth, with a tranquil but surprising taste.

5. Add 2 tablespoons of pure sweet cinnamon to the top of your drink concoction. Stir well & allow the cinnamon to blend perfectly.

TIP 1: It is important to let your "China Doll Iced Tea" steep and blend together in a COOL refrigerator for 4 days straight! Also, stir your drink mixture early in the morning, during the day, and at night during days of saturation. It is also very important to taste your creative masterpiece because you will notice every day that the overall taste will become smoother and smoother.

TIP 2: Remember that my specialty drinks always give you the opportunity to EXPERIMENT while having FUN! So after Day 2… if you want a little more "CHINA DOLL KICK," then carefully add JUST a LITTLE more Glenlivet. Stir and continue to steep for 2 more days.

Did I mention Ginger Beer Fun Cubes? Go to a novelty or party store and purchase multiple ice cube trays of crazy & unique designs of your choice (stars, palm trees, fruits, animals, words, erotica, etc.). Add Reed's Extra Ginger Beer (This beverage is non-alcoholic!) to your party ice cube trays and freeze. Pre-store as many Ginger Beer Fun Cubes as you want.

HOW TO SERVE: Stir your "China Doll Iced Tea" creative masterpiece very thoroughly in the fusion drink jar.

1. Serve 1/2 full in a rock glass for the gentlemen & serve 1/2 full in a goblet glass for the ladies.
2. Garnish with 2 or 3 fresh lemon slices.
3. Drink neat or add 3 Ginger Beer Fun Cubes.

TIP 3: Always keep your "China Doll Iced Tea" refrigerated. And remember that it is always BEST served with a group of special family & friends who want to have a FUN TIME!!!

Serves 15 to 20 people.

STRAWBERRY PASSIONATE KISS EUPHORIA

(Main Liquor Ingredients: 2 Bottles-(Liter) of Silver (Plata) Tequila or 2 Bottles-(Liter) of 1800 Coconut Tequila, 1 Bottle (750 ml) of Strawberry Daiquiri *Non-Alcoholic* & 1 Bottle (200 ml) of Strawberry Liqueur)

OPTION #1: Pour a 1-liter bottle of Silver (Plata) Tequila in a large glass fusion drink jar. BUT…do not surpass the ¾ full measurement of your fusion drink jar.

---OR---

OPTION #2: For you "Coconut Lovers" or "Adventurous Drink Explorers," pour a 1-liter bottle of 1800 Coconut Tequila in a large glass fusion drink jar.

After choosing **Option #1** or **Option #2**, stem 5-8 cartons of fresh Earliglow or sweet Louisiana strawberries; wash in cool water and drain thoroughly. Cut ½ of your strawberries into halves and fill ½ of your fusion drink jar with both cut and whole strawberries. Stir! (**Note:** Save all remaining strawberries for your Sparkling Strawberry Cider-Apple Fun Cubes!)

Once again depending on your option selection, pour ½ a liter bottle of Silver (Plata) Tequila or ½ a liter bottle of 1800 Coconut in the large glass fusion drink jar.

1. Stir and allow all the ingredients to blend together. Close the lid of your fusion drink jar and store at room temperature in a safe and secure location of your kitchen for 3 days!

2. Stir your "Strawberry Passionate Kiss Euphoria" early in the morning, during the day, and at night during days of saturation. It is also very important to taste your mixture for increasing smoothness.

3. **DAY 3:** Add 750 ml bottle of Strawberry Daiquiri (non-alcoholic) to your drink mixture. Then add 1 bottle of Strawberry Liqueur (200 ml). Allow your creative masterpiece to steep and blend for another 2 days!

4. SUPER CHILL your entire fusion drink mixture for a minimum of 6 hours before serving!

    NOTE: For additional pleasure and fun, try the variations that follow in order to make Sparkling Strawberry Cider-Apple Fun Cubes & French Mango Berry Fun Cubes!

5. Fill your blender with all remaining strawberries and puree-mix them in the blender. Your blender should be a little over ½ to ¾ full with strawberry puree. Next, fill the blender up with Sparkling Apple Cider. Continue puree-blending and test for taste. Add your Sparkling Strawberry Cider Apple Puree to your favorite novelty ice cube trays of crazy designs and freeze. Pre-store as many Sparkling Strawberry Cider-Apple Fun Cubes as you want.

6. Fill your blender with 3 peeled and chopped mango chunks and puree-mix in the blender. Your blender should be a little over ¼ to ½ full with mango puree. Next, fill the blender up with French Berry Lemonade. Continue blending and tasting. Add your French Mango Berry Puree to your ice cube trays of crazy designs and freeze. Pre-Store as many French Mango Berry Fun Cubes as you want.

HOW TO SERVE:
Slowly stir your "Strawberry Passionate Kiss Euphoria" creative masterpiece thoroughly in the fusion drink jar.

OPTION #1: Serve your cocktail in a ¾ full highball glass for the ladies & serve in ¾ full lowball glass for the gentlemen. Add 2 Sparkling Strawberry Cider Apple-Fun Cubes, one French Mango Berry Fun Cube & two fresh strawberry slices.

OPTION #2: Serve your "Strawberry Passionate Kiss Euphoria" in a 2 oz shot glass super-chilled & do a shot with a group of fantastic people! Make crazy drink toasts & do multiple continuous group shots!!!

OPTION #3: Strawberry Snow Cones -- shave some ice with a snow cone maker; if you don't have one, use your blender to blend a good supply of micro-fine shaved ice.

Use an ice cream scoop to roll a ball of shaved ice. The shaved ice should be able to sit perfectly on top of a small plastic or disposable paper cup.

Next, carve a small hole in the center of your shaved ice ball. With a turkey baster, extract a good amount of your "Strawberry Passionate Kiss Euphoria" & carefully coat your shaved ice ball until YOU personally say "STOP!"

TIP 1: Always keep your "Strawberry Passionate Kiss Euphoria" refrigerated, and remember that it is BEST served with a group of special family & friends who are celebrating life to the fullest!

FUN TIP: The "Strawberry Passionate Kiss Euphoria" shot is the perfect "ice breaker" between two flirty individuals who want to get to know one another more personally...while being intimately close.

Serves 20 to 30 people.

LE COGNAC DE PÊCHE

(Main Liquor Ingredients: 2 Bottles-(Liter) of Courvoisier VS & 2 Bottles (750 ml) of Pallini Peachchello White Peach Liqueur)

1. Wash 3 to 4 lbs. of fresh, sweet, plump peaches in cool water, then peel. Cut each individual peach into four equal quarters. Remove the peach seeds. Then fill your fusion drink jar ½ full with peach slices.

2. Add 1 bottle (liter) of Courvoisier VS & 1 bottle (750 ml) of Pallini Peachchello White Peach Liqueur in a large glass fusion drink jar. DO NOT surpass the ¾ full measurement of your fusion drink jar. Stir slowly.

3. Add another ¼ bottle of Courvoisier VS & ½ bottle (750 ml) of Pallini Peachchello White Peach Liqueur to your drink mixture. Continue stirring while testing for taste.

4. IT IS VERY IMPORTANT TO TASTE TEST!! Make Sure that the Courvoisier VS and the Pallini Peachchello White Peach Liqueur are blending harmoniously.

TIP 1: The ultimate goal is to create a very delicious peach cognac. You will not be able to taste the final overall flavor of the peach cognac in one day. Your creative masterpiece will need time to steep & blend in order to reach its best taste. BE PATIENT!!!

5. Add another ½ bottle of Pallini Peachchello White Peach Liqueur and ¼ of a liter bottle of Courvoisier VS to your mixture.

6. Your "Le Cognac de Pêche" mixture should almost fill your fusion drink jar. BUT…feel free to add as many fresh peach slices as you want without overfilling.

7. Close the lid of your fusion drink jar and store at room temperature in a safe and secure area of your kitchen for 5 DAYS! Allow your drink mixture to steep and blend for the entire time!!

8. Stir your cocktail mixture early in the morning, during the day, and at night during days of saturation. Don't forget to test taste for smoothness each day.

9. SUPER CHILL your entire creative masterpiece for a minimum of 6 hours before serving!

   NOTE: For Sparkling Peach Fun Cubes & Peach-Grape Fun Cubes, follow the steps listed below!

10. Fill your blender up with all remaining peach slices and puree them. Your blender should be a little over ½ to ¾ full with peach puree. Next, fill the blender with 100% Sparkling Peach Juice. Continue to blend while tasting. Add your 100% Sparkling Peach Juice Puree to your favorite party ice cube trays and freeze. Pre-store as many Sparkling Peach Fun Cubes as you want.

                                   ---OR---

11. Fill your blender with all remaining peach slices and puree them in a blender. Your blender should be a little over ½ to ¾ full with peach puree. Next, fill the blender with Sparkling White Grape Juice. Continue blending and tasting. Add your Sparkling Peach-Grape puree to your favorite ice cube trays of crazy designs and freeze. Pre-store as many Sparkling Peach-Grape Fun Cubes as you want.

HOW TO SERVE:
Slowly stir your "Le Cognac de Pêche" creative masterpiece very thoroughly in the fusion drink jar.

OPTION #1: Serve your exotic cocktail ¼ full in a glass snifter for the gentlemen & serve ¼ full in a small, neat cognac glass for the ladies. Give your guests the option of adding 2 Sparkling Peach Fun Cubes OR 2 Sparkling Peach-Grape Fun Cubes to their "Le Cognac de Pêche."

OPTION #2: For a delicious breakfast cocktail, fill a champagne flute ¾ full with your favorite chilled Brut Semi-Sweet Champagne, then fill your Champagne glass ¼ more with your "Le Cognac de Pêche." Give your champagne glass slight multiple twirls.

FUN TIP: Cut a small peach slice, quickly dip it in the Pallini Peachchello White Peach Liqueur, and lightly coat the peach slice with pure sweet cinnamon & brown sugar. Attach the peach slice to your champagne glass.

OPTION #3: Dinner Dessert Cocktail -- You will need the use of a small Mason jar. Take some peach slices from your "Le Cognac de Pêche" fusion jar and place in your Mason jar. Add a little of the cocktail mixture to the Mason jar. Roll one scoop of fresh vanilla ice cream and place in your Mason jar. Slightly coat your vanilla ice cream with the drink mixture. Roll one more scoop of vanilla ice cream and place in the Mason jar. Coat the ice cream with the "Le Cognac de Pêche." Top off your dessert creation with peach slices that have been quickly dipped in the Pallini Peachchello White Peach Liqueur; lightly coat the peach slices with pure sweet cinnamon & brown sugar. Add long sweet cinnamon sticks.

TIP 2: The "Le Cognac de Pêche" is also a perfect "ice breaker" & "conversation enhancer" while conducting business deals over lunch or dinner!

FUN TIP: The "Le Cognac de Pêche" Ice Cream Dessert is meant to be enjoyed by two individuals who are attracted to one another. All you need is enjoyable conversation and some good music of your choice!!

Serves 20 to 30 people.

TRÉ'S MAGICAL LOVE POTION FOR PASSIONATE CLOSET FREAKS

(Main Liquor Ingredients: 1 Bottle-(Liter) of Grey Goose La Poire Vodka and 1 Bottle (750 ml) of Cuervo Authentic Mango Margarita Mix Non-Alcoholic)

1. Start with pre-made **Sparkling Strawberry Cider-Apple Fun Cubes**. Fill your blender with 2 ½ cartons of fresh & sweet strawberries (stemmed & washed); puree your strawberries in the blender. (**Note**: Save a handful of strawberries for strawberry petal slices.)

2. Next, add almost ½ bottle of Sparkling Apple Cider to the mixture. Continue blending and tasting. Add Sparkling Strawberry Cider Apple puree to your novelty ice cube trays and freeze. Pre-store as many Sparkling Strawberry Cider-Apple Fun Cubes as you want.

3. It is time to make the pre-made Sparkling Mango Apple Fun Cubes! Fill your blender up with peeled and chopped mango chunks; puree in the blender. (**Note:** Use 3 sweet mangos, but save ¼ of a mango for use as mango petal slices.)

4. Fill the blender with almost ½ bottle of Sparkling Apple Cider. Continue to blend and taste. Add Sparkling Mango Apple Puree to your novelty ice cube trays and freeze. Pre-store as many Sparkling Mango Apple Fun Cubes as you want.

5. Pour 3-4 oz of Grey Goose La Poire Vodka; 2 oz of Cuervo Authentic Mango Margarita Mix (non-alcoholic); a splash of sweet

pineapple juice & a splash of fresh cranberry juice in a shaker (everything should be pre-chilled). Add Sparking Mango Apple Fun Cubes & Sparkling Strawberry Cider-Apple Fun Cubes. Shake well until SUPER-CHILLED & taste!

TIP 1: Add another splash of Cuervo Authentic Mango Margarita Mix (non-alcoholic) if you would like more of a mango taste!!

HOW TO SERVE:
Serve your "Tré's Magical Love Potion for Passionate Closet Freaks" in a martini glass for the ladies or in a rock glass for the gentlemen. Add fresh strawberry slices to your "Love Potion" creative masterpiece; then attach a fresh mango slice to the side of your martini or rock glass.

Finally, add 2 Sparkling Strawberry Cider-Apple Fun Cubes & 1 Sparkling Mango Apple Fun Cube.

FUN TIP 1: "Tré's Magical Love Potion for Passionate Closet Freaks" is BEST enjoyed by a group of FUN-LOVING & spirited women celebrating "Girls Night Out" to the FULLEST!!!

FUN TIP 2: For the highest quality of pleasurable gratification between 2 or more individuals, "Tré's Magical Love Potion for Passionate Closet Freaks" is also best enjoyed AFTER MIDNIGHT in an intimate & secluded setting!!!

Serves 1 person.

A SENSUAL HEART'S WET DREAM

(Main Liquor Ingredients: 1 Bottle-(Liter) of Grey Goose La Poire Vodka; 1 Bottle (750 ml) of Inniskillin Pearl Vidal Icewine or Jackson-Triggs Vidal Icewine & 1 Bottle (200 ml) of Rose's Pomegranate Twist Infusion)

1. Place a small quantity of fresh & sweet red grapes in a small plastic container. Then add Rose's Pomegranate Twist Infusion. The red grapes should be thoroughly submerged in the Pomegranate Twist Infusion. Soak & refrigerate your mixture for 1 full day!

2. Remove the red grapes from the plastic container & place in a Ziploc plastic bag. Freeze your Pomegranate Red Grapes before serving!

3. Pour 3 oz of pre-chilled Grey Goose La Poire Vodka and 2.5 oz of Inniskillin Pearl Vidal Icewine, (Jackson-Triggs Vidal Icewine works as well!) in the shaker. Slowly stir & taste (with everything pre-chilled).

TIP 1: Add another splash of Icewine if you choose to give your "A Sensual Heart's Wet Dream" creative masterpiece a little more Icewine flavor.

HOW TO SERVE:
Slowly pour your "A Sensual Heart's Wet Dream" ¾ full in a martini glass for BOTH ladies & gentlemen. Add 3 frozen Pomegranate Red Grapes to your delicious cocktail & slowly stir.

FUN TIP: "A Sensual Heart's Wet Dream" is IDEAL for a group of people who wish to enjoy themselves at an event, family get-together, or after hours function with good friends or significant others!

Serves 1 person.

You Don't Have to Be a Mixologist to Party and have a Good Time!

ÄÑ Å-P-P-Ł-É-Ľ-Ï-Ć-İ-Ö-Ú-Ş M Ę Ļ Ó Ď Í Ç M. Ī. Ń. Đ. F Û Û Č K

(Main Liquor Ingredients: 1 Bottle (375 ml) of Bombay Sapphire Gin; 1 Bottle (750 ml) of Bacardi Gold Rum; 1 Bottle (750 ml) of 1800 Silver Tequila; 1 Bottle (750 ml) of Reyka Vodka; 1 Bottle (750 ml) of Berentzen Apple Liqueur; and 2 Bottles (12 oz) of Sweet & Crisp Hard Apple Cider)

1. Wash in cool water and peel 2-3 lbs. of sweet & seasonal crisp apples. Cut each individual apple into two equal halves. Remove the apples cores. Fill your large fusion drink jar ½ full with apple slices.

2. Pour 1 Bottle (750 ml) of Berentzen Apple Liqueur; 1 Bottle (750 ml) of Bacardi Gold Rum; 1 Bottle (750 ml) of Reyka Vodka; 1 Bottle (375 ml) of Bombay Sapphire Gin; 1 Bottle (750 ml) of 1800 Silver Tequila & 2 Bottles (12 oz) of a sweet & crisp hard apple cider into a large glass fusion drink jar. Stir slowly, then taste. You will notice that your creative masterpiece has a smooth transitional apple taste!

3. Add ¼ to ½ bottle of Trader Joe's Blue Organic Raw Agave Sweetener & continue stirring slowly. Also add ½ bottle to ¾ bottle (16 oz) of cherry cola to your mixture.

4. For best results, allow your drink mixture to refrigerate for 3 days--or at least for a minimum of 6 hours before serving!

TIP 1: You will NOT be able to taste the final overall flavor of your "ÄÑ Å-P-P-Ł-É-Ł-Ï-Ć-İ-Ö-Ú-Ş M Ę Ļ Ó Ď Í Ç M. Ï. Ń. Đ. F Û Û Č K" cocktail in one day. It will need time to STEEP & BLEND for overall best taste. SO PLEASE BE PATIENT!!

1. Be sure to stir your creative masterpiece early in the morning, during the day, and again in the evening during days of saturation.

2. Next comes your **Sparkling Apple-Ginger Fun Cubes**! Fill your shaker half full with 100% Sparkling Apple Cider Juice and fill the other half of the shaker with Reed's Extra Ginger Brew. Shake and add Sparkling Apple-Ginger Juice to your novelty ice cube trays with crazy designs and freeze. Pre-store as many Sparkling Apple-Ginger Fun Cubes as you want!

HOW TO SERVE:

1. Stir Your "ÄÑ-Å-P-P-Ł-É-Ł-Ï-Ć-İ-Ö-Ú-Ş M Ę Ļ Ó Ď Í Ç M. Ï. Ń. Đ. F Û Û Č K" Creative Masterpiece thoroughly before serving.

2. Serve ¾ full in a highball glass for both the gentlemen & the ladies.

FUN TIP: This delightful cocktail is best served to get your party amped like there is NO TOMORROW—and from BEGINNING to END!! All you need to bring is your high level energy, some "FEEL GOOD" body pulsating music, an assortment of irresistible & delicious foods & a group of people who have NO FEAR when it comes to having a great time!!!

Serves 20 to 30 people.

ANGELIC LUST
(AN ANGEL'S SEXUAL CRAVING OF THE HUMAN BODY)

(Main Liquor Ingredients: 1 Bottle-(Liter) of Hangar 1 Vodka; 1 Bottle (750 ml) of Bacardi Gold Rum; and 1 Bottle (750 ml) of Cuervo Authentic Mango Margarita Mix (non-alcoholic)

1. Purchase the Porn Industry's #1 ranked sexual condom--"Crown Condoms." OR...purchase your own favorite brand of condoms!! (www.CondomDepot.com)

2. **OPTION #1:** (For vodka fanatics) -- Pour 6 oz of pre-chilled Hangar 1 Vodka & 2.5 oz of Cuervo Authentic Mango Margarita Mix (non-alcoholic) in a shaker semi-filled with ice.

3. Shake well until SUPER-CHILLED & taste!

    TIP 1: For more mango flavor, add another splash of Cuervo Authentic Mango Margarita Mix (non-alcoholic).

---OR---

1. **OPTION #2:** (For rum fanatics) -- Pour 6 oz of pre-chilled Bacardi Gold Rum & 2.5 oz of Cuervo Authentic Mango Margarita Mix (non-alcoholic) in a shaker semi-filled with ice.

2. Shake well until SUPER-CHILLED & taste!
3. Add another splash of Cuervo Authentic Mango Margarita Mix (non-alcoholic) if you desire more mango taste.

HOW TO SERVE:
1. Pour your super-chilled "Angelic Lust" cocktail into multiple mini-shot glasses for both the ladies & gentlemen!

2. Place one Crown Condom package OR your favorite packaged condom on top of the shot glass & serve.

3. **Note**: Do NOT unwrap the condom! Save it for use later!!

FUN TIP 1: Shout "CHEERS!" with all your crazy & zany friends joining in the fun, remove the condom package from atop your "Angelic Lust" shot BEFORE drinking. Enjoy!! I don't care if you are a wild & crazy person or a shy and conservative bore…The "ANGELIC LUST"…WILL…TURN…YOU…OUT!!!

FUN TIP 2: With that said…if you are looking for a unique way to introduce yourself to someone special one-on-one…then the "Angelic Lust" is a bold conversation starter & the perfect drink for the occasion!!!

Serves 4 people.

DOMINICAN RUM FIESTA PUNCH
(TRÉ'S VENEZUELA AVENUE EXPERIENCE IN SANTO DOMINGO-D.R.)

(Main Liquor Ingredients: 1 Bottle (750 ml) of Brugal Anejo Rum & 1 Bottle (375 ml) of Sweet CoConut Rum)

1. Using a punch bowl, place 4 oz of sweet Maraschino cherries with syrup, 1 cup of diced fresh pineapples, & multiple circular orange slices.

2. Add 1 bottle (750 ml) of Brugal Anejo Rum; 2 cups of sweet coconut rum & ½ cup of red grenadine (everything should be pre-chilled).

3. Stir & add -- 2 cups of sweet pineapple juice, 1 cup of sweet orange juice & 2 cups of puree-mixed sweet watermelon juice (watermelon should be pureed in a blender). Refrigerate!

4. For delectable **Watermelon Fun Cubes**, make more watermelon puree & pour into your favorite novelty ice cube trays of crazy designs and freeze. Pre-store as many Watermelon Fun Cubes as you want.

5. BEFORE SERVING…add 1 cup of ginger beer (pre-chilled) to the punch bowl & stir!

HOW TO SERVE:
Serve in a rock glass filled with Watermelon Fun Cubes & fruit bites for both ladies and gentlemen.

Serves 12 to 16 people.

THE IRON MAN
(MR. STARK'S DRINK OF CHOICE)
VS.
THE KRYPTONITE
(NOT EVEN SUPERMAN CAN HANDLE THIS!!)

(Main Liquor Ingredients: 1 Bottle-(Liter) of Absolut Black 100 Proof Vodka & 1 Bottle (750 ml) of Tim Smith's Climax Moonshine)

1. "THE IRON MAN": Pour 3.5 oz of pre-chilled Absolut Black 100 Proof Vodka and 1.5 oz of pre-chilled Simply Lemonade in a shaker semi-filled with ice. Add a splash of lemon-lime soda and a tablespoon of Blue Organic Raw Agave Sweetener.

2. Shake well until SUPER-CHILLED & taste!

3. You may add another splash of Absolut Black 100 Proof Vodka OR another splash of lemon-lime soda & Agave Sweetener.

---AND---

4. "THE KRYPTONITE": Pour 2.5 oz of pre-chilled Tim Smith's Climax Moonshine and 1.5 oz of pre-chilled fresh & sweet lime juice in a shaker semi-filled with ice.

5. Shake well until SUPER-CHILLED & taste!!

6. Add another splash of lime juice if you would like more of a sweet lime taste.

7. Now, let's do some **Sparkling Watermelon-Grape Fun Cubes**! Fill your blender with seedless watermelon chunks and puree-mix them in the blender. Your blender should be ¾ full with watermelon puree. Next, fill the blender ¼ full with 100% Sparkling White Grape Juice. Continue blending and taste. Add your Sparkling Watermelon-Grape Puree to your novelty ice cube trays of crazy designs and freeze. Pre-store as many Sparkling Watermelon-Grape Fun Cubes as you want!

HOW TO SERVE:
1. Pour your "Iron Man" creative masterpiece into a shot glass for both ladies & gentlemen!

2. Pour your "The Kryptonite" creative masterpiece into a shot glass for both ladies & gentlemen!

3. Place two Sparkling Watermelon-Grape Fun Cubes in a third shot glass for both the ladies & the gentlemen!

FUN TIP1: Before the party begins…I believe that it is very important to loosen up everyone & get them prepared to go full throttle! I GUARANTEE that "The Iron Man vs. The Kryptonite" group shots can set the tempo for a VERY entertaining and fun evening!! Tasty food selections & good music are also a necessity!!!

FUN TIP 2: Do a group "CHEERS!!!" with all your personal guests at the party after engaging in a group shot of "The Iron Man," instantly followed by a group shot of "The Kryptonite" as a chaser. Finish off your two-shot party kick-off by sucking on your Sparkling Watermelon-Grape Fun Cubes.

"The Iron Man vs The Kryptonite" is the BIG BANG PARTY STARTER!!!

"The Iron Man" serves 2 people.
"The Kryptonite" serves 2 people.

TROPICAL BRAZILIAN BREEZE

(Main Liquor Ingredients: 2 Bottles-(Liter) of Courvoisier VS)

1. Wash 2-3 cartons of fresh & lusciously sweet Earliglow strawberries or sweet Louisiana strawberries: stem, dice in circular slices, and place in a large fusion drink jar. Wash 5 fresh & sweet kiwi fruit: peel, cut in circular slices & add to the fusion drink jar. Peel 1 sweet pineapple & 1 sweet mango, then dice into bite-sized chunks. **Note:** Save 2 cups of diced strawberries, kiwi fruit, pineapple & mango fruit bites.

2. Pour 1.5 liters of pre-chilled Courvoisier VS into a large glass fusion drink jar and stir.

3. Pour ¼ bottle (1.75 liters) of Simply Orange Juice (pulp free); ¼ bottle (1.75 liters) of sweet cranberry juice; ¼ can (1.36 liters) of Dole 100% Sweet Pineapple Juice; and ¼ bottle (1.89 liters) of V8 Mango Peach Splash into a large pitcher and stir. **Note:** All juices should be pre-chilled!

4. Add 6 oz of pre-chilled Acai Berry Juice (if you can find it), MIXED with a sweet-tasting fruit juice & stir. **Note:** Your "Brazilian Fruit Punch" should be equal to a 2 liter pitcher. If not, continue to add all the fruit juices in proportionate amounts until you reach the goal of 2 liters. Taste your delightful cocktail mixture; it should taste like the sweet and refreshing kiss of a Brazilian breeze!

5. Pour ½ pitcher of your "Brazilian Fruit Punch" into the fusion drink jar. Stir slowly and allow ALL the ingredients to blend together. Taste your full-bodied fusion drink creative masterpiece! Add 0.5 liter bottle of Courvoisier VS for a little something extra!

6. According to your taste, add another ¼ pitcher of your "Brazilian Fruit Punch." Taste continuously as you add more punch.

7. Refrigerate for several hours or for as long as you want. This will allow your luscious cocktail to have a more tropical and fruity taste! Your "Tropical Brazilian Breeze" is ready to serve!!!

8. Now, for **Brazilian Fruit Punch Fun Cubes**, Add the remainder of your "Brazilian Fruit Punch" to your novelty ice cube trays and freeze. Pre-store as many fun cubes as you want.

HOW TO SERVE:

1. Stir Your "Tropical Brazilian Breeze" creative masterpiece very thoroughly in the fusion drink jar before serving.

2. Serve Your "Tropical Brazilian Breeze" ¾ full in a cocktail glass for the ladies & ¾ full in a rock glass for the gentlemen. Add an even tablespoon of diced fruit bites that consists of kiwi fruit, strawberries, pineapples & mangos to each glass.

3. Finish off your "Tropical Brazilian Breeze" creative masterpiece by adding 3 Brazilian Fruit Punch Fun Cubes.

FUN TIP: The "Tropical Brazilian Breeze" is an appetizing and smooth-tasting cocktail for all occasions…and is meant to help you luxuriate in the never-ending fun times with fantastic friends & family!!

Serves 30 to 36 people.

DELICIOUS VANILIA CINNAMON GODIVA KISSES

(Main Liquor Ingredients: 1 Bottle (750 ml) of Godiva Dark Chocolate Liqueur or Godiva Caramel Liqueur; 1 Bottle-(Liter) of Absolut Vanilia Vodka & 1 Bottle (750 ml) of Rum Chata)

1. Pour 3 oz of Absolut Vanilia Vodka; 1.5 oz of Rum Chata & 2 oz of Godiva Chocolate Liqueur (everything should be pre-chilled) into a shaker semi-filled with ice. (You may choose to use either the Godiva Dark Chocolate Liqueur OR Godiva Caramel Liqueur!) SHAKE WELL UNTIL SUPER-CHILLED & TASTE!

2. Add another splash of Rum Chata if you would like more cinnamon flavor.

3. In a small pan, pour 3 oz of Rum Chata and 3 oz of your personal choice of Godiva Dark Chocolate Liqueur OR Godiva Caramel Liqueur in the pan also. Place the pan on a stove top burner and bring the mixture to a slow simmer. Slowly stir your drink concoction continuously until the texture starts to become slightly thicker. At that point, turn the burner off and cover your pan to help maintain the warmth of your Rum Chata-Godiva Liqueur Mix.

HOW TO SERVE:
OPTION #1: From your shaker…pour your "Delicious Vanilia Cinnamon Godiva Kisses" cocktail ¾ full in a martini glass for both ladies & gentlemen.

Serves 1 person.

OPTION #2: From your shaker…pour your "Delicious Vanilia Cinnamon Godiva Kisses" into a 2 oz or 3 oz shot glass SUPER-CHILLED for both the gentlemen & the ladies. **Serves 3 to 4 people.**

OPTION #3: Delicately dip the outer rim of a 2 oz or 3 oz shot glass in honey. Next, coat the honey-laced rim of the glass with cinnamon sugar.

1. From your shaker…fill the shot glasses ¾ full with your delectable creative masterpiece. Now…using a teaspoon, roll a small ball of vanilla ice cream & place the vanilla ice cream ball into the center of the top of the shot glass. Sprinkle a little cinnamon sugar on top of the vanilla ice cream ball.
2. Carve a small hole in the center of the vanilla ice cream ball & coat the center of the ball with the warm Rum Chata-Godiva Liqueur Mix set aside in Step 3! **Serves 4 to 6 people.**

FUN TIP: Your creative masterpiece is an EXCLUSIVE DESIGNER DESSERT DRINK…and is custom made to help you celebrate the marvelous times of life with cheerful & fun-loving people! Now…make a group toast with regard to "sincere happiness & fun craziness!" Enjoy your awesome dessert drink…but when you finish, don't forget to LICK the honey-cinnamon coated rim around your shot glass!!!

JUST FOR FUN: If you are in the presence of your heart's One True Desire…top off this very special moment with a SOFT…SOOTHING…PASSIONATE…KISS!!!

OPTION #4: "Godiva Cinnamon Kiss Ice Cream Cones"

1. Delicately dip the outside rim of a mini ice cream cone in honey. Next, coat the honey-laced rim of the cone with cinnamon sugar. With a small ice cream scoop, roll one small ball of ice cream from your choices of vanilla, banana, strawberry, or chocolate ice cream.
2. Place your ball of ice cream on top of your honey cinnamon-crusted cone.
3. Carve a small hole in the center of your ice cream ball & coat the center of the ice cream ball with warm Rum Chata-Godiva Liqueur Mix.
4. With a small ice cream scooper, roll a second ball of your favorite flavor of ice cream. Carefully place the second scoop of ice cream on top of the first. **Repeat Step 3 above!**

FUN TIP: Sprinkle a little cinnamon sugar on top of your "Godiva Cinnamon Kiss Ice Cream Cone!" **Serves 6 to 10 people.**

EFFERVESCENT GLOW
(KOOL TIMES IN A KOOL KLUB-LIKE ATMOSPHERE)

(Main Liquor Ingredients: 2 Bottles (750 ml) of Kinky Pink Liqueur (Mango-Blood Orange-Passion Fruit Flavored); 2 Bottles (750 ml) of Kinky Blue Liqueur (Tropical-Wild Berry Flavored); & 2 Bottles (750 ml) of a sweet effervescent Moscato)

1. Pour 2 bottles (750 ml) of pre-chilled Kinky Pink Liqueur (mango-blood orange-passion fruit flavored) in fusion drink jar #1.

2. Pour 2 bottles (750 ml) of pre-chilled Kinky Blue Liqueur (tropical-wild berry flavored) in fusion drink jar #2.

3. Wash 10 fresh & sweet kiwi fruit; peel & cut in circular slices. Wash 4 cartons of fresh & lusciously sweet Earliglow strawberries or sweet Louisiana strawberries; stem & dice in circular slices. Peel 1 sweet pineapple & 2 sweet mangos; dice into bite-sized chunks. Wash 4 fresh & sweet ripe oranges and cut into wedges.

4. Place half of the kiwi fruit slices, diced strawberries, pineapple & mango bites, and orange wedges into the fusion drink jar filled with Kinky Pink Liqueur. Stir continuously!

5. Place the other half of your kiwi fruit slices, diced strawberries, pineapple & mango bites, and orange wedges into the fusion drink jar filled with Kinky Blue Liqueur. Stir continuously!

6. Refrigerate both fusion drink jars of Kinky Pink Liqueur and

Kinky Blue Liqueur for a minimal of 2 hours or up to 1 full day before serving. (**Note:** This will allow the fruit to marinate to perfection with both Kinky Pink Liqueur and Kinky Blue Liqueur, respectively.)

TIP 1: Anticipate how many people will be attending your social event. Go Online, find the BEST DEAL from various websites & wholesalers, and buy multi-colored blinking Glow Cubes for Cocktails, Party Mini-Glow Sticks used for visual decorations in the drink cocktails, and multiple-sized party glow sticks used for visual decorations around your head, neck, arms, wrists and other unique body parts of your choice. Also, shop for items for enhancing the visual ambiance & setting of your event. Finally, purchase multi-colored party 60-watt light bulbs to round out your visual decorations!!!

FUN TIP: Devise a crazy & uniquely colorful lighting scheme in the section of your house or party venue where people will be dancing to the pulsating beats of good music, devouring savory food assortments, and enjoying the "KOOL TIMES IN A KLUB-LIKE ATMOSPHERE" with their tasty "Effervescent Glow" cocktail. People absolutely LOVE to be teleported into a new and creative FANTASY WORLD of pleasure!!

HOW TO SERVE:
As people enter your social event, give them the multi-colored & multi-sized glow sticks to wear around their heads, necks, arms and other unique body parts of their choice. The glow sticks will provide an amazing degree of illumination under the multi-colored 60-watt light bulbs.

1. Next…slowly stir BOTH versions of your "Effervescent Glow" cocktail (Kinky Pink Liqueur and Kinky Blue Liqueur) very thoroughly in the fusion drink jar.

2. Pour 1 bottle (750 ml) of a sweet effervescent Moscato into the fusion drink jar filled with fruit & Kinky Pink Liqueur. Continue stirring. Add another ½ bottle or LESS of Moscato if you would like more of its presence and taste in your "Effervescent Glow" creative masterpiece.

3. Repeat Step 2 above exactly for your Kinky Blue Liqueur as well! (**Note:** You have up to one hour to enjoy that fresh & crisp effervescent taste once you open the bottles of Moscato & mix them with your "Effervescent Glow" creative masterpieces!)

4. Pre-set 20 blinking Glow Cubes to full bright & non-blinking illumination. Place 10 blinking Glow Cubes in each fusion drink jar.

5. In a central location at your social event, place both variations of your "Effervescent Glow" cocktail for all to see and marvel at. Activate all of your party mini-glow sticks & stylishly place them next to your "Effervescent Glow" creative masterpieces.

6. Serve your cocktails ¾ full in a martini glass for the ladies & serve ¾ full in a rock glass for the gentlemen.

FUN TIP: Add an illuminated party mini-glow stick to each "Effervescent Glow" cocktail served!!!

JUST FOR FUN: MAKE IT AN UNFORGETTABLE WILD NIGHT OF PLEASURE with captivating surroundings, hypnotic & body-banging music, tasty foods, and charming & appreciative outgoing people…all enjoying the alluring taste of "Effervescent Glow"!!!

"Kinky Pink Effervescent Glow" serves 20 to 30 people.
"Kinky Blue Effervescent Glow" serves 20 to 30 people.

CRAZY...ZANY...CoCo-LoCo CHILLED... CARIBBEAN-POP-SHOTS
(THE FRIDAY NITE SPECIAL)

(Main Liquor Ingredients: 1 Bottle-(Liter) of Cruzan Coconut Rum & 1 Bottle-(Liter) of 1800 Coconut Tequila)

1. For **Coco Peach-Mango Fun Cubes**, add Vita Coco 100% pure coconut water with fresh peach & mango bites to your novelty ice cube trays with crazy designs and freeze. Pre-store as many Coco Peach-Mango Fun Cubes as you want!

2. Making sure that everything is pre-chilled...Pour 3 oz of Cruzan Coconut Rum; 3 oz of 1800 Coconut Tequila; 1.5 oz of Dole's pulp-free sweet pineapple juice; and a splash of Rose's Red Grenadine in a shaker filled with Coco Peach-Mango Fun Cubes. SHAKE WELL UNTIL SUPER-CHILLED & TASTE!!!

3. Add another splash of Cruzan Coconut Rum if you would like more of a Coconut Rum taste.

---OR---

1. Add another splash of 1800 Coconut Tequila if you would like more of a Coconut Tequila taste.

HOW TO SERVE:
1. **OPTION #1:** Serve your "CRAZY...ZANY...CoCo-LoCo CHILLED...CARIBBEAN-POP-SHOTS" in a 3 oz shot glass SUPER-CHILLED!!! Do a group shot with an eclectic gathering of terrific crazy-zany individuals whom you truly enjoy being around!!!

   Serves 2 people.

2. **OPTION #2:** Serve your "CRAZY...ZANY...CoCo-LoCo CHILLED...CARIBBEAN-POP-SHOTS" ¾ full in a lowball glass for both ladies & gentlemen.
   Add 3 Coco Peach-Mango Fun Cubes.

   Serves 1 person.

   WHEN EVERY NIGHT IS A FRIDAY NITE......LET'S GET IT STARTED WITH SOME "CRAZY...ZANY...CoCo-LoCo CHILLED...CARIBBEAN-POP-SHOTS"!

Part II
Santo Domingo Euphoria

Una Loca Aventura Épica En La República Dominicana
(A Crazy Epic Adventure in the Dominican Republic)

GETTING READY

I'M ALL ALONE, standing on a plush, velvety-red mini-platform. All I'm wearing are my sleek, dark black Calvin Klein Euro-cut boxer briefs with devilish-red trim, a black Calvin Klein designer tank top, and a pair of black Armani ankle socks.

Three 12-foot tall Tuscan wall mirrors surround me, and I am illuminated from above by hovering micro-light beams. Staring at myself in the mirrors, I slowly take off my tank top. All I am wearing now are my boxer briefs and ankle socks. My intensive workout regimen has worked to perfection, along with my four-week "Full-Body Detox Cleanse" because I feel great and I am looking sensational! In case you're wondering, I have a lean athletic physique and my caramel-brown skin is glowing.

I Am Ready To Embark!

A live band is starting to perform and a lone male singer's passionate voice begins crooning a slow-burning Brazilian love ballad in Portuguese. The response is quick and explosive because women are shouting, slapping palms, screaming, whistling, and obviously having a wonderful time! Suddenly, I hear an energetic and sexy, "Hiiiiii, Tré!" followed by two other flirtatious voices calling out, "Tréeeeeeé!....Tréeeeeeé!" and "Helloooo Tré!" These exclamations were all exuberantly expressed in seductive and enticing international English accents.

I turn around and immediately start smiling because a globally diverse crew of three tall, vivacious women in their early thirties—all strikingly beautiful—had just burst into my posh dressing room unannounced. They were all wearing the edgy and sophisticated new Italian lingerie called "Peccaminosa Angelica Ragazza" (Sinful Angelic Girl). Although I didn't recognize who these extremely attractive women were, I knew they were all personal guests of Mr. and Mrs. Monahan. And since the Monahans were my all-time favorite clients and good friends as well, I was more than happy to make their acquaintance. For many years the Monahans had been very supportive of me with regard to all of my professional projects in the liquor industry.

I stepped off the mini-platform, laid my tank top on the white Ottoman sofa, and greeted my new friends who were all joyfully holding martini glasses filled with tasty red libations. The chic walk-in closet aka dressing room that we were all standing in looked like a luxurious night club tailor-made for only two people to enjoy discreetly. Next to the white Ottoman, there was an elegant glass table decorated with scented white candles, white roses, and a bottle of champagne. The entire room was lit up in a light green hue, while each wall was neatly stacked with multiple racks of stylish, high-end designer clothing for both men and women. In addition, there were trendy hats, boutique jewelry and accessories, and ladies shoes that retailed at no less than $1000 per pair.

The captivating blonde of the group, who was six feet tall in her caged high-heel Manolo Blahniks, quickly brushed aside the friendly handshake I'd offered her, while shaking her head. "Ohhhhh no, Tré!" she scolded. "You have to be more inter-personal than that with us because we three girls will only accept hugs and kisses on the cheeks from a handsome man like yourself! So loosen up!" She said as she twirled her "killa" orange chiffon, ankle-length lingerie outfit at me. Her "bad girl" attire was very complimentary to her four-pack abs, upper-chest area and lower "V-line" in a sensual but tasteful manner. I also loved how she creatively accessorized herself with an orange stone necklace and bracelet set accented by orange party glow sticks wrapped around her wrists, waist, and mid-thigh area. We gave each other hugs and kisses on both cheeks. My new blonde friend exhaled, "God…you smell incredibly good, Tré!" This spontaneous remark caused her two lovely friends to purr, "Mee-ow!" as they directed a cat claw wave toward me. Then my new friend said excitedly, "Tré…it is a pleasure to finally meet you because I've heard all about you."

    Noticing that I was quietly bewildered as to who she was, my blonde friend chuckled as she went on. "Tré, my name is Minka Vanderweghe and I am the legal consultant for Mr. Monahan's two boutique clothing stores and restaurant chill lounge. I am also his wife's business lawyer for her interior design company. The reason why I know all about you is because I've attended several of your High Themed Special Events as a personal guest of the Monahans."

    I nodded my head with a smile on my face. "Thank you," I replied, "and it is a pleasure to meet you Minka Vanderweghe."

    "No, the pleasure is all mine!" she responded as she took a sip from her martini.

    Next I hear a sweet, pouty voice say to me, "Isn't it a pleasure to meet me too, Tré?"

    I turned my attention to my other new friend who is a 5-foot, 10-inch drop dead gorgeous Asian cutie with a beautiful sun-kissed skin tone, sharp brown eyes, and an edgy auburn-red hair style. My heart rate starts elevating because my new Asian delight was "rocking" a plum-colored chiffon Peccaminosa Angelica Ragazza lingerie dress that was free-flowing and hovering just above her peach shaped "mid-derriere." The lingerie dress was extremely flattering to her perky upper chest and also her lower "V-line" region, revealing her plum-colored semi-sheer thong underwear. Peccaminosa Angelica Ragazza only makes tasteful and provocatively innovative lingerie for the sexy woman's body.

    I also noticed how her Christian Louboutin jewelry-adorned high heels illuminated the room like a sparkling diamond. My new Asian friend was doing her thing! I also loved the way she accessorized herself with shining jewelry bracelets while also wearing double twisted plum-colored party glow sticks around her forehead, upper right arm, and around her tightly contoured waistline.

It had taken me less than half a second to check her out completely, and without hesitation, we both warmly welcomed each other with hugs and kisses on the cheeks. As we were hugging, I could feel my inquisitive friend sniffing around my neck. She smiled at me, looked over at Minka and said, "Girl, you are right! Tré smells GOOD!" Then she squeezed my arms and lower waist while making the flirty comment, "And… he's firm, too!" At this point, all the lovely ladies in the room purred seductively and acted out another "Meow" cat claw hand gesture.

"Tré, this is Dr. Mai Sakakorn from Thailand," Minka says to me. "And she has been practicing trauma surgery here in the United States for the last four years." Completely caught off guard, I looked towards Dr. Sakakorn with an astonished smile on my face.

"Wow," I responded surprised, "that's really impressive Dr. Sakakorn!"

"Thank you, Tré," she said, smiling as she took a sip from her drink. "But relax….don't be so formal with my name. Just call me Dr. Mai or Miz Saka-Saka!" she said as she shook her hips twice and squeezed my smiling face.

We all erupted in laughter following Dr. Mai's humorous little comment. I asked Dr. Mai how she knew the Monahans. She replied excitedly, "I just bought a new mansion, so Ariel Santiago-Monahan is currently designing my bedroom as well as my outdoor meditation flower patio in a Neo-Colombian style."

"Good choice," I replied, "because Ariel Santiago is very talented and has unbelievable vision."

"Speaking of unbelievable vision, Tré I am really happy to meet you because I was a big fan of your 'Seven Deadly Sins Halloween Event' last year when you had seven girls body painted and placed on exhibit for everyone to see. Then you created these f---ing imaginative fusion drinks based on your interpretation of the Seven Deadly Sins. I had such an unbelievable time," she went on enthusiastically, "that till this day Minka and I still talk about that event."

I graciously thanked Dr. Mai for her warm support, but without any hesitation with regard to capturing my absolute, undivided attention, my third new friend made her presence known by greeting me with two simple words: "Hellooo Tré!" Her unique and sexy "proper" English accent, garnished with a twist of sultriness, was music to my ears. I immediately shifted my focus towards this 5-foot, 8-inch mocha-brown ravishing goddess. Her arousing athletic curves, piercing hazel eyes, and bushy-kinky, jet-black hair with brown highlights, were so flattering to the eyes that it took all of my willpower NOT to embarrass myself with respect to controlling certain body parts. She was boldly wearing a one-piece "mind teasing" dark blue sheer Peccaminosa Angelica Ragazza lingerie outfit with cleverly placed see-through embroidery patterns.

This sexy woman radiated extreme confidence because her lingerie outfit Voguish-ly hugged her well-proportioned, tan bosom along with her curvy "V-line" candy store. She was the very image of superior fashion sleekness. I also loved how she accessorized her entire lingerie outfit with bright blue glow sticks while strutting around in her blue Aperlai high heels that retail at $1000. After a quick scan, I replied, "Well…Hello to you Chef Cyn." An animated Chef Cyn gave me a big hug, grabbed me by the face with soft, gentle hands, and kissed me on the forehead. "Bless your heart," she responded while staring directly into my eyes. "You really know who I am?" she asked.

"Yes, but it took me a second to recognize you without your chef's uniform."

Everyone burst out laughing as Chef Cyn said, "Oh Stop!" and slapped me on the shoulder. Then she took a sip of her martini and posed with her right hand on her hip. Facing her, I went on to say, "You are Chef Cynthia Le Roux from South Africa, owner of the world famous South African-South American fusion cuisine restaurant called Só Afrikan Cocina. The Monahans adore your spot and I've brought many of my best clients to your restaurant as well."

Chef Cyn winked at me and said, "I appreciate your support Tré, and tonight we are all extremely happy to support you and your very entertaining event. Even though this is actually my first time coming to one of your Special Events, I must admit that I'm L-O-V-I-N- your N-A-U-G-H-T-Y side!"

Minka joined in by shouting, "Yeah…Tré! You set up a world where hard working professional women like us can feel FREE and liberated in a fun and exciting way!"

At that point, Dr. Mai, Minka, and Chef Cyn all raised their martini glasses and offered a toast. A super-animated Chef Cyn said, "Tré…I don't know what's in this delicious tasting 'Sensual Heart's Wet Dream,' but what I do know is that right now your drink is making me feel like partying *and* shopping for expensive clothes!" They all purred and waved in unison.

"Did someone "purr" for some more of Tré's 'Angelic Lust' mini-shots?" someone asked in a deep, debonair voice. We all turned around to see one of the male bartenders, dressed in a black, fitted, and sleeveless designer tuxedo, enter the room with a full tray of drinks. Chef Cyn, Dr. Mai, and Minka dart towards the bartender as each grabs an "Angelic Lust" mini-shot. The mini-shot glasses were all topped off with an unwrapped glow-in-the-dark condom for decoration. Dr. Mai shrieked with obvious bashfulness. "Tré…what are we supposed to do with these rainbow colored "glow-in-the-dark" condoms?" she queried.

Never one to miss out on a zestfully wicked comment, I replied, "That's why it's called 'Angelic Lust.' Just use your imagination in a dark room with someone special."

The entire room detonated into hysterical and uncontrollable laughter. In response, Chef Cyn flirtatiously yelled, "Uhhhhh…naughtiness with a sharp sense of humor, I see." Then, on cue, Minka, Chef Cyn, and Dr. Mai do an 'Angelic Lust' group shot with a loud and crazy cheer. Pure pleasure was written all over their faces.

Hearing the high octane commotion, Ariel Santiago-Monahan burst into the room speaking rapidly in a distinctly Colombian accent. "Chicas! What are you all doing back here with Tré?" she gently scolded. "Don't you know that I have been looking all over for you guys for the last ten minutes! You are going to miss out! Elise and her wife, Francisca, are about to begin their Exotic Dance Show with their prized troupe of international dancers, all body-painted in bright, ultra-violet colors."

"Whaaaat?" A blown away Minka and Chef Cyn say at the same time, their mouths and eyes wide open. Everyone slowly turns towards me as I smile and nod my head. "Don't miss out," I say to all of them, "because when you come to one of my events, I'm always going to give you an experience that you'll never forget."

Mr. Monahan walked in the room with my new custom-made white vacation dress shorts, trendy white button-up shirt, and also my white Panama Jack hat, all tailor-made for the tropics. "Yes ladies…you are missing out on quite an experience," he said in a distinct Bostonian accent, "because this event was created for me and my wife Ariel's thirty-five most beloved customers. So while you are here trying to seduce our client, Tré, the other thirty-two ladies are all over the Boutique Store, buying up all the top-selling women's apparel, exquisite high heels, and the first limited edition of the 'Peccaminosa Angelica Ragazza' lingerie line which you are currently wearing." He went on to say, "Everything is discounted at sixty percent off…so I suggest that you three ladies start shopping before we sell out the entire store." Mr. Monahan concluded his remarks with an F.Y.I. "Before you head for the store, I should warn you that Elise and Francisca's team of dancers have been instructed to be very interactive with everyone they see shopping."

"Yeah! This is my type of party, and I'm not going to miss out. Come on chicas…let's go!" Dr. Mai, overcome by a fit of excitement, shouted to everyone. Chef Cyn, Dr. Mai, and Minka wished me well with hugs and kisses on the cheeks. Meanwhile the bartender began escorting my three new friends out of the room. But before leaving, Dr. Mai said to Ariel in Spanish, "Tré es tannnn hermoso y inteligente." By way of response, Minka and Chef Cyn giggle and high-five each other. Chef Cyn next asked Ariel: "El tiene una esposa o cualquier niños?"

Finally Minka looked directly at me with a devilish smirk on her face, then turned towards Ariel and said in an enticing and steamy voice, "Yo amaría por eso picante caramelo despertarse en mi cama cada mañana como mi hombre." Dr. Mai, Chef Cyn, and Minka giggle once again, high-five each other and yell out "Girl…Yes…Yes…Yes…YES!" At this point Ariel shook her head, a wicked smile spreading across her face as she said to them: "HELLOOOOO LADIES! Tré is multi-lingual and Spanish is his second strongest language! As a matter of fact, in two days he's leaving for Santo Domingo, Dominican Republic to visit his native Spanish-speaking friends. That is why he is here in the dressing room to pick up his specially made clothes for the trip."

The cheers and giggles came to a screeching halt. Fanning herself with one hand, Minka spoke first. "I'm so embarrassed! No way, Ariel… you're joking with us."

Ariel replied laughing, "I warned you." Looking over at me, she asked me to repeat everything the ladies had said, except this time in English. Mr. Monahan was helping me put on my new white dress shorts as I looked directly into Dr. Mai's Eyes. "Dr. Mai thinks that I am sooooo cute and Intelligent," I said while proceeding to thank a wide-eyed Dr. Mai for her expressive compliments. Then, while Mr. Monahan buttons up my shirt, I next look into Chef Cyn's eyes and say, "You were asking Ariel if I have a wife or any kids. And the answer is no." Feeling slightly uncomfortable, Chef Cyn placed one hand over her mouth. As Mr. Monahan looks me over, evaluating my new outfit for style and taste, I look towards a blushing and unnerved Minka. I then say in a playfully seductive way: "Minka…Minka…MINKA! Everyone…Minka made it perfectly clear to all of us that she would LOVE for this sexy and spicy "caramelo" to wake up next to her—in her bed—every single morning as her one and only man!" As Mr. Monahan placed my white Panama Jack hat on my head, I gave the three ladies a little irresistible twist of my hips while they stood there silently for a moment, eyeing me down from head to toe, no doubt pondering…and wondering!

Ariel interrupted the moment of silence by urging the male bartender to promptly escort the ladies back to the boutique sales floor. As the trio headed down the corridor, the Monahans and I thoroughly enjoyed overhearing them talk enthusiastically about how they just couldn't believe that I understood everything they were saying about me in Spanish. They were also just as animated about how much fun they were having this evening! It always makes me feel appreciated when hard working people take the time out of their busy lives to come out and enjoy themselves for a couple of hours at one of my Special Events!

For the next half hour or so I was all alone with the well-dressed Monahans who were critiquing my latest outfit for their final approval. They were both fully dedicated to making sure that my appearance was always trendy and cutting edge, and particularly so with respect to my upcoming trip to Santo Domingo. Mr. Richard Monahan is a 57-year-old "fashionisto" millionaire from Boston while his wife Ariel Santiago-Monahan is a 27-year-old creative multi-millionaire "Chocolate Delight" from Colombia. After a thorough inspection of me modeling my new attire, Mr. Monahan and Ariel high-fived each other and shouted, "Sí (yes)!" Apparently, my purchases and taste had met with their professional approval.

"When Galilea sees you in this outfit, Tré, she is going to want to forget about being *Just Friends*," Ariel warned me. "So, you better be ready because Galilea is going to attack you with that strong Latina passion!"

As Ariel is speaking, I trance out slightly into a deep train of thought before replying, "Ariel, like I always say, Galilea and I are really close friends and nothing more. But you know what? I'm ready for however Galilea wants to take our friendship." Ariel quietly stares at me with that "You-just-don't-know-what-you-are-about-to-get-yourself-into" look! Then she smiles, hugs me, kisses me on the cheek and thanks me for helping her and her husband execute an electrifying event for their top-tier business clients.

"You are always hugging and kissing Tré. Is it because he's a younger man?" Mr. Monahan playfully teased Ariel. She smiled, then coyly replied, "Tal vez! Yo sugiero que tú continuas tomando tu tarde noche medicina, viejo papi lindo." (Maybe! I suggest that you continue taking your late night medicine, handsome Old Daddy). Enjoying the sharpness of Ariel's naughtiness, I let out a "Whooo…whooo!" And Mr. Monahan, like a champ, fires back, "Mr. Viagra and I are alert, and we are definitely ready for you tonight, dear." Ariel giggled, kissed Mr. Monahan on the lips and sashayed toward the door. However, she paused briefly to make me promise that I will definitely take advantage of my opportunity to enjoy my special time with Galilea in Santo Domingo.

I promise her that I will. Next, Ariel tells me that she wants to see plenty of photos of Galilea and I having a good time because she thinks that we would make a cute couple. She then wishes me "safe travels" and blows me a kiss as she exits the room to make sure that her VIP's are all having the time of their lives shopping and spending money!

I get undressed as Mr. Monahan neatly irons and packs up my purchases in separate lavender gift boxes. Then he carefully puts my Panama Jack hat in a fitted tan hat box. As I dress back into my Euro-cut shark-grey suit, Mr. Monahan meticulously places my prized merchandise boxes into a black and gold boutique carry-on bag. He slaps me on the shoulder, hands me my bag, and tells me to follow him over to his restaurant chill lounge so we can talk. Before we exit the dressing room, he grabs a fuchsia-pink and black boutique travel bag sitting on a glass table near the door. We follow the loud DJ-selected music pulsating into the main area of the boutique store. At that moment it was amazing to see how the Monahans and I had transformed a clothing store into a lively and posh chill lounge specifically detailed for the amusement of the Monahans' special guests.

We lit the majority of the Boutique Store with apple-red lighting except for the small stage area which was surrounded by white and black leather ottomans, small couches, and small tables with ornamental chairs. Each table exhibited a set-up of green apple-scented candles, bouquets of green rose blooms, and fusion mini-jars of my "Applelicious Melodic Mind Fuuck" cocktail filled with green apples and illuminating green glow sticks. The area is "halo-lit" with a cool sky-blue lighting scheme for visual elegance.

The energy level of my three favorite ladies is vibrant as they parade around half dressed, trying on expensive jeans, shirts, dresses, high heels, boots, jewelry, and also the newly unveiled "Peccaminosa Angelica Ragazza" lingerie line. Meanwhile a sexy female DJ keeps the atmosphere insane with frenzied music beats. A team of muscular male bartenders dressed in black sleeveless designer tuxedos are roaming around serving my creative drink concoctions—the "Angelic Lust," an "Applelicious Melodic Mind Fuuck," and "A Sensual Heart's Wet Dream."

As Mr. Monahan and I walk towards the stage area, Elise and Francisca's international crew of body-painted dancers come out and perform to the body-shaking, baby-making beats of the live DJ. Excited, screaming women rush the stage area while attempting to try on their new designer picks. As instructed, the dancers are out for the kill. They are gyrating their nimble body parts for the delight of the free-spirited, adventurous women who exhibit a thirst for happiness and freedom. The dancers are so aggressively interactive that they begin helping the VIP clientele to try on their new clothing. Some of the dancers break away from the stage area to dance with half-naked women who are avidly searching the racks for more clothing. On that note, Mr. Monahan and I exit the boutique store through a connecting door to enter his very popular restaurant chill lounge. This jewel is known for its delicious Colombian foods, colorful drink concoctions, and relaxing music.

Mr. Monahan and I sit at the only available booth in his entire restaurant so we can talk privately. He graciously tells me how much he appreciates me for supporting his Boutique Stores by purchasing outfits for my excursions and business travel in the U.S. and around the world. "No problem," I reply, "because you and Ariel always make sure that I represent myself with class and style." Mr. Monahan winked at me, a huge grin on his face. He also expressed gratitude for our genuine friendship, recalling how many times over the years I had given his customers first dibs on samples of the latest liquor innovations I was brand-imaging for the market. In the same spirit, I also acknowledged his and Ariel's support in buying my new liquor labels by the caseload, which provided invaluable support for me as a liquor consultant.

Mr. Monahan next shifted the topic of our conversation to something that we both loved to talk about—exciting travel. "So Tré…I can't believe that in two days you are going to be in the beautiful city of Santo Domingo," Mr. Monahan said playfully, pretending to be envious. "I know you are excited to see all your friends, but I also know that you are especially fired up to see a certain very special young lady by the name of Señora Galilea 'Gigi' Melendez."

I pondered his statement for a moment, feeling excitement surge inside me. I took a deep breath. "Yes, I am," I replied, "but due to the strict travel requirements placed on all Dominicans by the U.S. government, Gigi has been unable to come visit me here in the States. Because of that, we can only see each other once a year, and that's when I can take a break from work to travel to Santo Domingo to spend time with her."

Mr. Monahan grimaced. "Once a year is one year too long Tré, because you and Galilea are really close friends!"

I nod my head knowingly as he asks me what I am planning to do with Gigi during our vacation time. I tell him that it is my intention to show Gigi the time of her life over the next couple of days. "Because right now she is a nervous wreck," I confided. Mr. Monahan was taken aback by my shocking remark, but continued to listen attentively as I explained that Gigi was about to leave her immediate family and a very good job in the D.R. for a new dream job and career in the country of South Africa. She would be leaving very soon, I told him. "And in case you're wondering, she also has my full support," I added. Mr. Monahan expressed agreement, saying that my decision to support Gigi was a wise one which would give her a shot at a richer and more fulfilling life in the long run.

"Anyway..." I roared, clapping my hands to break up a somber moment, "that's all in the future, Gigi and I are going to take advantage of the present!" I went on to tell him about my plans so far which included reservations for us to dine at an exclusive restaurant with a breathtaking view. "Then we're going to the hottest Merengue Dance Club in Santo Domingo so Gigi can teach me how to Merengue!" I said, excited. "All I can tell you Mr. Monahan is that Gigi and I are going to do all the things that give us pleasure and enjoyment non-stop for six days and five nights! Or until we both pass out from severe exhaustion!"

Caught off guard by my free-spirited comments, he erupted joyfully, "Que caliente, Tré (That's hot, Tré)! You are always full of surprises!"

"Speaking of surprises," I said, "I almost forgot to mention that I've scheduled a surprise full body massage for Galilea and I to enjoy together because Gigi loves to be spontaneous."

All of a sudden Mr. Monahan placed the fuchsia-pink and black boutique travel bag on our table. "Speaking of a super surprise," he smiled, "I almost forgot to give you this gift bag that you ordered for Galilea, and that my wife Ariel and I have been putting together for her over the last seven months."

I immediately unzipped Gigi's gift bag with widening eyes and a gigantic smile on my face. I repeatedly thanked Mr. Monahan. "I really love the gift package," I say enthusiastically, "and it was definitely worth the wait because you guys have helped me to put together an absolutely memorable going away present that's going to touch Gigi's heart in an unforgettable way." I went on to tell him that he and Ariel had fulfilled my exact intentions by creating a memory that Gigi could always cherish. As we continued talking, Mr. Monahan's chill lounge Manager, Vanessa, came over to our table with a bottle of the new 1800 Coconut Tequila and a tray filled with three colorful mini-shots. "Thank You Tré for showing me how to make your 'CRAZY...ZANY...CoCo-LoCo CHILLED...CARIBBEAN-POP-SHOTS' by using the 1800 Coconut," Vanessa said with excitement. "Cause Boo, these are soooooo GOOOOD!" Next, she passed everyone a mini-shot and we all did a loud cheer as we threw back our shots. Mr. Monahan looked at me with a gleam in his eye as he said: "Tré, You did it again...I really have fallen in love with this Coconut Tequila!" Just then Mr. Monahan grabbed the 1800 Coconut Tequila bottle, gazed at

Vanessa, and asked her to order five cases! A jubilant Vanessa nodded her approval, scooped up our empty shot glasses, kissed me on the forehead, and floated away.

Mr. Monahan next asked me if I was going to pack a bottle of 1800 Coconut Tequila for my upcoming trip to the D.R. "I want to," I told him, "but airline passengers can't travel with oversized liquor bottles in their carry-on bags because TSA screening agents are very alert and restrictive. And besides, all TSA would do is confiscate my new bottle so they could drink it later for their own personal enjoyment." Mr. Monahan chuckled as I leaned back in my booth, contemplating. Thoughtfully, I looked over at him and said, "I was really hoping to make a surprise 1800 Coconut Fusion Drink for Gigi, her family, and friends before I leave Santo Domingo. It would be another nice going away present for her because Gigi simply adores all of my drink creations."

Thinking over my comment, Mr. Monahan suggests that I pack the bottle of 1800 Coconut in my suitcase. "Oh, nooooo!" I respond instantly, afraid that the bottle will burst and ruin all of my new clothing! I also express to him that my suitcase is already close to the seventy-five pound weight limit, and that I am still packing.

Mr. Monahan then boasted that when he and Ariel travel the world, he always takes along a bottle of his favorite $150 champagne! "And that's not all," he continued to taunt me, "Ariel brings her favorite $200 bottle of Chilean Red Wine." Knowing how luggage shifts around during flight, I was puzzled by his statement.

"How are you guys able to do that without the champagne and wine bottles colliding and exploding in your suitcase?" I asked. A smirking Mr. Monahan graciously reminded me that Ariel is an Interior Designer who knows how to pack and ship expensive things all over the world. Rubbing it in, Mr. Monahan tells me that packing two liquor bottles in a suitcase is easy work for Ariel, and more importantly, she is able to do so in a manner that avoids any unforeseen mishaps.

He then leaned toward me with a serious demeanor. "Listen up, Tré," he said, "how many 1800 Coconut bottles do you want to take?" Without hesitation I respond that I would like to take two bottles. Mr. Monahan slaps his right hand on the table and replies, "Excellent!" He went on to tell me, "After our event tonight, come over to the house and drop off your two bottles and I'll have Ariel carefully wrap them for you.

Then first thing tomorrow morning while you are out, come back over to the Boutique Store so you can pick them up. Ariel will be more than happy to show you the best way of packing them securely!"

DÍA UNO
(DAY ONE)
Tré is in Santoo Domingooo, Bebé!

I'M IN MY five-star, beautifully decorated hotel room with a stunning view of the Malecón section of Santo Domingo. The view also affords me a jaw-dropping panorama of the sparkling blue Caribbean Sea cutting through sapphire blue skies. Currently, I am in a frenzy while unpacking my things and ironing out my outfit for the evening because within the next couple of hours I will be attending a live music concert with Gigi.

Three days before, Gigi had called to ask if I wanted to go to the Pitbull and Enrique Iglesias concert. Being a fan of both, I'd heard all the way back in the States how excited the entire City of Santo Domingo was about the concert. "Let's make it an epic night," I told Gigi, "so hurry up and buy the tickets before the concert sells out!" I also promised that I would reimburse her for both tickets because the night is on me. After I finished unpacking and ironing my clothes, I called a couple of good friends from Santo Domingo to let them know that I'd arrived safely. I also made plans to hang out with them so they could show me around their city over the next couple of days because my time in Santo Domingo, unfortunately, was going to be too short.

I took a cold shower to help rejuvenate my body. I was feeling somewhat fatigued because I had arrived at the airport at 3:30 a.m. in order to allow sufficient time to get checked in and then undergo screening by airport security. I'd then boarded my flight to Santo Domingo at 5:30 a.m. So I promptly got dressed, exited my room, and headed down to the hotel café. I ordered a glass of homemade coconut water-mango juice along with a small but delicious fruit bowl. Feeling thoroughly revitalized after my five-minute power snack, I kept it moving. While hurrying outside to catch a taxi to the concert, I looked around and saw a friendly, average-built, baby-faced taxi driver smiling at me as he cheerfully waited beside his taxi. The right passenger side door of his clean and freshly scented vehicle was open. I walked over to him and asked him in Spanish if he could please take me to the Enrique and Pitbull concert.

Surprisingly, the taxi driver responded in perfect English with a slight Dominican accent. "Come on…let's go," he said to me, "because you are going to be late mi mano (my brothá)!" We shake hands, I hop in the taxi, and my soon-to-be new friend closed my door and zoomed off into the early evening traffic. At the first opportunity, I introduced myself and also thanked him for taking me to the concert on such short notice. "I'm always at your service and bienvenido (welcome) to my beautiful city of Santo Domingo, Tré," he said enthusiastically. Staring out the passenger side windows, I was enjoying the marvelous sights of the city. I looked towards the front of the taxi and asked in Spanish, "Brothá, what is your name?" The driver looked back at me through his hanging rear view mirror with a super-sized smile on his face. "My name is Henry," he told me, "but we native Spanish speakers pronounce my name as 'Enri' because the 'H' is silent."

Enri complimented me on my Spanish-speaking skill, and urged me to keep up the good work. As he effortlessly maneuvered his way through the growing rush hour traffic, we talked cordially about my hectic career in the liquor industry, which led to him offering me expert advice about what I should do for fun while in Santo Domingo. He handed me his business card and insisted that I call him whenever I needed a ride to anywhere. "No matter if it is early morning, mid-day, or late at night, I am your personal go-to guy who guarantees you will always get to your destination safely, on time, and with the best rates in all of Santo Domingo!" Impressed by Enri's professionalism and hospitality, I was receiving nothing but positive vibes from him as a person. I didn't even bother to think twice about it before promising that I would be calling him very soon.

Enri nodded his head in appreciation and asked me who I was taking to the concert. I tell him that I am meeting up with my good friend Galilea, who loves it when I call her Gigi. "Gigi…that is a cute and unique name. Do you have a picture of her?" Enri replied with curiosity. "Of course I do, and I'm the only person that Gigi allows to call her by that name," I replied boastfully. Enri laughed. I reached into my pocket and pulled out my small point and shoot camera. Scrolling rapidly through the hundreds and hundreds of photos, I heard Enri mumble something as he abruptly slowed down. I looked up to find that we'd run into some unexpected bad traffic, either stemming from an accident or from the mass of people flocking to the Pitbull & Enrique Iglesias concert. I checked the time on my smartphone only to discover that the concert would be starting in just twenty-five short minutes, and I honestly had no idea how far I was from the outdoor arena!

Enri apparently sensed that I was becoming a little anxious. "Don't you worry, Tré!" he reassured me. "When you ride with me, I guarantee that I will get you to your destination on time—me entiendes (understand me)? Now show me a picture of Galilea." Relaxing now, I handed him my camera so he could scroll through the photos of Gigi as he accelerated ferociously through the heavy traffic with no sign of distress. Enri started checking out the photos and instantly swerved toward a group of honking cars heading in our immediate direction. Realizing that we were heading for a deadly crash, Enri gracefully maneuvered us back into the appropriate lane as if he didn't have a care in the world. Still looking at multiple photos of Gigi while driving, Enri roared: "DIOS MÍO (MY GOD)! Is she your girlfriend? Man…Tré, you should marry her!"

Trying to remain calm after almost being obliterated by four cars, one truck, and two motor bikes, I laugh and reply, "We are just very good friends, but Gigi is extremely beautiful, classy, intelligent, and artsy. She's just a very well-rounded girl, so I definitely enjoy our time together whenever I'm in town." Enri gives me back my camera, shaking his head. "So…what's the problem?" Reminiscing in silence for a few seconds, I lean towards Enri and say, "It's a little complicated between us. And besides, she is about to move to South Africa because of a new job."

Enri was obviously not one to entertain any illogical excuses. "Well, move to South Africa with her and marry her, Tré!" he replied sharply. Meanwhile Gigi started "blowing up" my phone with a series of calls and text messages. But when I answered, I couldn't understand her because she was speaking to me in Spanish. She was also calling me from an area near the outdoor arena where the background noise and loud music was making it impossible to hear her. To make matters worse, since my smartphone was serviced through a U.S. phone carrier and I was an hour and a half south of Miami—in the middle of the Caribbean—my calls kept getting "dropped." Although I was urgently trying to make a sustainable phone connection with Gigi, with Enri driving through one dead zone after another, I could literally see the battery life in my smartphone steadily draining from a seventy-five percent energy level down to five percent emergency power. Not panicking, I abruptly stopped trying to call Gigi back because I knew that once my phone died and shut down, it would be impossible for me and Gigi to find each other at a concert where more than 50,000 people were gathered!

 I handed Enri Gigi's phone number and asked him to please call her. Once she was on the phone Enri tried to calm her nerves by explaining what was happening. He also told her that we were only five minutes away and where to meet us. Gigi relayed a message to me through Enri that the concert was about to start in fifteen minutes, that the arena was jam-packed, and that the tickets she'd purchased were for seats located in a section right next to the front of the stage. As if that wasn't enough pressure, Gigi repeated that we needed to hurry up because the front stage section was fast becoming standing room only!

 Enri glanced back at me, giving me the thumbs up signal as he suavely replied to Gigi in Spanish: "Tré says no problem my love! He'll see you in a couple of minutes." "How tall is Gigi?" Enri asked as he gazed at me through his hanging rear view mirror. I answer that she is about 5-foot, five inches tall. "I hope that you are in real good physical shape," he said with concern.

 "Why?" I asked, slightly thrown off by his comment. "Listen, Tré," Enri responded, "if you do not find a good area where she can clearly see Pitbull and Enrique performing, then like most men with their girlfriends near the front stage, you are going to have to put Gigi on top of your shoulders for this three-and-a-half-hour long concert! If you do not, Gigi is going to be extremely angry and upset with you for arriving late. The show is about to begin in less than ten minutes and we are still not there yet."

 Enri paused and turned to glance at me before he went on. "Tré if I were you," he told me, "when you get there, take Señora Galilea by the hand and force your way as close as you can to a good area that she likes.

But if she is unable to have a nice view of the front stage, then mi mano (my brothá), my personal advice to you is to go as long as you can with Gigi enjoying the concert sitting on your shoulders. Understand me?" He addressed me in Spanish.

"I understand," I said, nodding my head while Enri quickly called Gigi to tell her to meet me at his taxi. Just then we see Gigi instantly appear out of a massive human sea of enthusiastic music fanatics. As she walked toward Enri's taxi, he turned to me mesmerized. "DIOS MÍO TRÉ," he exclaimed, "ELLA ES TANNNNN PICANTE-CALIENTE" (MY GOD TRÉ, SHE IS SOOOOO SPICY-HOT)! I excitedly nod my head in agreement. Before I could open my door to exit, Enri informed me that he would be coming back after the concert to pick up his daughters, and that he would be happy to give Gigi a ride home and then drop me off at my hotel. Enri then pointed to an isolated area of the parking lot that would be easy to find. This would be the designated spot where he would hook up with us and his two daughters after the show. I thank him for all of his help and generosity.

Exiting the taxi to run over and greet Gigi, I can hear Enri calling out to me through his open window to have fun tonight and to make sure that I dance with Gigi all night long because "Dominicanas" (Dominican women) want to marry a man who knows how to move his body in a passionate and sensual way. I give Enri a thumbs up and began focusing all of my attention on Gigi, who is running towards me shouting, "Hola Tré! Hola Tré!" Not having seen her for almost a year, I had to admit that Gigi's Intoxicating beauty still had a "spellbinding" effect on me. She was the vision of a sexy ballerina with glistening reddish-brown skin, with dark golden-brown Asian eyes accented by kissable, full-blossomed lips and medium-length straight hair (parted in the middle) that was the color of almonds.

Gigi and I embrace as I swing her body three feet into the air because I am so happy to see her after twelve long months! When I gently set her back down, I automatically took note of her trademark sense of chic-ness. Gigi was "killing it" by wearing a pair of tight, mid-thigh, white designer shorts and a Voguish form-fitting white shirt with a shimmering pink butterfly emblem. She then chose to "rock" her outfit with a set of dressy, French-designed white sneakers. Gigi looked directly into my eyes with an infectious smile on her face before she started giving me that "You're late, Tré!" demeanor! However, today was obviously an exception because we were so overcome with joy that we began hugging, caressing, and kissing each other on the cheeks. Following our warm greetings, I handed Gigi the money for the tickets. After checking our section number, I asked her about the fastest way to get there. She pointed towards the main entrance of the arena which was "stacked and packed" full of amped up music lovers rushing to their seats. I take Gigi's hand as we dart through a sea of people. It was as if I was back in New York City forcing my way through a busy Grand Central Station subway terminal.

As we got closer to the front stage area, I continued to overpower people by moving them out of our way. I felt bad, but all I could do was to repeatedly say, "Disculpa Nos" (Excuse us)! in a very loud and aggressive voice in response to the unfamiliar Spanish words that everyone was directing at me that I couldn't understand. The show was about to start and Pitbull's band was now performing. Gigi and I finally arrived at our assigned section, pushing as close as we could to the jam-packed front stage area. I looked around at Gigi and I noticed that she was unable to find a clear view of the stage because the majority of the guys in our section had their girlfriends on top of their shoulders.

Feverishly looking around for an open area where Gigi could see better, I noticed this slim-figured guy with a protruding "baby gut" standing next to us. He was easily and comfortably drinking two beers while shouldering his very attractive, full-figured girlfriend who clearly outweighed him by seventy pounds! All I could say was that this guy must have some type of reserve tank of herculean strength because what he was doing seemed impossible.

Suddenly Pitbull burst onto the stage and the entire crowd erupted in explosive delirium! People were cheering, clapping, screaming, spraying water guns and throwing colored confetti all over the place. Gigi began jumping up and down because she was desperately trying to see Pitbull. So I grabbed her, stooped down, and told her to sit on my shoulders. Gigi's frown suddenly lit up into a beaming smile. I mirrored her happy smile with one of my own. "Tré…you don't have to do this," Gigi protested. "Yes I do," I replied, "because I promised you we were going to do it strong tonight! Está Bien Hermosa" (Okay Beautiful)? I responded. "Está Bien, Lindo," (Okay, Handsome) she replied, still smiling. Then she climbed onto my shoulders as I lifted her up. What was so cool was that there was a group of really nice guys standing next to me who made sure Gigi didn't fall off as I raised her up. Once I got my balance, people started cheering and patting me on my back.

You should have seen the look on my face! I'm not even going to lie because I loved having two strong and soft bronzed legs wrapped around my neck. And my God! Gigi's legs were smelling soooo good because she had meticulously babied them with a floral-scented lotion. I took full advantage by massaging her calves and shins, so Gigi was feeling really comfortable sitting atop my shoulders. She was moving and grooving her lower body around my shoulders non-stop to the pulsating sounds of "Mr. 305!" There is a reason why Pitbull is a global music icon, and tonight did not prove to be a disappointment as he electrified an arena of 50,000 plus fans like a true virtuoso of his craft. Standing close to the front stage area made it impossible for Gigi and I to communicate with each other because the live music plus the crowd noise was deafening. All we could do was vibe together while listening to some damn good music being performed by Pitbull!

After almost an hour and a half of Pitbull's high energy excitement, while I kept up a relentless dance pace with Gigi on my shoulders, I slowly began to realize that the current temperature where we were standing was more than 100 degrees Fahrenheit! Mixed in with the suffocating tropical humidity, the heat was causing me to sweat through my clothes. In fact, the entire crowd was drenched in sweat and pushing towards exhaustion. Guys were struggling to support their girlfriends on their shoulders. Meanwhile, given the humidity and the lotion lacing Gigi's legs, she was becoming too slick for me to properly hold on to.

The situation became seriously apparent to me as I stood staring at the thin legs of the slim guy who was somehow still holding up his thick girlfriend with the generous curves. All of a sudden his legs just buckled beneath him, causing both him and his girlfriend to come crashing down hard! The eight beers he'd drunk combined with the severe heat were just too much and had finally taken its unforgiving toll. But what this man had done physically for almost two hours straight was an unbelievable feat in my eyes!

Thankfully, someone got the attention of a team of patrolling first-aid nurses. The nurses immediately began reviving the guy with fresh water and hand fans. Then, with the assistance of his girlfriend, they walked him over to the first-aid station for additional treatment. The nurses were busy all over the concert grounds, aiding people who were either physically exhausted or badly dehydrated. Gigi leaned down from her perch on my shoulders, placed her pouty lips near my right ear and said something to me that I couldn't hear at first because of Pitbull's "killa" performance which had fans going berserk. She asked if I was okay. "Yes," I replied, "but I need some water because I'm thirsty."

Gigi rubbed my chin, then signaled a beverage vendor to come over. He quickly handed her a bottle of water and a beer which she had ordered for herself. I gulped down the bottled water in seconds and Gigi quickly bought me another. Always the nurturing one, Gigi personally gave me sips of water so that my hands could remain firmly locked around her lower thighs. That being said, I'm not even going to front. The water was NOT rejuvenating me. My body was in the "red zone" stage of breaking down and crashing altogether from physical fatigue!

As I've said before, I engage in a very disciplined, year-round exercise regimen, but when you're dancing around in the middle of an airless tropical heat blast, with a 130-pound woman gyrating on top of your shoulders for two hours, the outcome is going to be pulverizing to your body. Still, I was refusing to break mentally. Instead, I was praying for Enrique Iglesias to hurry up on stage and start performing some of his world famous romantic Latin love ballads. Enrique was going to be my excuse to put Gigi down and ask her for a slow dance. I don't need to tell you that I was looking forward very much to the wonderful relief of having Gigi off of my shoulders. Just at that moment Pitbull finished his set and exited the stage. The live music smoothly transitioned into an ultra-mellow tempo, and the crowd exploded into a frenzy of deafening cheers and screams, myself included because I was yelling repeatedly "Muchas Gracias a Dios" (Thank You God)! God had indeed heard my pleas for help because, all of a sudden, Enrique Iglesias slowly began rising from beneath the stage area. Then, like a lion on the prowl, he smoothly strutted across the stage. You should have seen the grin on my face. But sometimes I wonder if God has a wicked sense of humor because exactly forty-five seconds after Pitbull left the stage, he returned to his beloved fans wearing a new outfit. He and Enrique Iglesias then begin to perform thirty minutes of explosive, high octane, world famous, "azz- shaking" musical hits together NON-STOP!

Although deeply disappointed, I dug deep and found that second level of energy from within. I decided to embrace this awesome moment of being on a Caribbean island at a "kick azz" concert with my alluring friend. Gigi was the ultimate motivational remedy, and I happily drew all of my inspiration from her beauty and grace, which was allowing me to celebrate longer, stronger, and harder. I got into my musical groove trance and danced while Gigi was still gyrating all over my shoulders. The entire arena, including me, were all cheering, dancing, and singing. It was an epic concert and hands down one of the greatest that I had ever witnessed. Pitbull finally exited the stage to an ear-shattering standing ovation and Enrique began singing one of his slow songs. At this point people started to dance the Merengue to the slow, rhythmic, seductive beat of Enrique's aphrodisiac-laced vocals.

Hot Steamy Night + Great Vibes + Romantic Music + Liquor = An Epic Exhausting Night of Fun!

In my case, I was verbally thanking God and Jesus Christ out loud for their divine and merciful intervention because my body was at the final one percent reserve energy level before automatic shutdown. I quickly got Gigi's attention. "You owe me a dance," I told her. Gigi rubbed both sides of my cheeks and leaned down head first. I could see her, upside down, smiling at me as she replied, "Yes, Tré…I've been waiting to dance with you all night long." She slid down my back, and I could instantly feel my energy level powering back up. On the dance floor, she started off with a slow Merengue dance maneuver, but I smoothly transitioned us into a slow dance by pulling her up into my chest. I whispered softly to Gigi: "Just relax and let me lead you because I'm showing you how we do it back in the States." Gigi looked at me without saying a word. She lay her head on my chest and softly serenaded me with Enrique Iglesias as her back-up singer.

Following my lead with ease, Gigi needed no help in showing off her exceptional dancing ability. But from time to time, I couldn't resist showing her off to a nearby group of dancing couples by maneuvering her through a series of intricate, seductive, crowd-pleasing twirls. I even captured a "devilish edge" by dancing with Gigi with my arms securely wrapped around her shoulders and petite, huggable waistline. To my amazement, the people closest to us began observing and imitating our dance moves.

We danced uninterrupted, with only eyes for each other, until the end of the concert. When Enrique concluded his final set, we just stood silently on the dance floor smiling at each other. "Gracias, Tré," Gigi said as she softly kissed me on both my cheeks. It was just at that moment that I began to sense a very obvious and awkward moment between us. Although Gigi continued smiling, I noticed that her doe eyes were glistening. I'd known Gigi for almost six years and she had never looked at me in this way before.

We silently stared at one another with flirtatious smiles on our faces—until we almost got run over by a tsunami wave of super-hyped, drunk, and exhausted fans who were all in a mad rush to go home! Gigi yelled at them in Spanish as I grabbed her by the hand and guided her NYC style through a maze of impatient people. In a span of thirty seconds flat we arrived at the designated area where Enri and his two daughters were patiently waiting for us. When I first saw the two young women, both in their mid-twenties, I was thinking like, "Wow!" They were both so attractive.

I was also thinking that Enri must have been a teenage father because he looked more like an older brother of about thirty-five years old or so. I warmly introduced Gigi to Enri and his two girls. All three of them reciprocated the love by cheerfully introducing themselves as Enri, Maria, and Tatiana. After our friendly pleasantries, Enri told everyone to get inside the taxi after which he swiftly drove off so we could beat the mass exodus of the post-concert crowd.

"How was the concert?" Enri asked moments later. Then for twenty minutes straight, Tatiana, Maria, and I all ecstatically described to him how Pitbull and Enrique both gave memorable and incredible performances. Enri slapped his steering wheel three times out of disappointment as he said in Spanish: "I knew that I should have gone to that concert!" Maria answered him back in English. "We told you to go, Enri! Next time maybe you will listen to us!" However, I found it very unusual that the usually bubbly Gigi was just sitting quietly to herself while the rest of us were having an entertaining conversation in both English and Spanish. Next, Enri asked if anyone was hungry, because if so, we could all go have a bite to eat at a popular late night

Dominican diner.

Gigi finally broke her silence. "No," she responded, saying it was getting late and she had to be at work at 6:30 a.m. in the morning. Hearing this, I was very disappointed because if she was visiting me back in the States, I would have stayed out all night with her and WILLFULLY suffered the consequences of going to work tired. Especially since we had not seen each other in almost a year!

When we arrived at Gigi's home, she got out of the taxi so fast that I was unable to get out and open her door. She then walked over to Enri, and was about to pay him. "Gigi," I called out, interrupting her, "I'll take care of everything."

"Thank you Tré for a fantastic evening. I will call you tomorrow, está bien (okay)?" she said as she wished all of us a good evening. "And thank you Enri for the ride," she said as she abruptly walked away. As she headed down her front walkway, Gigi's older brother Jaime opened the front door and escorted her inside. However, very quickly Jaime returned to the taxi, looked inside, and saw me. He waved and yelled out, "Qué pasa, Tré" (What's up, Tré)? I waved at him and he returned to the house. Maria, who was sitting in the front passenger seat, hopped in the back and purposely sandwiched me between herself and Tatiana.

Enri decided to take me and his daughters to a very famous late night café located near the Caribbean Sea. As we were riding along on an unbelievable moonlit night, Enri looked through his rear view mirror at me and said: "Tré, I see why Gigi is only your friend and not your girlfriend!"

Maria responded to her father's comment with a frown. "She was really cold," she said accusingly. "She didn't even give you a goodbye hug and kiss!" Meanwhile Tatiana looked over at me sympathetically. "I know that if I hadn't seen you in almost a year, I would have given you nothing but "abrazos y besos" (hugs and kisses), she told me.

Maria placed her hand on my left arm, smiled and asked, "Tréeeeé… are you single?" Enri quickly interrupted. "Stop! Stop messing with me Tati and Mari… I'm serious!" he said to his high-spirited daughters. Paying no attention to their father, Tatiana and Maria sandwich me in tighter, to the point where I am forced to put my arms around them. "Yes, I am single," I say charmingly in Spanish.

"Okay…okayyy!" Tatiana responds sweetly. Then we all started laughing because of Enri's discomfort. Maria looked at her father. "Enri…please turn the music up and ignore us," she said to her father. Enri mumbled something before turning up the volume on a local Merengue station while giving me a look that said, "Take it easy, Bebé! They may look like my younger sisters but they are still my daughters."

Hanging out with Tatiana, Maria, and Enri was actually brightening up my evening because I was still slightly perplexed about why Gigi had acted so strangely after having such a great time with me at the concert. But I was never one to dwell on negative energy because my motto is "Keep it movin'!" So I simply refused to let Gigi or anything or anybody "poison pill" my well-deserved vacation.

We were dining at a prestigious late night café that was super-busy. It actually felt like we were in lower Manhattan during a crazy midday luncheon. I was rehydrating my body by eating a delicious bowl of melons. I was also drinking a large glass of coconut water mixed with slices of passion fruit. Meanwhile Enri, Maria, and Tatiana were "chowing down" on a deluxe Dominican pizza known as the "El Cuarto Carne" (The Four Meats). It consisted of hamburger, fish, pork sausage, and smoked turkey. My companions generously offered me as much pizza as I could eat, but I only ate one slice. I actually could have eaten more of the tasty treat, but I don't like eating heavy foods late at night. I hate it when my stomach feels like a loaded bag of rocks while I am lying in bed trying to sleep.

I was always taught that great food, great people, and great conversation can go a long way, no matter where you are in this world. So I was very grateful for my newfound friends who cared enough to share their time and a delicious meal with me. Enri even told me that if I ever needed anything while in Santo Domingo, he and his daughters would do their best to assist me.

"As a matter of fact, I do need some assistance," I said without a second thought. "I want to make Gigi a Strawberry Tequila Fusion Drink as a going away present because she is relocating to South Africa, and I need help finding the ingredients because I don't know where to shop."

Tatiana rolled her eyes. "You should not make her anything Tré, because she might not appreciate your thoughtful gift," she said.

Enri shook his head. "Tati…mind your own business and be quiet," he scolded his hot-blooded daughter. Immediately, Maria and I began laughing at this big brother-little sister interaction. Maria asked me what exactly I was looking for, and I explained that I needed to purchase fresh strawberries, a bottle of strawberry liqueur, a blender, ice trays, sparkling apple cider and a fusion drink jar. But it was difficult for me to explain what a fusion drink jar is in Spanish, so I uploaded a photo of it on my smartphone.

"It's going to be difficult to find everything you need Tré, because here in Santo Domingo these things are not as convenient as in the United States," Tatiana told me. "But we will start looking as soon as businesses begin opening for the morning hours." Thanking everyone for their help, I also indicated to them that I was hoping to create my fusion masterpiece by tomorrow evening because it was going to require a minimum of three days to steep and blend. Pondering what I'd just said, Maria responded by telling me to go talk to the Night Manager at my hotel. Enri agreed, telling me that once I have a list of the stores, he will be available anytime tomorrow to take me anywhere I need to go to make my purchases.

At around 1:30 in the morning, Enri and his daughters dropped me off safely in front of my hotel. As I got out of the taxi, Tatiana and Maria sent me off with hugs and kisses to my cheeks. Maria thoughtfully handed me her to-go box of leftover pizza to eat later. I paid Enri for the ride, thanked everyone for a beautiful evening of sharing, and headed inside my hotel. Entering the hotel lobby, I see the very beautiful Night Manager, Serena Reynaldo, diligently performing her managerial duties. The lobby is empty, but the caressing sounds of Latin jazz fill the entire space with musical ambiance.

I approached Serena who was wearing her usual effervescent smile.

"Buenas noches, Tré!" she greeted me.

"Buenos días y como estas, Serena!" I reply amusingly by making reference to the fact that the new day is already beginning. Serena, who is bi-lingual, laughed. "Yes…It is indeed the early morning and I am doing fine, gracias." Resuming her activities, Serena observed, "Tré… you were out late."

"Yes…because I went to the big Pitbull and Enrique Iglesias concert with my friend Gigi," I said. Serena immediately stopped what she was doing and looked at me with dark, piercing eyes. She paused for a milli-second, her mouth hanging wide open. "Oh, my God! I wanted to go to that concert…soooo bad!" she shrieked. "How was it?"

Shaking my head, I reply, "Serena, it was one of the best concerts I have ever been to in my entire life. Both Pitbull's and Enrique's performances pushed everyone to the breaking point of sheer exhaustion!" Serena sighed as she told me that she couldn't go to the concert because she had to work the night shift while her husband works during the day. Always the mischievous one, I show no mercy in teasing Serena about how she missed out on a musical experience for the ages. Doing her best to fight off her disappointment, Serena shushed me playfully, "Stop, Tré! You are making me feel bad!"

At that point we both started laughing because Serena knew I was only joking with her. With that said, I started cheering Serena up by showing her some of the photos I had taken at the concert. She excitedly scrolled through them, her enthusiasm written all over her face. I tell Serena that I will gladly e-mail her the photos when I return to the States.

"Yes! Yes! Please send me your photos. Thank You, Tré!" Serena said in rapid Spanish, her excitement bubbling over as she grabbed my hand. She then complimented me on my command of Spanish and kindly expressed to me that if I ever needed her assistance during my stay, please let her know. Thanking Serena, I confided that I did need her help immediately in locating the ingredients I needed to create a Strawberry Tequila Fusion Drink for my friend Gigi. I tell her that I need to purchase these supplies by tomorrow evening. Otherwise, my surprise gift will be doomed never to happen! Admitting to Serena that my Spanish is not perfectly fluent, I wrote down everything I needed on a piece of paper, with explanations written in both English and Spanish. Seeing the baffled look on Serena's face as she read the list, I pulled out my smartphone and uploaded the necessary images.

Once she comprehended everything I needed, Serena gazed at me with an admiring smile on her face. "How lovely, Tré!" she said sweetly. "You are an extraordinary man! In my personal opinion, making a creative gift for a woman that you care about is the precious key to unlocking her heart," Serena said sincerely as she went on. "And even though you say that you and Gigi are just good friends, I have a strong feeling that she is really going to ADORE your gift!"

Going over my list again, I emphasize to Serena that I have to get started on my project tomorrow! She then honestly confided to me that she personally did not know where to find all of the required items, but that she did know a person who might be able to help me. She told me she would contact me the next morning with the necessary information. But before I headed off to my room, Serena told me that my Strawberry Tequila Fusion Drink sounded delicious, and that she definitely wanted to try it because she had never tasted a custom-made, original cocktail before.

I wished Serena a good night, and as I was walking away I noticed that she was frantically looking at her watch. She'd suddenly realized that she didn't have enough time to place her lunch order and have it delivered within the next fifteen minutes. In other words, she'd been talking to me for almost an hour, and now she didn't have enough time to eat her lunch. I felt bad, so I walked back over to Serena and offered her my pizza. She was delighted as she confessed that pizza was her favorite nighttime snack. I then said my "final" goodbyes only to return five minutes later with two plastic cups filled with ice and a bottle of 1800 Coconut Tequila. I really wanted Serena to taste a sample of the drink I was going to create for Gigi. So we both did a chilled shot and she was blown away into a "mellow-euphoria!" Serena couldn't believe what she had just tasted and promised she was going to do everything she could to help me to make my deadline.

The moment I returned to my room, my body reminded me of just how sore I was, how exhausted I was, and how jet-lagged I was! So I called room service and asked them to bring me a couple of bags of ice. I began filling up my tub with cold water and the two bags of ice which had been delivered to my door almost instantly. I took a couple of Ibuprofen and performed a few stretches to help loosen up my muscles. Finally, I soaked myself from head to toe in an ice water bath until I couldn't feel my body anymore. After bathing in the Arctic waters of my bathtub, I went to bed and slept like a "bebé" for three and a half hours!

DÍA DOS
(DAY TWO)

I WOKE UP re-energized and decided to walk down to the Malecón section of the city where I began to take colorful abstract photos of the sun rising above the tropical waters of the Caribbean Sea. Then I headed back to my hotel and strolled through an empty lobby. All of a sudden I heard someone calling my name. I turned to see a smiling Serena walking towards me. "You are up and out early this morning, Tré," she greeted me. "Are you leaving to go somewhere?" Serena asked.

"I got up about an hour ago and I went to the Malecón to take some photos of the sunrise," I replied.

"I am so happy that I saw you before leaving to go home Tré," Serena told me. "Because I wanted to tell you that I've found someone who can help you."

Overcome with relief, I immediately began expressing my gratitude. Serena graciously acknowledged my sincerity with a smile followed by an invitation to accompany her to an empty kitchen area where a chef was busy looking over his notes and tasting different bowls of bright red strawberries. Serena turned to me. "Tré…I want to introduce you to Chef Rafael, my husband."

Chef Rafael and I shook hands and exchanged salutations. I lean back and smile in admiration as Chef Rafael and Serena hug each other because they make such a cute couple. Chef Rafael continued studying the notes that I had given to Serena last night. He looked up at me and said in flawless English, "Tré…I believe that we can help you find all the things that you need so you can make this fascinating Strawberry Tequila." He went on to show me around while pointing out his wide selection of fusion jars.

Next, the Chef escorted Serena and I over to a table and fed us luscious red strawberries that looked like irresistible red candies straight from heaven. Serena purred, "Deliciosa!" Turning to me, the Chef wanted to know if these were sweet enough for my drink concoction. I closed my eyes and jubilantly shouted: "Yes! These strawberries are perfect! They are super-juicy and bursting with sweetness!" Chef Rafael nodded as he informed me that these are the sweetest strawberries in all of the Dominican Republic. He also indicated that he personally uses them to make his own very popular strawberry white-vanilla wedding cakes.

Continuing to review my notes, the Chef stopped to gaze at me with a grin. "Tré! We have everything you need, mi mano," he assured me. "It will be our pleasure to assist you! Now...can I please say that Serena and I are also wondering if you can do a very important favor for us?"

"Sure, mi mano! How can I help?" I responded without hesitation. He walked over to me. "Tré...we are in the process of preparing for a highly important Summer Party Event for our hotel owners and fellow colleagues," he said. "The event will take place in three days and Serena and I were both hoping that you could also make another Strawberry Fusion Drink for our event." The Chef went on enthusiastically, "We really want to surprise everybody with your imaginative drink. From what Serena has been saying about you, your Strawberry Tequila is going to capture everyone's attention and hopefully help them to have an unforgettable time."

Feeling flattered, I tell Serena and Chef Rafael, "Yes! I like being the one who can put people in the mood to party like crazed maniacs all night long!" They both laughed. Serena whispered something to her husband, but all I could hear was the word "coco" (coconut). She turned to smile at me and asked if I could make the Strawberry Fusion Drink with my two bottles of 1800 Coconut? I drew in a deep breath and stood there silently for a moment. "What's wrong, Tré?" Chef Rafael asked with a concerned look. I slowly reply, "Yes, I can do it, but there could be a problem because I was planning to use the two bottles myself, and unfortunately, those are the only ones I have."

Serena's and Chef Rafael's smiles quickly evaporated. Desperate for a solution, I began thinking out loud. "We need to find a place here in Santo Domingo that sells it," I said, "but I know that this is impossible because the 1800 Coconut was just released in certain parts of the United States. So I am one hundred percent positive that you guys don't have it here yet." They nod their heads in agreement. An idea suddenly hit me and I asked the Chef if 1800 Silver is sold at the hotel? He answered yes, but that he would prefer for me to use the 1800 Coconut because this morning Serena—who wasn't even a Tequila drinker—couldn't stop talking about how delicious it tasted. I had to agree. The 1800 Coconut did have an amazing taste!

"Wait a minute!" Serena suddenly interrupted our train of thought. "Let's call your cousin Marlin in Miami and have her buy the 1800 Coconut. She can ship it to us today along with a case of our favorite German Riesling." Chef Rafael lit up with a smile, kissed his beautiful and brainy wife, and told us that he was just about to call his cousin today because he drank their last bottle of German Riesling the night before. Patting me on the shoulder, he went on to explain, "Marlin works in the American Airlines International Shipping Department located in Miami, and she sends us things all the time at a cheap rate, and sometimes for free."

Serena reminded her husband that since this is on behalf of their special event, she could charge all costs for making the drink to the hotel. Hearing Serena's comment, I got a flash. "You know what? I'll make two different variations of my Tequila Fusion Drink for the hotel using both the 1800 Coconut and the 1800 Silver. Then I am going to make two more 1800 Strawberry-Coconut Fusion Tequilas—one for myself and the other one for you guys for helping me out."

Chef Rafael's eyes brighten as he begins thanking me. Serena, who was totally caught off guard, had a different response. "Tré...you don't have to do this," she said.

"No problema, Fam!" I reply. "I would love to do this for you guys!" I say enthusiastically in Spanish. I next tell Serena to please have Marlin to purchase and send us four bottles of the 1800 Coconut, four bottles of Strawberry Daiquiri Mix, and four bottles of Strawberry Liqueur. Serena writes everything down and then asks Chef Rafael if the hotel has the rest of the ingredients I will need.

"Yes...Don't worry about anything Tré," he replied.

Reminding both of them that I have to have everything by tonight, they both reassure me that there's no cause for worry. I still had one important concern though. I expressed to them that I needed access to a kitchen because my room at the hotel was not equipped to make four

Fusion Drinks. Serena immediately chimed in: "I was already thinking about this Tré, and I began checking into it. So my solution is, as of right now, I'm going to upgrade you to an executive suite that overlooks the Malecón for no additional charge," Serena informed me as she went on. "Your suite will have a fully furnished kitchen, a Jacuzzi, bigger beds, and more space to move around in. And guess what else Tré?" she asked with a sparkle in her eyes. "You can stay there until you leave Santo Domingo four days from now!"

Serena didn't stop there. She went further to inform me that my suite would be located two corridors away from a newly-wed couple, the only guests presently on the executive floor. She also told me that I would have access to everything I needed as if I were staying in my own house. "When your liquor products arrive later on today, I will bring them up along with the other things on your list," Serena concluded. I was absolutely blown away as I gave her a big hug and shook her husband's hand.

Chef Rafael reconfirmed that all the ingredients I needed would be brought to my suite by early evening. I paused as I shook his hand. "May I ask for one more last thing?" I asked looking at both of them. "Sure...ask me anything, Tré!" Serena responded with curiosity. I went on to explain that creating Four Fusion Drinks by myself was going to take me the entire night. Looking directly at Serena, I say innocently, "Serena...I know that you work nights, but do you think that you would be able to help me...please?" Just then the Chef quickly interrupted me, his face stern as he grabbed me by the shoulder. "Tré...are you trying to spend the night with my wife?" he growled, staring me down like a crazy man!

Thoroughly taken aback, but maintaining my composure, I reply, "No...no...no...I wasn't trying to suggest that!"

But Chef Rafael roars: "Yes! Yes, you are Tré! I know what you are trying to do!"

Shaking my head in disbelief, I continued to counteract his accusations. "No...I wasn't," I repeated with sincerity.

All of a sudden, Chef Rafael breaks out with a huge and mischievous grin on his face. He and Serena both start laughing. "Don't mind my husband, Tré," Serena warns me a bit late. "He likes to tease people. That's why I married him because he always makes me laugh."

Chef Rafael hugged me. "I'm just joking with you, Tré...of course you can spend the night with my wife!" he said.

"COMO" (What)? Serena shrieks, and we all started laughing. Afterwards, I tell Serena that, with her help, we should be able to finish everything in about an hour and a half maximum. After agreeing that we will meet at my suite at about 12:30 a.m., I said my goodbyes and began preparing myself for a fun-filled outing with two beautiful Dominican friends.

My new executive suite, compliments of Serena, looked like an upscale and luxurious condo with a sun deck overlooking the breathtaking Caribbean Sea. Once I got situated, I immediately showered, changed clothes, grabbed my backpack (that was already pre-packed with everything I could possibly need for a day of relaxation and fun), especially my trademark toiletries to help keep a young man looking and smelling fresh!

Walking through the hotel lobby, I was unexpectedly assaulted with big warm hugs and kisses from my good friends Yolanda (Yoly) and Jessyca (Jessy)! We were all so incredibly happy to finally be in each other's presence again after not having seen each other since last summer. Like I said, I can only fly out to the Dominican Republic once a year, and Jessy and Yoly are unable to visit me in the States because they have not been able to obtain a U.S. Non-Immigrant Visa.

Would you believe that Dominicans have an easier time boarding a very inexpensive flight to Spain—a trip of eight to ten hours—versus getting on a flight to Miami, Florida which is less than ninety minutes away! Jessy, Yoly and I exit the hotel, hop into Jessy's black and red Fiat convertible, and zoom off into the Malecón's busy afternoon traffic. As Jessy easily maneuvers us through the dangerous "no holds barred" traffic, we all begin catching up on everything currently happening in our lives. I love hanging out with Jessy and Yoly because they are both highly intelligent and free-spirited women with the will to live their lives to the fullest. They were both instrumental in helping me improve my Spanish comprehension skills. I was also very helpful to both of them in enhancing their fluency with English.

Next, Jessy began explaining to me that the plan for the day is to go shopping at the Azul Mall, visit a couple of Santo Domingo historical museums, walk through the "Zona Colonial" (Colonial Zone), explore

"Trés Ojos Park" (Three Eyes Park), and tour some of the island's most scenic areas where I can take some really "kool azz" photos. Yoly suddenly turned around from her front passenger seat and screamed, "And then for your big surprise tonight Tré, we are going to finish the night off with you in pure Dominican fashion by going to an "invitation only" pool party where there will be good food, a great DJ, and fantastic people!" I am obviously excited as I ask who is having the party. Yoly and Jessy both tell me that it's a guy by the name of Marco.

Finally, we arrive at the Azul Mall and shop for over two hours! Yoly and Jessy help me find sweet Dominican dark chocolate bars for my family and friends back home in the States. Just in case you didn't know, Dominican chocolate is one of the best-tasting chocolates in the world. Discovering good Dominican chocolate here in the United States is extremely difficult, and that is one of the main reasons why it makes a wonderful personal gift for your loved ones.

Next, Jessy and Yoly help me to pick out a nice form-fitting shirt and a pair of shorts designed by a local fashion designer so I can "stunt and represent" at Marco's pool party. Then I assisted them in choosing "caliente-hot" but classy evening swimwear that would guarantee that the spotlight at the pool party would focus exclusively on them. Yoly and Jessy already had the bodies, the faces, the vibrant personalities— and now they had the two-piece bikini outfits that were going to have everyone turning their heads tonight. After leaving the Azul Mall, we began touring historical areas and popular museums all over the city of Santo Domingo. Everywhere we went I took photos because I love capturing and sharing vivid memories of my adventures with my friends and family. In addition, Jessy and Yoly were excellent hostesses because wherever we went they would always provide me with background knowledge about the D.R. with regard to its people, art, cuisine, and cultural influences.

Next, Jessy drove us over to Trés Ojos Park. If you've never been here to this beautiful island, you have to visit the fantastic National Park because it is indeed one of the Dominican Republic's hidden treasures. The sights are gorgeous and overwhelming—and a photographer's paradise. Trés Ojos Park is a limestone underground cave with a series of lakes that are a fluorescent dark green. Once you walk underground into the cave, you next have to travel by a small boat where a guy pulls on a straight line of rope connected to the other side of the cavern. The sole responsibility of this strong man is to tow you, in a boat that seats eight people, safely to a new area of the cave where you can resume walking once again. As Yoly, Jessy and I were effortlessly being towed in the small boat, I began noticing giant stone encrypted "pictograms" covering high, unreachable areas of the cave. Yoly informed me that the Taíno Native Indians used to live here, and she began teaching me about their history. I always enjoy learning about the unique histories of Native Indians from various parts of the world because I have Native American ancestry on both sides of my family.

For our next adventure, Jessy and Yoly drove me to a surprise area of Santo Domingo that offered a phenomenal aerial view of the entire city as well as the Caribbean Sea. Jessy parked her car on a hillside safe zone and I walked a couple of steps away to take in the incredible view. I begin firing away with my camera while Yoly and Jessy start removing chairs and a giant-sized picnic basket from the trunk of Jessy's Fiat. The divine smell of one of my all-time favorite dishes suddenly hits me. I close my eyes in pure euphoria as I take in the aroma of Jessy's signature Dominican Chicken with stewed vegetables and rice.

Taught by her 85-year-old "abuela" or grandmother, Jessy has perfected the secret recipe by grilling her herb-seasoned chicken first, thereby incorporating a flavorful charcoal-smoke taste and tenderness. Then she finishes off her Dominican Chicken masterpiece by frying it for approximately eight minutes. Overcome with happiness, I start hugging Yoly and Jessy at the same time. The expression on their faces were priceless because I knew that, deep down, they were thrilled to put a smile on my face too.

"Remember your promise, Tré?" Jessy reminded me. "When Yoly and I come to visit you in the States one day, you have to barbecue for us your specialty cuisine of Blackened-Smoked Turkey Wings, Smoked-Grilled Chicken Wings and your Herbal-Buttered Grilled Corn."

"Just hurry up and get your papers so I can throw you two the greatest BBQ Fiesta you've ever had!" I reply overzealously.

Yoly chimes in, "At your barbecue fiesta, are you going to help us find a good hard-working single man, Tré? You know we both want to get married someday."

In response, I wrapped my arms around both Yoly and Jessy. "Don't worry...I will still be single by the time you guys come visit me," I reply flirtatiously. "I have no issues with marrying and being a good husband to both of you!" Jessy and Yoly both yell out in unison, "Tré! Tú estas tannnnnnnn LOCO!" (Tré! You are sooooo CRAZY!) We all started laughing.

Jessy hooked her Ipod into her car's sound system and started playing some mellow tropical music. Relaxing to the beats, I was surprised when Yoly pulled out a bottle of Veuve Clicquot Champagne. She graciously poured everyone a glass. I smile and say, "Gracias!" because I was flattered by both Jessy's and Yoly's genuine acts of kindness. After that we all sat down in our portable lawn chairs, facing the panorama of Santo Domingo. Jessy stared at both of us and with a broad smile on her face as she spoke. "A good friend from America once taught me," she began her toast, "to always share a good meal with a bottle of good champagne in the presence of special friends and family." She paused for a moment before continuing, "Because drinking champagne with these exceptional people is the only way to truly celebrate life's incredible moments of happiness."

We Toast To Happiness...To Our Friendship...And To Life!!

I thank Jessy for her beautiful words as we all began feasting and conversing while offering more champagne toasts in own little world of "paraíso" (paradise). Next we head over to Jessy and Yoly's apartment. We all shower separately and change clothes. Yoly and Jessy dress up in their new evening swimwear outfits and they look "killa-chic!" Having always been taught to take no prisoners when it comes to fashion and style, I made sure that I was "Stuntin" in my new shirt and shorts outfit. Glancing at the time on my smartphone, I tell Jessy and Yoly that I have to get back to my hotel by 12:30 a.m. Feeling disappointed, Yoly asked why I had to leave so early. After explaining the situation, she understood but insisted that she and Jessy still wanted to hang out with me after I finished making my Strawberry Tequila Fusion Drinks.

In addition, Jessy and Yoly offered to come up to my hotel suite to help assist Serena and I so I could finish up faster. I also knew that the main reason why they wanted to help me out was because they were both super fans of my drink creations. Over the years, Yoly and Jessy loved the fact that I always took the time to email them new and exciting cocktail recipes to try out. They also told me repeatedly that they were tired of going to different night clubs in Santo Domingo because none of the local bartenders knew how to impress them with original and exotic drink creations like I could. In fact, every Saturday night they would call me and complain that the only thing that local bartenders could do well was to serve cold El Presidente beer! That being said, I began teaching them how to make their own mixed cocktails.

Just as Jessy sat massaging her long contoured legs with a golden-shimmer lotion, she hit upon a great idea. "Tré, there is a 24-hour grocery store by your hotel," she told me. "So after we leave the pool party, I want to go there and buy some groceries. I'm going to make us a light dinner dish in your hotel room while you guys work on the Strawberry Tequila Fusion Drinks." She was clearly excited as she went on. "We can drink, eat, listen to some cool music and also change clothes before going to a late night Merengue Club."

"Okay," I reply. "And could you please take me to a liquor store before we arrive at Marco's pool party? I want to express my gratitude for his invitation by presenting him with a gift from all of us," I told her.

Yoly became excited. "Tré, is it also because you want to show off one of your latest drink creations?" she asked.

I smile and reply nonchalantly in Spanish: "Perhaps…but I'm only going to tell you if you guys scream my name very loudly right now!" Yoly and Jessy abruptly stop what they're doing and scream, "TRÉ!" as they burst into laughter.

Later, at the liquor store, Jessy waited in the car because she had to make a phone call, while Yoly and I went inside to browse through the rum section of the store. That's when I discovered that the only rum sold in the entire store was Brugal Rum. Made in the D.R., Brugal Rum is one of the world's top tier rums. Very smooth in taste, it enjoys strong support and distribution throughout the Caribbean.

With Yoly's help, I chose Brugal Dark Rum for its superior taste and smoothness. Afterwards, we walked over to the drink mixtures section where I found a non-alcoholic Mango Margarita Mix. Yoly smiled and said, "Hmmmmm! I love mangos, but I never knew that there was a mango mix for drink creations! Tré…I am very curious, and I cannot wait to try out your new mango drink." Yoly hugged me as we walked over to another section of the store where I selected a good quality vodka.

After arriving at Marco's, it took us twenty minutes to find a parking spot because there were cars and motor-scooters lined up everywhere on both sides of the street. Although I was not familiar with the area, the middle class subdivision looked like a nice place. As we were getting out of the car, I could see groups of lively party aficionados walking in the direction of the pulsating high energy beats stemming from a live DJ.

Always the gentleman, I personally escorted Yoly and Jessy to the entrance gate, one on each arm, because I wanted them to look cute and not stumble in their high heels. I was floored as we came closer to the entrance because I could already see three medium-sized, irregularly shaped pools filled with ultra violet blue water that was built on a rustic stone base and surrounded by baby palm trees and a five-foot high waterfall. To the side of the pools was a giant-sized stone house of Spanish Colonial design, ideal for hosting indoor and outdoor special events. I was very impressed with how the whole area was embellished with red-scented candles, eye-catching red flowers and burning Tiki Torches.

As we neared the entrance to the party, I noticed that almost four hundred people dressed in brightly colored swimwear were already here! People of all different shapes and sizes were dancing, talking, swimming, drinking, and making out, while others were just playing it cool as the live DJ kept the music amped up. Just as we enter the party, Jessy and Yoly pause briefly for effect and locked arms with mine. Staring me down with a risqué little grin, Jessy slowly kissed me on my right cheek and Yoly provocatively "lick-kissed" me on my left cheek. Now I'm wearing two "glitter-glow" kisses on both sides of my face.

"We're just letting these 'malditas chicas' know that you are with us tonight!" Jessy says as she winks at me. Then Yoly says in Spanish, "Yeah Tré, you belong to us now!" They both started giggling among themselves as they yelled, "Holaaaa!" and gave each other high fives. Not fazed at all, I reply, "But I like those "malditas chicas" (bad bitches)!

Yoly quickly says, "Good! We can both show you that side too if you can handle us!"

"Girl…Tré just does not know what he has gotten himself into TONIGHT!" Jessy chimed in as they giggle, yell "Holaaa!" and high five each other again.

"Oh, really?" I retort sarcastically and smile. As we strolled around, scoping out the party, it was very obvious that everybody was checking us out. They certainly didn't know who the hell I was. But to see an absolute stranger with two Dominican bellísimas (beautiful women) dressed up in sexy evening outfits on both arms had definitely turned some heads! I could even see people in the pool and on the dance floor looking and stopping what they were doing. And if that wasn't enough, the female DJ began pointing at me with a huge grin on her face as I was escorting Jessy and Yoly around to the hypnotic sounds of her body-grooving trance music. In several instances during our stroll, guys were openly and boldly flirtatious with Jessy and Yoly. But of course my girls kept it moving as they refused to acknowledge the aggressive advances directed towards them.

Walking near the pool area, Yoly sees Marco and calls out to him. Of course he is busy entertaining a group of friends. Marco looked over in our direction, smiled and excused himself as he ran over to embrace and kiss Jessy and Yoly. He shook my hand and said, "You must be the infamous Tré."

"Yes, I am…and thank you for inviting me," I reply.

"Welcome my friend," Marco says. "Anybody who is a friend of Yolanda and Jessyca is a friend of mine, too."

Marco's graciousness reminded me of the gift we'd brought for him. "Jessy, Yoly and I all want to do a celebration toast with you," I told Marco. "So please allow me to create a special drink for you and twenty of your favorite people here at the party that you would like to toast with."

"I see you have the Brugal Rum. I love it!" a flattered Marco commented. He then looked around at Jessy and Yoly and said in Spanish, "Here is a man who respects our Dominican culture!"

I asked Marco to gather his select group of friends and meet me by the DJ's booth in twenty minutes. I also asked him to send over two bartenders to assist me. I then went inside Marco's marble bathroom to wash up before joining Jessy and Yoly at the bar, but suddenly realized that I had forgotten to set up my "Evening of Surprises" with Gigi that I planned to do the next day. I'd been so busy having a blast and hanging out with Jessy and Yoly that it had completely slipped my mind. Checking my phone, I noticed that Gigi hadn't attempted to call me either. I decided to call her from inside the bathroom because of the loud music and party chatter outside. When I dialed Gigi's number she answered on the first ring.

She was just about to call me, she told me, but immediately started complaining that it was too difficult to hear me because of the background noise blaring in her ear. She then asked where I was and I told her that I was at a pool party with a couple of my friends. She then said something but I couldn't understand her because of the loud music. Gigi began to talk louder as she asked me to move to a quieter area so we could hear one another. I indicated that I couldn't, and Gigi attempted to compensate by talking louder and faster into the phone. I could sense the agitation and frustration in Gigi's voice, so I attempted to keep her calm by doing my best to muffle out the loud noise in the background.

"You know that I will be leaving in a couple of days," I said to her, "so let's meet up tomorrow in the early evening since you told me you were going to be free the whole time I'm in Santo Domingo." Gigi replied by asking me to please forgive her for not seeing me today. She explained that she knew today was going to be impossible for us to get together because she had a long day ahead at work, followed by having to rush home to finish packing all of her important items to be shipped to Cape Town in a couple of days.

We continued to talk for a while even though it was still very difficult to hear each other clearly. However, I noticed that whenever Gigi was able to understand me, she was delightfully sweet. But when she couldn't, she became fiery and short-tempered, which was highly unusual for her. I interrupted her complaints about the noise and abruptly gave her the address of where to meet me tomorrow at 5 p.m. sharp. "Where are we going, Tré?" she asked, saying that she was unfamiliar with the area.

"Don't worry," I reassured her. "We are going to have a great time, and the address I just gave you is only a ten-minute taxi ride from your house." Now that she was aware of my plans, Gigi calmed down and became her normal adorable self again as she enthusiastically expressed to me how much she loved surprises. She wished me a good night and told me to enjoy the rest of the evening with my friends.

I hurried over to meet Jessy, Yoly, and my two assistants at the bar. Yoly eagerly asks, "Tré, we are all dying to know what we are going to create with the vodka, Mango Margarita Mix and the Brugal Rum?" Pausing in silence with a big smile on my face, I rub my hands together, embrace both of my lovely friends, then I say to everyone in Spanish: "Tonight we are going to make two variations of one of my favorite party drinks called 'The Angelic Lust'!"

Jessy looked at me wide-eyed and shouted, "Dios mío, Tré! Tú estás tannnn loco bebé!" (Oh my God, Tré! You are so crazy, baby!) Meanwhile Yoly and the two bartenders gazed at me with astonished eyes and expressive body language that said, "Wow!" Opening the bottles of liquor, I explained that "The Angelic Lust" is very easy to make, and more importantly, it is also one of my most anticipated fan favorites.

Jessy, Yoly, and the bartenders set up twenty-five mini-shot glasses on three silver serving trays and began filling four cocktail shakers with cubes of ice. While we were all prepping to execute our "Angelic Lust" cocktails, I tell everyone that the dark rum version of this seductive cocktail was originally taught to me by a gentleman named Doug Nixon. Mr. Nixon was a mentor to me when it came to making "kool kick azz" drinks back in the day when I was working for Major Brands, one of the best liquor distributors in the United States.

Nonetheless, I experimented on my own and came up with another creative version of "The Angelic Lust" by using vodka instead of rum. I also used a variety of tasty mixtures such as strawberry, peach, watermelon, and pineapple-coconut. Here at the pool party, I'd decided to give this drink my unique personal touch. So by the time I'd finished working my particular brand of magic, it wouldn't matter if you were an aficionado of rum or vodka. I grabbed the bottle of Mango Margarita Mix and let everyone take a whiff. At this point the two bartenders were looking at me as if I was a culinary chef on the Food Channel. The aromas permeating the air had them licking their lips in anticipation of a taste. While I was mixing the drinks, I noticed a waiter with a tray of fresh mangos and strawberries. I quickly told Yoly to please go grab the tray and bring it back to me. I then asked my assistants to chop up the mango slices and strawberries into small pieces, after which Jessy placed the colorful fruits into the mini-shot glasses.

Suddenly, one of the bartenders says to me in Spanglish: "This looks and smells incredible…we want to try some too." I reply, "Con mucho placer" (with much pleasure) while thanking my two new friends. Now…with four shakers filled with both versions of the "Angelic Lust," Jessy and Yoly carefully filled twenty-nine mini-shot glasses without spilling one single drop. Then I shout, "IT'S GROUP SHOT TIME!" and we all did a toast.

Everyone eagerly tried both variations. Yoly closed her eyes, grabbed me by the arm, and said, "Delicioso, Tré! I love the smooth mango flavor!" After finishing their shots, the bartenders quickly became an animated duo who kept saying to me that they were rum drinkers but after trying my vodka version, their eyes were definitely open to something new with regard to the world of vodka. Meanwhile Jessy did another shot of the rum version by herself, indicating to me that she didn't know that Brugal Rum could mix so well with other products.

The two bartenders next grabbed the trays filled with our creative masterpieces and began walking towards the DJ booth. Jessy, Yoly, and I followed them, our arms locked. We were now making our grand entrance with the intention of creating a spectacle that would steal everyone's attention. The DJ spotted us walking around the pool area, heading towards her. She turned the music off and got ready to make the announcement over the microphone. In a very sultry voice, she asked the crowd of party fanatics to raise their glasses and get ready to wish Marco a big "Happy Birthday!" with a group toast.

I was caught off guard because Yoly and Jessy had failed to mention to me that the party I was attending was actually Marco's birthday celebration. Taking it in full stride, I was thankful that I had insisted on honoring Marco's invitation with a gift. We arrived at the DJ's booth where Marco was waiting for us along with his twenty closest friends and family members. As the bartenders passed out the drinks, I made sure to personally hand deliver one to the DJ as well. She smiled, blew me a kiss, and said: "Gracias Guapa" (Thank you, Beautiful)!

A tearful Marco grabbed the mic and thanked a massive crowd of almost 500 people for coming out to celebrate with him. Everyone began cheering and singing "Feliz Cumpleaños" while doing multiple happy birthday toasts in Marco's honor. "Fire up the music!" Marco shouted to the DJ after our toast. The DJ screamed over the mic, put on a Trance-Bachata music mix, and everybody went INSANE with invigorated energy!

I didn't know the song, but Yoly and Jessy immediately led me out onto the dance floor. People were dancing EVERYWHERE—including the three swimming pools! Sandwiched between Jessy and Yoly's shapely, rotating hips, I was dancing hard and feeling "charged up" with limitless energy as we danced song after song non-stop! While we were dancing, guys would try to cut in or sometimes ask permission to dance with Jessy and Yoly, but they would refuse all of these unflattering requests by simply pointing at me. After having their hearts crushed and horny little egos deflated, some of these guys automatically made me the target of their rejected frowns. Without a care in the world, I would fire back at them with a look that said: "Whatevá!" or "Come with it!"

That being said, guys were becoming so bold about their chance to meet Jessy and Yoly that a few of them respectfully pulled me aside to ask if either one or the other was my wife, girlfriend, sister or cousin! They also communicated that they were eager to meet whoever was single, while requesting my blessings. If I felt that the guy was on point and sincere, I would let them know that Jessy, Yoly, and I were only good friends. Then I would relay their personal request back to Yoly or Jessy.

In the meantime, my beautiful friends would always smile at me for trying to hook them up. Once the introductions were made, however, I minded my own business. Even if I was curious about what was being said, it was impossible for me to hear because the DJ was now blasting Old School Hip-Hop over free-flowing Merengue beats. In fact, she was damn near driving the entire neighborhood into an uncontrollable frenzy. But usually, after five minutes of conversation, Jessy or Yoly would shut the poor guy down and he would end up walking away nursing his hurt feelings. Somehow they always returned to me and the three of us would resume dancing together.

My Secret Crush

The party was "sizzling" and I love seeing people caught up in the moment. But as I was dancing, I caught the vibe that someone was dancing all up on me! Looking around, I was trying to scope out who was hovering around me and touching my butt! I even began sensing body heat immediately followed by something silky smooth whisking me on the back of the neck.

The dance floor was jam-packed, so it was almost impossible to spot the culprit. But as I looked around again I noticed that Yoly and Jessy were not reacting to anything unusual. They were both in their own little worlds. So without missing a beat, I started dancing backwards with the intention of physically pushing the Mystery Person off of me.

But when I did, nobody was there!

Thinking that I was probably just imagining things, I continued dancing. But then it happened again. This time I knew I felt something or somebody caressing my butt, and immediately concluded that someone had decided to "cop a feel." I quickly executed a dance move by turning myself round in a circular motion. Once again I saw nothing unusual, just 500 or more men and women dancing at a blistering pace. So I continued dancing as if nothing had happened. What else could I do? And then, to my amazement, it happened once again. But there was a difference this time. I could feel someone's warm breath and soft strands of hair massaging the back of my neck. I even saw two hands suddenly reach over my shoulder and quickly disappear as my Mystery Person sensually grind-ed their body into my ass!

Suddenly I began yelling, "Hell the fuck NOOOO! I know that no muthafuckiń guy is trying to freak me down out here in the middle of the dance floor like I'm his chick!" Ironically, nobody could hear what I was saying because my voice was drowned out by the loud music. I looked up to see Yoly and Jessy still dancing with me. They weren't even paying me any attention. So I tell myself that I am going to do a side step towards Jessy and Yoly, turn my body at a 90 degree angle, and unload violently with the full force of my right shoulder and elbow into the freaky person's face and chest in one vicious motion. I was going to put him on the ground in front of everyone at the pool party. Then I was going to proceed to whip his "azz!"

Moving to the pulsating beats of the DJ, I did a side step towards Jessy and Yoly, braced my body, turned around, and immediately called a halt to my actions. It was NOT a guy who was "grindiń" on me in a freaky way. It was a 6-foot 2-inch blonde Dominicana goddess decked out in high heels and wearing a chic yellow summer dress! Her skin tone was cinnamon-kissed by the tropical sun, her eyes were aqua blue, and her lips were peachy and lush. I stared into her eyes in awe as she flirtatiously began dancing in a back-stepping motion toward her group of friends comprised of five girls and six guys who were talking, smoking, and drinking in the middle of the dance floor. I thought contritely to myself: She was just trying to have a good time on the dance floor, but none of her friends wanted to dance with her. So she decided to dance with me.

Then Yoly grabbed me by the arm and I resumed dancing with her and Jessy. Two minutes later I detected a pleasurable fragrance fondling my olfactory senses, followed by someone dancing seductively in the area of my lower torso. This time I got with the program. I moved in closer, backing it up butt first, and felt my blonde cutie all over me. She definitely obliged by pulling me in even closer. Let's just say that we were absolutely giving each other what we both wanted. I had no problem sharing the "azz-sets" with my new dance partner as the DJ continued to mix up her "killa" beats. By now I had a strong desire to have some face time with this bold Dominicana, so I turned round in perfect rhythm to the DJ's pulsating beats, but my free-spirited cutie coquettishly retreated to rejoin her non-dancing, boring friends. I suspected that one of the guys in the group had to be her boyfriend.

Once again I'm going at it with Jessy and Yoly on the dance floor when I began to feel the presence of my blonde goddess. This time Yoly and Jessy noticed her and started smiling. Just then the music shifted to a slower pace, giving people a chance to catch their breath while the DJ began talking to the crowd over the mic. "Oh my God, Tré! I think you have just found your future Dominicana wife! That girl was all over you, and she even had a cute little naughty smile on her face the whole time," Yoly and Jessy said almost in unison.

"Como?" I feigned surprise as I turned around to see my Dominican cutie talking with her group of friends.

"Tré…You should go talk to her! Don't you think she's pretty?" Jessy said excitedly.

"Yes! But I believe that she is with her man," I say in Spanish.

"No, I don't think so, Tré," Yoly quickly says. "I think that she likes you, and you should say something to her before it's too late."

"But what if she doesn't understand me because of my Spanish? Or what if she doesn't sabe Inglés?" I reply.

Yoly pondered my questions for a milli-second, grabbed Jessy's hand, and promptly announced: "We will go talk to her and see if she is single."

Jessy inconspicuously got her attention. She smiled and walked over to Jessy and Yoly. All three then walked away from me, went into a huddle, and began having a private conversation. As they were talking, all three would point or gesture toward me from time to time. Soon they were staring and smiling at me too. It seemed like I was waiting for an eternity. But all I could do was act as if I was unfazed by maintaining a cool and urbane aura about myself. But on the inside, I felt like I was being tortured because I was wondering what the hell they were saying about me. I was also dying to know if the blonde bombshell had a man or if she was interested in meeting me.

After ten minutes of feeling like a nude statue on display for their exclusive examination and pleasure, I saw everyone exchanging phone numbers, hugging and saying their farewells. I also noticed that my Dominican cutie started "sashaying" towards me, but I was still unsure about what she was going to say or how she was going to react. A couple of seconds later she said, "Hello, Tré" in English with a very sexy Dominican accent, all while shooting a warm thrill through me with her radiant eyes and beautiful smile.

"Hooolaaaa!" I responded expressively as she abruptly passed me by and rejoined her friends. Yoly and Jessy then walked over to me. "You were right, Tré. She has a boyfriend," Yoly said.

"I knew it," I replied, shaking my head. "But what were you guys talking about for so long?"

"Just girl talk!" Yoly said innocently. "We were mainly talking about you, Tré!"

"Yes…she wanted to know ALL about you, but she is a faithful girl to her boyfriend," Jessy chimed in. "Yoly and I both like her because she is really a nice person."

"What's her name?" I asked out of sheer curiosity.

"Lea," Jessy replied.

I asked why everyone was exchanging phone numbers.

"Ohhh! Lea wants to hang out with us sometime when she is not spending time with her boyfriend," Yoly confided. "We also complimented her on her outfit, and she told us that her parents own a clothing boutique and that she will be happy to give both Jessy and I store discounts."

Jessy hugged me and said, "When Lea travels to the United States one day, you will be the first person she calls." Slightly perplexed, I reply, "How is she going to call me when she didn't ask me for my phone number?" Jessy grabbed both sides of my face with her hands and playfully yells: "Come on, Tré. Give us some credit. We gave Lea your phone number, silly!"

I humorously yell out in Spanish: "Muuuuuuuuy bien! I will be ready and waiting for her too!" Then we all explode with laughter. Lea glanced in our direction and gave me the thumbs up. I smiled back at her and she blew me a kiss.

Just in case you were wondering, Lea did unexpectedly reach out to me eight months later. Her first series of messages were energetic and bubbly. She informed me that she had just received a temporary visa to visit the States. More importantly, she confided that within three days she would be in the U.S. visiting relatives in Florida and NYC while touring several colleges she was considering for work on her Master's Degree. She also urged me to make arrangements for us to get together before her visa expired. Lea sent me several other messages that were thoughtful, cheerful, and sometimes a little anxious because she had already arrived in the States and wanted me to know that she was willing to fly out to any city to meet me or that perhaps I could meet her in New York because she was looking forward to seeing me.

Lea's final communication to me was a very long, sad, and upset message asking why I wasn't responding and why my phone was constantly going to voicemail. She was very emotional as she explained that at first she thought she had dialed the wrong phone number, but then she checked with Jessy and Yoly several times to verify that the number was the correct one. She also accused me of being very rude for not responding to her. Lea was almost in tears as she recorded her message. "Tré…" she said, "your friends Yoly and Jessy are always telling me that you are a good person that I should really try to get to know…." But then she teared up at the end of her message as she told me she was at the airport, preparing to head back home to Santo Domingo.

I still regret the irony of this extremely unfortunate and embarrassing situation to this day. I was in Costa Rica doing an Ecotourism Tour for the entire time that Lea was in the States. Therefore, I wasn't able to receive any of her voicemails until I landed in Dallas-Fort Worth, Texas at three o'clock in the morning. I listened to them while waiting in a long line of people being processed through U.S. Customs.

After clearing Customs, I immediately put in a call to her at about 4 a.m. A sleepy Lea picked up the phone and I apologized with all my heart. Lea was still a bit upset, but thrilled that I had called her to apologize. She listened attentively to me as I put forth my best effort to communicate with her in her native language because she only spoke intermediate level English. She told me that she had just arrived in Santo Domingo earlier that night. As gently as I could, I expressed to her that she should have told me that she was coming so we could have made plans to meet without having any issues. In a more enthusiastic and cheerful voice, Lea confessed that she was only trying to surprise me, but that she now realized her honest mistake. After talking the situation over calmly, I made her a promise. "Lea…the next time you travel back to the States, we are going to meet, okay?" I assured her. "I promise I will show you around…and when I come back to Santo Domingo next year, you will have to show me your city." She responded with an enthusiastic, "Sí." Then she thanked me and we said our goodbyes.

Back at Marco's epic birthday bash, Jessy grabbed me by my arm and said: "Tré, we can go now. I want to stop by the store so I can cook us a light evening meal to eat while you work on your Fusion Drinks. Then we will all go back out to the Merengue Club." I followed her lead. As we exited the premises I wrapped my arms around Jessy and Yoly's shoulders. Yoly turned to look at me. "Tré, you owe us an incredible time when we come to visit you in the States," she told me.

"Yes, I know," I answered back in Spanish with a broad grin on my face.

Ain't Nothin' But a Merengue Party!

It's 11:30 p.m. and Jessy, Yoly, and I are wandering around a 24-hour neighborhood grocery store. We head over to the fresh meat and fish department as Jessy asks me if my hotel room is furnished with a kitchen stove and cooking utensils. I enthusiastically reply yes, then go on to explain to both of them that my executive suite is state of the art. Yoly smiles as Jessy tells the butcher to package up an order of fish fillets to go.

"Tré, Jessy is going to make her famous Fish Fritter 'Morditos'

(Small Bites)!" Yoly says excitedly. The Morditos is one of Jessy's best dishes, personally taught to her by her grandmother, and it tastes soooo delicious! Jessy next directs Yoly and me to pick up the necessary ingredients for her tasty treat. We do as instructed, and I even scoop up a couple of bottles of chilled Moscato. I explain to Yoly that Moscato goes well with fish, and it is also the perfect dessert drink after an appetizing light meal.

Yoly and I join Jessy at the check-out counter where they were about to pay for all of our groceries, but I insisted on paying. It was the only respectful thing to do on my part because I was feeling blessed and thankful for everything that they'd done for me. Especially after our epic day of fun and excitement. And the night was still young!

We arrived back at my hotel at around 12:15 in the morning. The lobby was empty except for a few people lounging around and talking. I didn't see Serena anywhere, so we took the elevator up to the Executive Suite level. As Yoly, Jessy, and I arrived at my floor, Jessy yells out: "Tré! You are so lucky to be in such a great hotel!" We were all surprised at how loudly her voice echoed down the hallways before she could even finish her statement. Yoly turned quickly to shush her. "Quiet girl!" she told Jessy. "People are probably sleeping." A shocked Jessy immediately began apologizing multiple times.

"It's really okay," I interrupted her. "Don't worry about it because ten of the twelve suites on this floor are unoccupied, except for me and a newlywed couple celebrating their honeymoon night. And I seriously doubt that they are asleep right now if you know what I mean." I punctuated my statement with a naughty sexual gesture. Jessy and Yoly erupted in hysterical laughter. Then Jessy says: "Tré, tú estas tan loco Papi!" (Tré, you are so crazy, Cool Daddy!) Not to be outdone, Yoly adds, "Yes, they are definitely making a honeymoon baby!"

Following a good laugh, I led the girls to my section of the floor. All of a sudden, we started hearing Merengue music playing. Yoly says, "Somebody is having a party."

"The music must be coming from a new couple on the floor, or maybe it's the newlyweds getting it on?" I reply.

"Tré…" Jessy interrupts me, "who makes love to fast-tempo Merengue? The guy will climax too quickly or pass out from a heart attack if he's dealing with a Dominicana in bed, especially when the beats are never-ending 'picante-caliente' (spicy-hot) like this song."

"Poooor favor, noooo" (Pleassseee, noooo)! Yoly screamed because Jessy was making us laugh so hard that they dropped their bags of groceries. Recouping our sanity, we continued walking in the direction of the Merengue musical source. As we turned a corner, I began seeing light beams shooting through a partially open door. "What the hell...?" I say as I drop my bag of groceries.

"What's wrong?" Jessy asks.

"That's my room!" I reply.

Jessy and Yoly exchange concerned looks as they ask in unison: "Who is in your room, Tré?"

"I don't know...but wait here!"

I grab one of the bottles of Moscato from Yoly's grocery bag, and like a "stealth assassin" I quietly maneuver my way through the open door, ready to "bang!" But to my wonderful surprise, I see the lovely Serena washing bowls of fresh strawberries in the kitchen sink. Serena didn't see me because her back was turned as she grooved to the sounds of upbeat Merengue music. My frown immediately evaporated into a smile as I placed the bottle of Moscato on the dining room table.

I was overcome with excitement because Serena and her husband had delivered on everything they had promised. Serena already had the dining room table laid out with Fusion Drink Jars; bottles of 1800 Coconut and 1800 Silver Tequila; Strawberry Liqueur; sparkling apple cider; Strawberry Daiquiri Mix; and they even somehow found crazy custom-design ice trays so I could make my "Sparkling Strawberry Cider-Apple Fun Cubes." A few seconds later, Yoly and Jessy burst into the room ready to fight. Then they saw that I was okay.

Meanwhile Serena heard us talking and turned to greet us with a warm and infectious smile as she turned the music off.

"Sounds like you're having a fiesta, Serena," I say to her.

"I was...and all by myself, Tré," she says, placing her hands on her hips. "Nobody else is on this floor, so it's party time for me."

"I heard that!" I chuckle. "I'm with you, Serena!"

She began to reflect for a brief moment. "Besides, I seriously doubt that the newlyweds are sleeping on their honeymoon night. God knows that my honeymoon night turned into three days straight of intense, suffocating passion! No sleep and no contact with anybody! Me and my husband just couldn't get enough of one another!" We all started laughing, whistling, and hollering!

Serena then told me that she'd come early expecting to find me in my suite. "I hope that you don't mind that I started washing the strawberries?" she said politely.

"Nooo!" I reply as we greet each other with a hug and kisses on the cheeks. Serena also volunteered that she could stay as long as I needed her to because another Night Manager was covering for her. I thank Serena and then pause to properly introduce her to my two good friends. Almost immediately, Jessy and Yoly began checking out my hotel suite. They loved the combo kitchen and dining area, the marble floors in the bedroom, the spacious Jacuzzi in the living room, and they positively went insane over the walkout patio that overlooked the Malecón and the Caribbean Sea shimmering under a full moon.

I grabbed my notes and started organizing all the liquor products on the dining table. Upon my request, Serena, Jessy, and Yoly gathered around me. I tell them to pay close attention so they can learn, up close and personally, how to make the "Strawberry Passionate Kiss Euphoria." I also explain that I want them to be able to create this exotic cocktail all on their own so they can one day present it as a special gift to their close family and friends. I also tell my new "mad scientists" about the world of cocktails and that my father was the one who showed me how to make this terrific Fusion Drink. However, I later experimented and added my own unique creative touch.

I went further to explain that the "Strawberry Passionate Kiss Euphoria" can be utilized to make small shots or as a cocktail because it is the ultimate party libation that can fire up party people to "go hard" when they're celebrating. Jessy then excused herself in order to start cooking up her special dish for all of us to enjoy. "Thank you so much," Serena said, "because I haven't eaten my lunch yet." Yoly and Jessy shriek, "Lunch?"

"Yes, because I work nights!" Serena explained.

I cracked open a bottle of Moscato, put the other bottle in the refrigerator, and grabbed four wine glasses from the kitchen. Serena filled our glasses, using the entire bottle of Moscato. Jessy came out of the kitchen to join us, an apron wrapped around her waist. We then do a group toast to good health, to new friends, and to making it a fun night of drinking and dining on great food.

"Salud!" Everyone yells out as we down our last toast and Jessy returns to the kitchen to start cleaning the fish and peeling vegetables. She turns on the stove's top burner and coats a cast iron skillet with cooking oil as Serena flips through the music channels on the flat screen TV until she finds a station featuring Merengue music videos. Thanks to Jessy and Serena, our Merengue party was starting to heat up!

Suddenly I felt inspired to open up all of the draperies to give everyone a marvelous view of the moonlight raining down magical beams all over the Malecón and on the Caribbean Sea. I also began lighting scented candles located throughout the suite. I explained to the ladies that flaming scented candles put me in a creative mood when I am designing Special Events, writing scripts, or concocting new drink recipes. Serena, Yoly, and Jessy concurred as they indicated to me that they needed to go to a creative space as well. After we finished washing and drying the strawberries, Yoly and I cut one bowl into perfect halves, leaving the remainder uncut.

Noticing that I had been given two blenders for my personal use, courtesy of Serena, I tell her and Yoly that we are now going to make multiple trays of "Sparkling Strawberry Cider-Apple Fun Cubes." Yoly and Serena looked at me as if I was from planet Jupiter before they both started telling me that they had never heard of this before. I explained to them that the "Sparkling Strawberry Cider-Apple Fun Cubes" were a creation from my "Madd Diabolical Creative Mind" because I want all of my cocktails to stand out with a signature of originality and ecstasy.

As instructed, Serena and Yoly fill each blender one-half full with sparkling apple cider. Then they add another one-quarter of strawberries so that both blenders are three-quarters full. I pushed the puree button and the blenders roared like charging lionesses for five minutes straight, creating a glistening, valentine-red mixture. I give Serena and Yoly a sample taste. Their eyes roll back in their heads with delight.

"Tré! I can't believe how magnificent this tastes!" Serena shakes her head as she snaps out of her blissful spell.

"I know," I quipped, winking at her.

Next, we grab all of the Crazy Design Ice Trays and I instruct my two eager protégés to fill them up. Not one to leave anybody hanging, I catered a sample to Jessy in the kitchen while she was seasoning her

Fish Fritter "Morditos" and dancing to the Merengue videos blaring on all TV screens. In the end, we made sixteen trays of sparkling cubes and put them in the freezer. Afterwards, we filled all four fusion drink jars one-half full with both whole and cut strawberry halves. All of sudden, a famous new Merengue song comes on. Jessy quickly washes her hands and hollers out: "Turn up the music! Esa es mi Canción!" (That's my song!)

Jessy, Yoly, and Serena all started clapping and shouting Spanish words that I didn't understand as they began dancing around the giant TV screen which was crowded with people dancing and having a blast! Jessy darts over to me, grabs my hand, and yells: "Come on Tré! We are going to teach you how to dance the Merengue the Dominican way, so you don't dance like an American gringo no more!"

"Let's go! Show me ALL your moves, Bebé!" I said confidently as I took her up on her challenge. Suddenly, I found myself boldly dancing with all three "chicas" at once. I love up-tempo Merengue because it's fast and free flowing. Even though I didn't know or understand all the correct moves, I felt very comfortable doing *my* thing. The scene reminded me of my college days when I was living in "Da Chi" (Chicago). One night I decided to go to my first Techno-Trance Club with a group of my international friends. Later that evening, I met a tall, very attractive red-head named Heather who made it her mission to teach me how to dance by wearing my "azz" out on the dance floor. We danced till the club closed at 5:30 in the morning!

After that experience, I was always "game" to "body shake" with the best of them. It makes no difference whether I'm totally clueless or not about the proper steps for a particular dance technique because I always "do it strong!" As we all danced around the living room floor (while watching the dancers in the music video at the same time), I was gradually able to connect to the rhythm and movement of the song. Following their lead, my ears instantly became addicted to the hypnotic and pulsating beats.

The song that was playing was right up my alley because I love grooving to frenetic, upbeat music. While we were dancing, everyone was laughing and shouting "dance-off" challenges to one another. This particular Merengue song went on for fifteen minutes! When it finally ended, we immediately began swigging down the rest of the Moscato to quench our thirst. Taking a couple of minutes to cool down, Jessy resumed grilling her fish treats.

I tell Yoly and Serena that we are going to make a total of four "Strawberry Passionate Kiss Euphoria" Fusion Drinks (three drinks made with the 1800 Coconut Tequila and one using the 1800 Silver Tequila). I instruct Yoly to pour two bottles of 1800 Silver Tequila into fusion jar number one, and to also start mixing and stirring the fresh strawberries already placed inside the jar. I then ask Serena to repeat the same process by pouring the 1800 Coconut Tequila in the remaining three fusion jars. I explained to my helpers that normally I would allow the fresh strawberries and Tequila to steep and blend for three days at room temperature before adding the Strawberry Liqueur and Strawberry Margarita Mix. But because of my short stay in the D.R., I decided to add them to all four fusion jars immediately.

As Serena and Yoly diligently performed their duties by stirring the drink concoctions, they almost lost it. The strawberry aroma was absolutely exquisite! I reminded them once again that it is very important to always celebrate good times with good people. They acknowledge my heartfelt words as they start filling two cocktail shakers with the "Sparkling Strawberry Cider-Apple Fun Cubes." I next pour and separate both versions of my "Strawberry Passionate Kiss Euphoria" into individual cocktail shakers. Yoly and Serena started shaking them up while I line up six mini-shot glasses. Once chilled, they fill up the shot glasses. My excited helpers quickly devour both versions of the cocktail. "My God, Tré. We did it! We did it!" they shout as they assault me with hugs!

"We did it, Tré! We did it! This is sooooo GOOD! Your father would be proud! Incredible!" Serena continued to shout. Suddenly, I heard Jessy's pleading voice coming from the kitchen. "Come on guys… don't forget to take care of the chef!" she shouts out to us. Never one to slight a good friend, I grab Jessy's two shots and teasingly place them on the kitchen counter for her to see as she expertly performed her duties. It was truly magnificent to see her hard at work creating her food masterpiece. By this time she had the entire suite smelling like a gourmet's Utopia. I hand delivered a shot to her rosy lips as she turned to me. "Yaaaaaa! Ya! Ya! Ya! Ya! Ya! Ya! That's good! Ohhhh, Tré…yes, the coconut mixes divinely with the strawberry!" Acknowledging Jessy's positive comment, I personally hand delivered the second version to her smiling lips. Jessy's eyes blinked several times as she murmured: "Hmmmmm! That's good, too!"

She paused, looked at me with a twinkle in her eyes, and whispered: "Sí…Dios….sííííí!" (Yes…God….yessss!) With a grin on my face, I ask, "What's wrong?" Jessy takes her apron off and says, "Tré…you just don't know what your drinks are doing to my body right now. My body feels so, so, so good! And I also feel so "caliente" (hot) on the inside!" She says with a sensuous sigh. I lean my head slightly toward her and calmly say: "I don't know what you are talking about Jessy." Then with a devilish look on my face, I finish with a warning: "Never underestimate the power of my drinks."

Jessy looked at me, and the next thing I know, another famous Merengue song comes on. I met Jessy and Yoly on the floor in front of the TV screen and we cranked up the music full blast. Once again we started doing it hard. All at once I started to feel a little nervous as I became aware of a situation at the door. I quickly alerted Yoly and Jessy, who were both totally oblivious that Serena was now at the front door talking to security. We all stopped dancing because we were very curious about what was happening. Then Serena escorted a distinguished-looking older man into the room.

He placed his walkie-talkie on the dining table, Serena took him by the hand, and they walked towards us animated with positive energy. Then suddenly they started dancing. Jessy, Yoly, and I all felt relieved as we got back into our zone. But I have to admit that our new guest was putting us all to shame. The Distinguished Old Gentleman's moves were sensational as he executed intricate Merengue steps with youthful vitality and precision. He easily guided Serena through a series of smooth Merengue transitions that were suave, graceful, and classy—even if they were borderline kinky! It was an unbelievable performance too exquisite to describe! As I moved nearer the couple in order to view The Old Gentleman's class act up closer, I began to notice how gracefully he was aging. He was handsome, well-built, full of life, and well-groomed. I thought to myself that he must have been handpicked by God himself to become a dancer! Don't get me wrong, Serena was a magnificent dancer as well, but this old guy was giving her everything she could handle and more!

Yoly, Jessy, and I had to stop dancing because Serena and the Distinguished Gentleman were going so hard that they literally retired us from the dance floor! The older man's face revealed nothing but an easy and tranquil smile, while Serena was starting to get a bit winded. Thrilled by the spectacle in front of us, Yoly, Jessy, and I started clapping, cheering, and yelling "Va! Va! Va!" (Go! Go! Go!) at the top of our lungs. After dancing for what seemed like an eternity, Serena stopped for a time out because she was just plain out of gas. The Distinguished Old Gentleman bowed his head and kissed Serena's hands as she kissed him on the cheeks. The old guy winked at me, smiled, and extended his fist toward me for a friendly "pound."

Then, very suavely, he focused his attention on Jessy and Yoly as he bowed to them, kissed their hands, and flashed a smile that showcased his perfect white teeth. Enamored by his charm, Jessy and Yoly both blushed giddily, saying: "How cute! He is soooo romantic." Like a Smooth Latino 007, the Distinguished Gentleman guided Jessy and Yoly by their waists to the patio balcony. Still in the mood for fun, Jessy fanned herself with her hands and said: "My God Yoly! What is he about to do to us?"

"I don't know…I don't know!" Yoly replied enthusiastically.

The next thing I know, Serena and I are watching Jessy, Yoly and this Dominican assassin dancing The Merengue out under the stars glistening down from above the outdoor balcony. While Serena and I could see by Jessy and Yoly's faces that they were giving their all to the dance, this 70-year-old man showed no form of tension or fatigue on his face—only a blissful smile. He was literally attacking both of them with an entire arsenal of close-quarter Merengue movements that frankly seemed unreal. "I can't believe what this guy is doing!" Serena and I kept repeating to each other. "This is crazy! Not even in their wildest dreams would anyone ever believe what we are seeing!"

It was a stunning visual masterpiece as the Distinguished Gentleman stepped back in time to become a 25-year-old BEAST right in front of our eyes. As the music came to an end 20 minutes later, he bowed coolly to his young dance partners who were both huffing and puffing for air. Then he locked arms with Yoly and Jessy and escorted them back inside the suite. At that point, Serena walked over and said: "Everyone, I want to present to you my very dear friend…Señor Fernando." Though confident and fearless on the dance floor, Señor Fernando appeared to be a very down-to-earth and humble man as he smiled, nodded his head, and looked down at the floor while Serena was introducing him.

Serena hugged her good friend as she said to us in Spanish: "Mr. Fernando is 72-years-young and I adore this man soooo much with all my heart, including his beautiful 50-year-old wife!" That being said, everyone laughed and cheered. Suddenly, Jessy said in a loud animated voice: "Señor Fernando, I am so impressed because you are the best dancer that I have *ever* danced with!" Meanwhile Yoly began playfully checking him out with her seductive eyes, but he flashed a shy smile and waved her off.

Serena giggled as she told us that her good friend and his young wife owned a very prestigious dance studio here in Santa Domingo. We also learned that they are professional dancers who travel all over the Caribbean because they love to teach dance. "Me and my husband take dance classes with them two times a week," Serena confided. After Mr. Fernando generously passed out business cards to us that included five free dance lessons, I shook his hand and Yoly and Jessy attacked him with big warm hugs and kisses as Serena escorted him to the front door.

"I'm tired…I want to relax my feet and thighs because they are sore," Yoly said as she turned on the Jacuzzi.

"Girl, save me a spot. I'm going to join you," Serena quickly responded.

I tell them to make themselves comfortable. In the meantime, Yoly goes to wash up in the bathroom and walks back into the living room with a towel wrapped around her. Then she hopped into the Jacuzzi and started exhaling with pure relief. Jessy is hard at work in the kitchen once again and she yells out to us: "Give me ten more minutes to finish cooking our meal!"

"Hurry up! We're ready to eat!" Yoly, Serena, and I all shout back sarcastically.

Serena changed the Music Channel and tuned in to some soothing Latin jazz. Then she sat on the edge of the Jacuzzi with her skirt slightly raised and allowed the rushing water to massage her feet, calves, and thighs. While the ladies relaxed, I decided to finish up with the Strawberry Tequila Fusion Drinks. After performing a taste test, I immediately began to smile. All I could think about now was the ecstatic smile on Gigi's face once she tasted my special gift. I was sure she would cherish my surprise treat so much that she would literally fall to pieces. It also gave me a great feeling inside to make Gigi feel extra special because of our special friendship over the years.

Moments after tasting Gigi's special drink, I felt fired up in anticipation of tomorrow's rendezvous with her. I was going to astonish her by giving her the ultimate female fantasy: a relaxing early evening spa treatment followed by a gourmet dinner at one of Santo Domingo's best restaurants. I planned to finish off the night at a popular Merengue club with drinks, dancing, and stimulating conversation. My priority for our special night was to make it an epic and unforgettable evening for both of us since I didn't know when we would have the chance to see each other again. I thought back to something my mom and dad would always say to me when I was growing up: "Enjoy every day like it's your birthday, and always celebrate life's special moments because you never know when the good times may come to an end!"

Jessy woke me up suddenly from my vivid daydream about my special night with Gigi by asking me to help her set the dining table out on the balcony. I did as I was instructed with only the moon and starlight overhead to keep me company, then called out to Yoly and Serena that it was time to eat. Displaying my best manners, I seated them in their respective patio chairs. Finally, our five-star chef appeared with her Blackened-Seasoned Fish Fritter "Morditos" and a giant Dominican vegetable salad. Serena, Yoly, and I go "Ouuuuuu!" and "Ahhhhhh!" as we take in the mouth-watering aromas of Jessy's food. Jessy placed our meal on the table and I seated her with a gentlemanly flourish. I next poured everyone a glass of chilled Moscato. After giving thanks to God for bringing us all together, we did a group toast and proceeded to enjoy our meal over warm and relaxed conversation.

Yoly, Serena, Jessy and I talked intimately about love, happiness, and family, as well as the passions that drive us to live our lives to the fullest. I hadn't felt so happy and blessed in a very long time. I was also feeling a special appreciation in being around authentic and endearing friends who didn't care about your profession or financial status or how you were viewed by other people. Jessy, Serena, and Yoly only cared about getting to know the real me and enjoying my company as a person.

At the conclusion of Jessy's fantastic meal, I poured everyone another round of shots of both versions of the "Strawberry Passionate Kiss Euphoria." We all swore that the blend was so smooth and tasty that none of us could detect any traces of alcohol. The Strawberry Tequila now tasted more and more like a mouth-watering piece of strawberry candy. We had all just turned our attention to the sun rising gloriously over the Caribbean Sea when an unnerved Serena glanced at her watch and cried out in Spanglish, "Oh, my God! Oh My God! It's 4 o'clock in the morning! I need to go! I have to get back to work! The time flew by too quickly and I lost track of time!"

Jessy and Yoly also began scrambling inside the suite for their belongings. Yoly looked at Jessy and said: "We have to hurry home, shower, change clothes and go straight to work, chica!"

"I can't believe that we have been talking for hours!" Jessy replied, shaking her head in disbelief.

Meanwhile Serena gave me a quick goodbye hug and told me that she would call me later to discuss making arrangements to pick up her Fusion Jars of Strawberry Tequila. The ladies all exchanged goodbyes, and Serena gave Jessy and Yoly her business card and told them to call her if they ever needed a good price on a room at the hotel. Just as Yoly and Jessy were about to walk out the door, I asked them to please stay for a couple more minutes. I promptly grab an empty bottle of the 1800 Coconut off the dining table and began filling it three-quarters full by using all three Fusion Drink Jars filled with the 1800 Coconut version of the "Strawberry Passionate Kiss Euphoria". Moving swiftly, I placed my camera on a tripod, set the timer, and focused on the sun hovering just above the rushing waves of the Caribbean Sea. Yoly, Jessy and I then do a series of crazy glamour shots. But even as we were posing, I could sense that my two beautiful friends were feeling a little sad because they began tearing up as they hugged me super tight!

I've had to say goodbye to many close friends from different parts of the world over the years, but it never gets any easier. Especially when you know that you won't see that person again for a very long time, or in some cases, ever again! After taking a series of outrageously entertaining photos, I walked Jessy and Yoly to the front door. They both told me they were going to miss me and promised they would one day visit me in the States. Then they rushed off towards the beeping elevator.

The Newlywed Honeymooners

Feeling super-juiced with energy, I showered, dressed and decided that I wanted to stroll around the city as well as get several more shots of the sunrise. I grabbed my 35mm camera and headed down to the lobby which was busy with new arrivals and other guests getting ready to go on their tours. As I strolled toward the front exit, I heard a friendly female voice say: "Good morning, Gringo American friend."

I turned round in bewilderment because I didn't know if this mysterious person was talking to me or not. My eyes scanned the hotel lobby until I saw a jovial, good-looking couple in their mid-twenties, smiling and waving at me. Absolutely puzzled, I pointed to myself and asked, "Are you talking to me?" I had no clue as to who they might be. "Yes, you my friend," the man said enthusiastically in English. I slowly approached the harmless looking couple with a smile on my face while desperately scrolling through my Rolodex of memories, trying to figure out if I actually knew them from somewhere.

Being me, I respect everyone, so I happily greeted the cheerful couple in Spanish. "Good morning," I said enthusiastically, "How are you? My name is Tré." Their response was not the one I was anticipating. They looked at me strangely as they talked amongst themselves for a full minute before the inquisitive man repeated my name. "Yes, my name is Tré," I said slowly in Spanish, making sure to articulate my words clearly. Now the young woman turned to me with a confused look as she said: "No…no…that can't be, dear. You say that your name is Tré?" Chuckling slightly now, I answer, "Yes!" Then I asked them what their names were. "My name is Sofia and this is my husband Oscar," the curious young woman replied as I shook hands with them. "Sofia, you have a very beautiful name and it's a pleasure to meet you too, Oscar," I said, smiling. "And as I said, my name is Tré."

Sofia and Oscar continued to stare at me before turning toward each other to engage in animated conversation. I overheard Sofia saying clearly to Oscar, "That poor kid! But why…?"

"No…no, Sofia, you can't ask him that," Oscar asserted. "He might be offended!"

At this point I interrupted them. "Ask me what? I can understand you."

Looking slightly ashamed, Sofia asked timidly, "Why did your parents name you after the number three? Nobody names their kids after a number like five, thirty-nine, or one hundred and twenty-six or a thousand! I don't understand this!"

I started laughing as Sophia and Oscar shot me a frustrated look that said: "What the hell, man?" I then told them that my actual name is Elson C. Williams III, but everyone calls me Tré because I am in fact number three! (The word "Tré" translates into the number three in Spanish, Portuguese, Italian and almost all other Romance Languages.)

Now, having finally grasped the concept that Tré is my nick name, Sofia and Oscar both exhaled, "Ahhhhhhhh!" as they started laughing. I also confessed that I am used to Romance Language speakers asking me this particular question.

"How did you know that I was American? Have we met?" I asked them.

"No," Sofia replied, looking at Oscar as they both started giggling, "but we've seen you before, Tré."

"Where did you guys see me?" I asked eagerly, overcome by curiosity.

Sofia's smile began to widen even more. "Last night…at your suite," she said.

"Como" (What)? I responded with surprise, a grin on my face.

"You were having a Grande Fiesta (Big Party) all night long that lasted into the early morning with three beautiful Dominican women, including the Night Manager of the hotel," a highly impressed Oscar asserted, pointing toward the front desk area. We all looked in that direction to see Serena checking in a long line of international hotel guests. Oscar continued: "You guys celebrated better and crazier than we did on our honeymoon night! Sofia and I should have come over for drinks."

Sofia shrieked, "Amor…don't say that!" Then she playfully hit Oscar on his arm. They eyed each other mischievously and giggled once again. Then they embraced while smiling at me. Sofia was finding it difficult to contain her laughter. "Please ignore my husband, Tré. But yes…we were both wondering what was going on because around 11 p.m. we saw hotel staff members constantly bringing up trays of strawberries, liquor, and cooking appliances to your room. Later, we heard the Night Manager singing and playing Merengue music because she left your front door open. Then Oscar and I heard you celebrating with your two other friends and making loud noises with electric blenders!"

All I could do was quietly listen in amazement as Oscar and Sofia tag teamed me in an effort to solicit more information about what was actually happening inside my hotel suite. I honestly was starting to feel bad because I didn't know if Serena, Yoly, Jessy, and I had actually ruined their honeymoon night. I feel like your honeymoon night should be that one magical time that happens at least once in your life! Understandably, a newlywed couple would want to have a perfect night of pure ecstasy and passionate lovemaking in a nice, quiet, romantic haven. Had we spoiled it for them? I desperately hoped not.

Interrupting my train of thought, Oscar chimed in, "We also heard the Jacuzzi, laughing, clapping, and a live tropical Merengue concert. It was as if Sofia and I were at a club." Oscar now started laughing again as he went on to tell me that he could even smell a delicious meal being prepared. Sofia closed her eyes for a second as she said excitedly: "Wow! That food smelled soooo good! And what about that cute old man, Oscar?"

"Yes…the dancing old man!" Oscar quickly replied. Just then Sofia interrupted. "Who was the old guy doing Merengue dancing on the patio balcony with those two attractive girls? It was as if he was putting on a show for all the Caribbean to see!" Sofia gushed excitedly. But all the time they were talking, I was thinking to myself: "It was your honeymoon night. You guys should have been "getting it in" and not worrying about what other people were doing. I know what I am going to be doing on my honeymoon night, and I guarantee you that I won't be focused on the outside world!"

Attempting to change the focus of this uncomfortable conversation, I say to Sofia and Oscar: "I feel terrible and I hope that I didn't ruin your special evening. Please allow me to take you guys out for breakfast right now. Have you eaten already?"

Oscar tells me that he and his wife will be happy to join me. I asked them to hold tight for a couple of minutes as I walked over to Serena who greeted me by saying: "Tré, you really don't know how tired I am."

I started laughing as I whispered, "Serena, you see that couple near the front entrance of the hotel?"

Serena looks and nods her head. "Yes, they're the newlywed couple on your floor," she informed me. Then I told her that they knew all about our noisy block party last night, "and I think we ruined their honeymoon night."

Serena looked at me with a nervous smile on her lips as I went on. "They heard everything…including you singing. They even saw Señor Fernando dancing on the patio balcony with Jessy and Yoly."

"Ohhhh God!" Serena exclaimed, blinking her astonished eyes at me. "But how Tré? How do they know these things?"

"I don't know," I said without a clue, which caused Serena to go into conniptions. "Jesus Christ! On your honeymoon night you're supposed to be trying or at least practicing on how to make a baby!"

"I know that's what I'm going to be doing when I get married one day," I say sarcastically.

Serena let out a high-pitched outburst, tapped me on the head, and looked over at Sofia and Oscar patiently waiting for me. "Serena, I'm going to take the couple out for breakfast because I feel so bad about last night. Can you please recommend a good breakfast spot?" Serena quickly jotted down an address. "Take a taxi to this place," she said, handing me a slip of paper. "It's me and Rafael's favorite breakfast diner."

Serena composed herself and gestured to Oscar and Sofia to come to the front desk. Then very calmly and very softly she whispered to them in Spanish: "Mr. and Mrs. Alverez, I understand that you guys had an unexpectedly interesting encounter last night. Am I correct?"

Sofia and Oscar both looked directly at Serena, then at each other, and finally back at Serena.

"Sí," Sofia replied softly.

"And because of that very unexpectedly interesting evening," Serena went on in Spanish, "I am going to give you guys a complimentary extra night and a complimentary bottle of champagne to help you celebrate your honeymoon all over again…if you know what I mean. Do you understand me?"

Oscar and Sofia's eyes lit up as they kissed. "Yes…we understand you," Oscar replied. The happy couple began thanking Serena profusely as she adjusted their reservations on the computer. Serena faced the couple again as she said very slowly: "Even though Tré and I didn't have anything to do with your unexpectedly interesting encounter last night, the hotel personally wants to wish you both a very good stay once again. And please…enjoy a wonderful breakfast with my friend Tré." Watching Serena operate with such finesse and charm, I didn't have to wonder why she was the hotel's Head Night Manager.

I called Enri the taxi driver and he took us to the breakfast diner recommended by Serena. This particular restaurant was indeed a hidden jewel for foreigners like me. The diner, which served a delicious breakfast 24-7, was full of happy and spirited customers relishing their meals. Oscar and Sofia proudly began teaching me about their authentic Dominican breakfast cuisine as we shared a hearty meal called "Mangú" or "The Three Hits," consisting of fried eggs, mashed plantains, fried salami, fried cheese and red onions. Our tasty breakfast also came with hash browns, buttered toast with homemade peach jam, a giant fruit bowl (mango, strawberries, kiwi and bananas), grilled turkey, spicy chorizo sausage links, and a pitcher of fresh orange juice. I was salivating while eating everything in sight because the fruit was bursting with fresh flavor. And the meat, seasoned with flavorful Caribbean spices, was light on the stomach.

While we were dining, I apologized once again for interrupting their honeymoon night. Oscar quickly replied: "My American friend, will you please stop apologizing!" Sofia joined in as well. "Yes, Tré, stop it because we fooled everyone last night!" I stopped eating with a baffled look on my face. "What do you mean when you say you fooled everyone?"

"Yes! The thing is Tré that most newlywed couples celebrate their wedding reception late into the evening with their family and friends. But Sofia and I decided to celebrate on our own terms by trying to have a baby as our wedding gift to ourselves. So the plan was to get started very early in the evening!" Sofia and Oscar smiled and kissed each other. Then with a big smile on her face, Sofia went on to explain. "You see, we premeditated an excuse in which I pretended to become ill with a terrible migraine at our wedding reception dinner. So we told everyone that we were leaving to get my medicine back at the hotel, and that I also wanted to relax for one hour before returning. But truthfully, we had no intentions of coming back. It was no problem for us because we both knew that our families and friends would go on celebrating into the late hours with or without us."

With a sly grin on my face, I continued eating and listening in silence.

"And besides, it really was good to get away because Sofia's parents don't get along with my parents. Especially Sofia's father! He has always thought that she could find a better man to marry!" Oscar asserted, slightly agitated.

"Give him time, Sweetheart. My father will finally one day see that we are perfect for each other," Sofia consoled her husband.

I patted Oscar on the shoulder. "I believe Sofia's father is acting totally normal to a certain degree," I added. "Sometimes fathers have a tendency to be extra hard on the man who is replacing him when it comes to their daughter's love."

Oscar nodded his appreciation as I continued to offer my sincere advice. "Oscar, you appear to be a very nice person, so it is important to keep working hard and building your life in a positive way. And trust me, Sofia's father will start to appreciate you more and more over time. It's all about proving yourself with him."

"Yes…my father will be coming around," Sofia agreed. "Oscar and I have been together for four years. We both have college degrees. We speak three languages. We both have good paying jobs. We love and respect one another. And we love doing adventurous things together! And Tré, we've also been saving to buy a small house for our future family."

Oscar and Sofia both stare at me suddenly and I stop eating with a puzzled look on my face. Then they smiled and kissed. There was a pause followed by dead silence at our booth as Oscar seemed to trance out for a moment. Then, he placed one arm around Sofia's shoulders. "We want to thank you, Tré…" he began.

"For what?" I interrupted.

Oscar continued in a loud and animated voice. "Because you had a wild night of excitement last night for the whole city of Santo Domingo to hear and enjoy!" He paused for a moment as we stared at each other in silence. Meanwhile I was feverishly trying to figure out where our conversation was headed. Suddenly Oscar winked at me and slapped the table top with gusto. He then explained that he was just trying to get a rise out of me.

"Yes, I know that you were joking Oscar," I said, still somewhat puzzled, "but what are you and Sofia really trying to tell me?"

Sofia took it upon herself to explain. "Basically, what Oscar is saying Tré is that your party last night was messing up our romantic ambiance," she said with a straight face. "But because we are spontaneous people, Oscar and I decided to be adventurous and naughty under the stars by trying to make a baby out on the patio balcony."

"Your loud music muffled our screams of ecstasy," Oscar eagerly joined in. "We were making so much noise that one would have thought that we were trying to kill each other," Oscar laughed good-naturedly as he continued. "Tré, Sofia and I were extremely thankful for your high energy Merengue music and cheers! As you and your friends were screaming 'Va…Va…Va' (Go…Go…Go), Sofia and I were pretending that you guys were cheering us on."

"Como" (What)? I roar as I started laughing along with them. "So that's how you and Sofia saw Señor Fernando dancing with my two friends outside on the patio," I said, finally putting it all together.

"Yes! And we were fully naked too, but no one saw us. It was one of the craziest things that Sofia and I have ever done before," Oscar went on excitedly. "And it felt soooooo good! Especially after abstaining from sex for six long months." Sofia's eyes were gleaming as she spoke. "We were caught up in the moment, so we didn't want to go inside and lose our intensity. It was really as if we were daring you and your friends to catch us. We felt racy, like we were playing with fire, and we got unbelievably turned on sexually for the whole world to see last night. It was definitely the best night that we've ever experienced together! Just incredible!" Sofia sighed with pleasure as she closed her eyes for a few seconds.

"Tré, a girl needs to be a little kinky from time to time," she went on, obviously enjoying herself. "When you first get married you have to keep things "picante" (spicy-hot) with your spouse!"

Meanwhile I sat there taking it all in. "I hear you…because I definitely will have no issues with keeping it "picante" with my future wife!" I said with passionate feeling.

"Sofia…" Oscar spoke softly to his new bride, "I think that last night we might have started a whole new and beautiful life out on the patio." Still exuberant from their erotic encounter on the balcony, Oscar leaned back in the booth and continued: "The thing that I remember most is my body trembling furiously. Then all of a sudden I began moaning extremely loud and uncontrollably. Sofia had to hold her hand over my mouth so you and your friends wouldn't hear me!"

Sofia giggled proudly and looked over at me. "Yes, Tré…after Oscar stopped trembling, he couldn't move his entire body for about ten minutes because he was paralyzed. So I just softly massaged him until he regained his consciousness and strength. We then quietly moved back inside our suite to finish enjoying the rest of our evening."

Shaking my head, I reply, "Okay…okay! That's enough you two. I'm very happy that I was able to help spice up your honeymoon night."

Oscar, who appeared to be very relaxed at this point, went on talking. "You know Tré," he confided, "Sofia and I had to abstain from one another for six brutal months, and that was one of the most challenging things that we've ever done. So with that said, nothing was going to stop us from enjoying our special night…if you know what I mean."

As I sat drinking my glass of orange juice, I took a good look at Oscar and Sofia, a playful smirk on my face. "Yes! I do know what you mean Oscar," I replied, "and I have to say that you guys certainly feel super comfortable hanging out with me!"

Sofia nodded her head. "Don't mind us, Tré," she tried to reassure me. "We are completely harmless, but we are known to act a little crazy from time to time because Oscar and I are free-spirited personalities." Sofia's smartphone beeped suddenly and she began checking her messages. "Thank you, God!" she exhaled. "Penelope, our wedding photographer, has sent us the wedding photos from last night. Look Oscar!" she said.

Helloooooooo Isabella

The couple immediately began scrolling through their wedding photos on Sofia's smartphone. The "wow" factor was clearly written all over their faces as they erupted with multiple exclamations of joy and surprise. Tearing up slightly, Sofia continued to repeat, "Penelope did an extraordinary job with our photos." She then grabbed me by my arm, overcome with excitement. "Come around to my side Tré," she instructed me. "We want you to see our wedding photos, too!"

After seating myself between Sofia and Oscar, I told them that they certainly made a beautiful couple, and that I wished them a wonderful and happy life together. After viewing a couple of photos of Sofia holding a beautiful bouquet of flowers, I turned to compliment her. "Sofia…you look absolutely stunning in your wedding dress!" I told her. Flattered by my words, Sofia batted her eyes, smiled and thanked me with a hug as I continued watching Oscar scroll through the photos.

I was genuinely impressed and amazed by Sofia and Oscar's day of matrimony because they had staged the perfect outdoor "Sunset Beach Wedding." Oscar told me that they had been planning their wedding day for more than a year and a half, adding that it was certainly well worth it in the end! Especially after he saw Sofia in her wedding dress for the first time as she walked toward him along the shoreline just as the sun was setting over the Caribbean Sea. Feeling inspired by their wedding pictures, I indicated to Oscar and Sofia that when I get married, I'm definitely going to have a beach wedding!

Sofia continued to scroll through hundreds of beautiful memories when I suddenly snatched her phone and yelled: "Hold it! Stop, Sofia!" The couple was somewhat taken aback by my aggressive behavior.

"What's wrong, Tré?" Oscar asked with concern.

I glanced up at him for only a milli-second as I continued backtracking through the photos. "I thought I saw something!" I said by way of explanation as they both stared at me. I began searching faster and faster, halting all at once because I finally found what I'd been looking for. My eyes went wide with surprise and curiosity as I stared at one photo, completely mesmerized. I gently set Sofia's phone back down on the table with its screen showcasing an image of the most beautiful girl I had ever seen. Dressed in a captivating, red form-fitting bridesmaid's dress, she was exotic and intoxicating. She was tall and sexy with athletic curves and flawless skin that shimmered like caramelized brown chocolate. But that was only the appetizer. For the entrée she offered long, wavy red hair, lips that were pouty and firm, perky and lovable cheeks and dark brown almond-shaped eyes that sparkled in the flaming sunlight.

"Who is this gorgeous woman?" I asked, directing my question to both Oscar and Sofia, an irrepressible smile on my face. My enthusiasm was so obvious that the people seated near us were intrigued and immediately started looking around to catch a glimpse of this striking beauty that they thought had just entered the room. Sofia gazed at me and smiled. "Take it easy, Papi," she said, attempting to calm me down. Oscar, on the other hand, started laughing as he announced that the "girl of my dreams" was Sofia's sister, Isabella. I gazed at Isabella's photo one more time then turned slowly to Sofia. "Much respect, Sofia," I told her, "but Isabella is gorgeous and her name fits perfectly."

Turning my head from side to side in overwhelming disbelief of Isabella's "eye-assaulting" beauty, I addictively continued to peruse photos of her interacting with other guests at Sofia and Oscar's wedding. Suddenly Sofia whacked me on my arm as she shrieked: "My God, Tré, I really do believe you have a thing for my sister!"

"Sí!" I replied, laughing. "I'm telling you guys the truth when I say that Isabella is the girl I've always wanted to meet. Is she married? Is she single?" I went on excitedly. Oscar quickly chimed in. "I told you Sofia," he agreed with me, "when Isabella fixes herself up, she is on the same level with you as far as looks go. But everyone has forgotten about her potential, including Isabella herself, because she has allowed that lifeless, unappreciative, and boring jerk to bring her standards down!"

"I know, Oscar…you're so right," Sofia shook her head in disgust. Turning to me, she went on. "Tré, we have both tried talking to Isabella about this man many times, but she doesn't listen anymore! Maybe she feels ashamed. Who knows?"

I was listening attentively as I continued to track Isabella's movements on Sofia's phone. At the same time I was trying to comprehend what Oscar and Sofia were talking about. I abruptly pulled myself away from Isabella's photos. "May I ask what exactly is going on with Isabella?" I said casually.

"Basically, Tré…" Oscar responded, "Isabella has been with the same guy since secondary school—almost eight years now. It's like they are practically married…but realistically, they are not married!"

"Como" (What)? I blurt out. "You mean this guy has been with Sofia's sister for eight years and still has not asked her to marry him? He sounds 'loco' to me. Something is obviously wrong with him!"

Sofia frowned as if in deep thought. "Yes Tré…and it's no good to be tied down unmarried with the same man for a long time because you are going to miss out on life." She paused, looked at me then pointed toward Oscar. "Like us for instance…we love each other because we learned how to be good people from our previous relationships. Experiencing life on multiple levels has shown Oscar and me the meaning of what true love is. In my opinion, Isabella still has never learned the authentic beauty of life because she has stayed with this Little Boy far too long."

Oscar interrupted angrily. "For the love of God! They don't even live with each other or have any kids together! Isabella can basically leave if she really wants to!"

"We want her to GO!" Sofia said boldly. "She has a college degree, a nice secure job, and she could get back to being her normal self again. Tré, I'm telling you that my sister can have any man her heart desires!"

Oscar tapped me on the arm as he began firing off again. "No one likes Isabella's boyfriend, and that includes both sides of our family, Tré. Even though her boyfriend has two degrees and a good paying job, he's very uneventfully dull and is NOT like you, Sofia or me. We are all outgoing, carefree people." Oscar paused to calm himself while I remained absorbed in my own thoughts. Sofia resumed scrolling through her wedding photos, pausing on a picture of Isabella posing beneath a gorgeous sunset.

"All he does is go to work and then to his mother's house because she is always cooking and cleaning for him, so he can relax on the couch and watch American sports all night long," Oscar exploded again, halting to take several deep breaths in an attempt to control his emotions. "And to be honest, Tré, Isabella's boyfriend doesn't even spend time with her anymore. Yet, she allows it! What a sad situation!"

Sofia's fiery anger was obvious as her hand gestures became frantic. "I don't like him Tré because he cheated on my sister in the past!" She raised her voice by several decibels as she continued: "In my eyes, a cheater is always a deviant and untrustworthy asshole!"

"Realmente" (Really)? I yelled out so loud that everyone in the diner began looking in our direction. I stared at Sofia mystified.

"Yes, Tré…but of course she accepted him again after he crawled on his stomach begging for forgiveness."

Oscar clinched his fist as he snarled, "That was her sign to move on with her life. But she didn't do it. I really believe that Isabella fears being single again after staying with one man for such a long period of time. I also know for a fact that she feels very uncomfortable about positive changes that would unquestionably make her a happier person."

We continued to look through the wedding photos when a more subdued Oscar commented: "Yesterday was the first time in a very long while since Sofia and I have both seen Isabella so carefree and full of life."

Meanwhile I was pondering the situation, thinking deeply about Isabella. "Sofia you just don't know," I heard myself saying spontaneously, "that I would do everything in my power for the opportunity to meet your sister Isabella before I leave Santo Domingo in the next couple of days." I paused thoughtfully for a moment to collect myself, to try to control my rapid-fire thoughts as the three of us quietly stared at a group wedding photo. Isabella was clearly the center of attention in the photo, though it was unintentional. This time I looked directly at Sofia as I spoke what was in my heart. "Sofia, if I could have a delicious, romantic dinner with Isabella, it would mean the world to me. All I need is five minutes alone with her and I promise you that I will make her forget about her pretend boyfriend! No problem at all!"

Totally caught off guard, Sofia's face mirrored elation as she laughingly replied, "Whoaaaa! Take it easy, Papi! Take it easy!"

But Oscar quickly intervened. "Don't get us wrong…we like you, Tré!" he chimed in. "And we would love to help make your romantic dream date become a reality with Isabella because we believe you are a good man. She needs to meet a person like you. But, you are asking for a miracle, mi mano, because Isabella doesn't listen to us anymore when it comes to trying to introduce her to a man who would love to show her a new fresh start in life."

Sofia nodded her head in agreement and hugged me. Oscar reached over sympathetically to give me a "pound." But I was undeterred as I pleaded with both of them. "Well…please…try one more time. And this time, make it happen!" I said boldly.

With that said, I paid the waitress for our fantastic Dominican breakfast. But before she could walk away, Sofia asked her to take photos of us with my 35mm camera and with our individual smartphones. With group photos, I always like to spice it up by sticking my tongue out, my personal trademark. It's just my way of making people smile as they reconnect mentally with good memories of me. The waitress as well as Oscar and Sofia were so caught off guard by my playful antics that they couldn't stop laughing when they started scrolling through the photos. We were making such a big commotion that everyone in the diner was constantly looking around to see what was going on with us as Oscar, Sofia, and I all walked out the front door laughing hysterically.

Rendezvous with Galilea!

I made it back to my hotel suite at around 12:30 in the afternoon, when my body suddenly just crashed from being awake and active for more than thirty-two hours! I was also starting to experience the slightly delayed effects of jet lag. I knew I had to get some rest because it was going to be a long and exciting late night-early morning rendezvous with Gigi. Enri the taxi driver was scheduled to pick me up at the hotel at around 4:30 p.m., and then he was going to take me to meet up with Gigi at 5 p.m. sharp. I told myself that I needed only two quality hours of sleep to recharge my body. Looking forward to doing it strong with Gigi, I began prepping my attire for the evening. So I ironed my stylish white dress shorts and my designer short sleeve shirt. Then I unpacked my Euro-style white dress shoes and my white Panama Jack hat. Before I took my "power nap," I wanted to make sure that I had everything laid out—including my designer under garments!

Next, I double checked to make sure that Gigi's surprise gift was ready for my final approval. With the help of the Monahans, owners of my favorite boutique, we had carefully put together the ultimate "going away gift package." The package included a cute, girly, fuchsia-pink & black boutique travel bag. What made this particular travel bag unique was that it had a solar power outlet from which Gigi could play all forms of electronic devices anywhere around the world. In addition, the Monahans and I had filled the travel bag with fuchsia-pink flip flops, summer hats, and designer shirts that were all tailor made to fit Gigi, giving her that "fashionista" edge for all of South Africa to see.

I had every intention of sending my ravishing Dominicana off in style! I was also hoping that she was ready for tonight because I know that I was. It was going to be an epic night of surprises for her. For starters, we were both going to be pampered with a full body massage at the best spa in all of Santo Domingo. Next, I had made a dinner reservation at a very prominent Italian-Dominican Fusion Restaurant where we could dine and converse in a comfortable atmosphere. Finally, Gigi and I were going to finish the night off at a Merengue club located in an area where we would have a serene and picturesque view of downtown Santo Domingo. This was the spot where I planned to challenge Gigi to a marathon "dance off." Of course we were also going to celebrate by doing lots of drink shots, dancing, and being free all night along until the early morning sunrise! I was well aware that it could be years before Gigi and I would have the opportunity to see each other again, or possibly never! So, no regrets after the fact for me. I wanted to live in the moment and share an entertaining night filled with priceless memories with her.

Having finished my preparations, I closed the draperies to shut out the sunlight, laid on top of my bed (because I wanted to feel the cool air blowing therapeutically over my severely energy-drained body), placed my smartphone on my chest, and fell asleep right way. But I woke up a couple of minutes later when I felt my phone vibrating. I was in a semi-groggy mental state, but I was still able to comprehend that it was Enri calling me. I answered my phone and Enri immediately began speaking in a frantic and concerned tone of voice. "Ohhhh, Tré! Thank God you finally answered your phone. Where have you been? I've been trying to get hold of you for the last two hours, but your phone kept ringing and going to your voicemail!"

Enri kept talking on and on at a super-fast pace in Spanish, much of which was incoherent to me. "What are you talking about, Enri?" I finally cut him off. "I've been in my hotel room all this time and I haven't received any of your calls until now," I told him. "All I did was lay down on my bed for a few moments. So what's wrong, mi mano?"

"I wanted to confirm that I am still picking you up, Tré! I didn't want to have to come all the way out in your direction if you don't need me because I will miss out on other potential customers," Enri replied in an exasperated voice.

"Yes, I still need a ride Enri," I reassured him. He seemed to calm down a bit. "Bueno, I'm headed your way now!" he told me. I paused, slightly confused by Enri's haste. "On your way now? But Enri, you're not scheduled to come until 4:30 p.m.," I quickly reminded him.

"I know…it's 4:15 now, Tré!" Enri shot back. I instantly hopped out of bed as I stared at my radio clock which read 4:15 p.m. I then opened all the draperies in my room, noticing that the sun was now hovering over an entirely different section of the Caribbean Sea. My heartbeat accelerated as I looked at my phone which told me that I had missed a total of ten calls, twenty text messages, and five voicemails from both Enri and Gigi! "Oh my God! Oh my God!" I began shouting over and over as I frantically turned on all the lights in my suite! Meanwhile Enri, who is still on the phone, hears me scrambling around and panicking. "What's Wrong Tré?" he asked, concerned.

"I was planning to take a two hour power nap and wake up at 2:20 p.m. sharp. But I overslept by two hours."

Enri tried to relax me. "Don't worry Tré!" he told me. "It was a good thing that I kept calling you."

I THANK Enri and indicate to him that I can't delay the time of my reservations for the Day Spa Salon or the Italian-Dominican Fusion Restaurant because my night of surprises for Gigi will be totally ruined!

"I know…I know," Enri says calmly.

Doing my best to keep a clear head, I tell Enri that the earliest I can be ready is 4:45 because I still have to shower and get dressed. "If we leave at 4:45, will Gigi and I still be able to make our 5 o'clock spa reservations?" I ask Enri.

Enri pauses and slowly responds, "Yesssssss….I think you guys can make it, but we will be pushing it because the rush hour traffic is terrible right now."

Calculating multiple scenarios, good and bad, about my evening with Gigi, I tell Enri I have to go. But before Enri hangs up he says quickly: "Tré…if you happen to get ready sooner, come on down to the hotel lobby and I will be there waiting for you."

After Enri ends our phone call, I immediately started listening to a series of Gigi's messages while trimming and lining my moustache and beard. Gigi's first message began with a very exuberant and sexy, "Good Afternoon, Tré!" Then she went on to tell me how much she loves surprises and how she couldn't wait to see me this evening. She ended with kisses and a reminder to call her as soon as I was free.

Gigi's second message was somewhat less enthusiastic. She was courteous but a little anxious, yet she still assured me that she was looking forward to seeing me this evening. She ended her call by asking me to confirm the time of our meeting. In her third message she sounded irritated and disappointed that she had not yet heard from me. However, it was her final message that she lost it. "I'm very confused and upset with you right now, Tré, because of your impolite non-responses to my messages," she began. "Why haven't you called me back…when you know that I want to see you tonight! I need to know if we are still meeting in one hour. Okay? Call me now and let me know if you still want to see me. Thank you!"

When I heard her final message, I knew I had a lot of explaining and making up to do. I'd never known Gigi to get that upset with me—and rightfully so. With that said, my heart began to pulsate faster and faster because I didn't want this innocent mishap to shatter our evening into a million pieces. Especially since I'd spent many months of careful planning in order to make this a night full of surprises and adventure!

I was so angry that I started cursing myself out! I couldn't believe that this was happening! And of all the people in the world, why was this happening to me tonight of all nights? Once I got all of the negative energy out of my system, I took a deep breath, relaxed, and called Gigi.

She picked up on the first half-ring and immediately began flipping out. "Why didn't you pick up the phone when I was calling you, Tré? And why didn't you call me back sooner? *What's wrong with you?* I'm your friend and you should not have treated me this way! I only wanted to make sure that we were still going out tonight! Tré…you know how much our friendship means to me…." Gigi went on talking relentlessly. I knew that I had to diffuse her quickly because I was running late.

"Gigi…please let me say something…" I calmly interrupted her emotional tantrum. "Gigi…can you please relax for a second and listen to me?" Suddenly she went silent. "Thank you, Galilea," I said softly, "and I am so sorry for not responding to your messages until now. Please believe me when I say that I was not ignoring you. Okay? Honestly, what happened was that I went back to my hotel to take a two-hour nap before meeting up with you, and my body just crashed and I overslept. That's why I missed your phone calls and text messages. In fact, it was my friend Enri the taxi driver who woke me up with constant phone calls," I pleaded with Gigi, hoping she would understand. On the other end of the phone line I could hear her sigh with relief. "It's okay, Tré. I accept your apology," Gigi said graciously. "Are we still meeting in thirty-five minutes?"

"Yes! And I can't wait to see you Gigi!" I responded with gusto. Thanks for understanding my situation," I said to her in Spanish.

Gigi's mood was definitely more cheerful now. She sounded like her old self as she purred: "Now that's what I like to hear, Tré! Do you think we can meet earlier at 4:45 p.m.? I am very anxious to see what my surprise is!"

"Oh, no, no, noooo!" I replied. "Because I am just about to shower and get dressed. I'll see you soon!"

"Don't worry, Tré," Gigi sighed. "I can wait until 5 o'clock. I'll let you go now." She hung up without saying goodbye.

I quickly took an ice cold shower to wake me up. Then I reached for my Orange Ginger Shower Gel to help re-energize my body. The thing that I love most about it is that it stimulates your entire body with its fresh zesty scent. It also attracts women to the point of flirtatiousness, making them want to touch and sniff your body up close and personal.

I don't know how I did it, but I was able to shower, dress, and groom myself into an irresistible, unstoppable assassin and meet Enri in the hotel lobby in eleven minutes! This gave me a solid twenty minutes to meet up with Gigi a little before 5 p.m. Enri reconfirmed to me that Gigi and I would l be able to make our spa reservation on time. No worries.

Enri roared through the streets of Santo Domingo like Mad Max! I have to tell you that driving (or just riding) in a car in the D.R. is the most dangerous and scariest experience I have ever had. How can you drive safely when you have motor bikes spread four-deep across the roadway that zoom unexpectedly into your lane with no regard to their own or anyone else's safety. Many drivers make up their own rules of the road as they speed along, zipping in and out of traffic. Moreover, the roadways themselves are very underdeveloped and hazardous without the presence of streets lights and road signs. Unfortunately, a lot of drivers play the deadly game of "chicken," swerving into your lane and meeting you head-on, only to dart back to their side of the road at the last second. The result is a lot of near misses and far too many horrible and tragic head-on collisions that cause the premature deaths of drivers, motorcyclists, and often innocent pedestrians.

That being said, I knew I was in safe hands. Enri made driving through rush hour traffic look easy as he zoomed in and out of lanes. I began rechecking Gigi's surprise package to make sure it had a nice visual flair. As I was reorganizing it, Enri asked me to look up. He then proceeded to tell me that if things went well with Gigi tonight, to please invite her to the free live Merengue concert near my hotel. I gave Enri the thumbs up and thanked him for his suggestion.

"Tré, this concert is going to be great," Enri assured me. "They have delicious food and drinks, sensational musical entertainment, and you will have the chance to meet authentic salt-of-the-earth Santo Dominicanos while celebrating in an unbelievable atmosphere," he said excitedly as he went on. "And, by the way, Tré…tonight you shouldn't have any problems having Gigi show you how to Merengue dance like a true Dominican."

"That sounds like a great idea, Enri," I laughed.

Next Enri tells me that all I have to do is follow the live Merengue music because the outdoor concert will be only five short blocks away from my hotel. Enri also offered me some personal safety tips just in case I decided to walk to the concert from my hotel, warning that the streets were dark and could serve as hiding places for robbers or thieves.

"So if you decide to walk Tré," he cautioned, "don't wear any jewelry and don't carry a lot of cash on you. Leave your cell phone in your hotel room."

"Okay," I replied as my ears perked up. Enri had certainly succeeded in capturing my immediate attention.

"But don't be afraid to walk there Tré, especially if Gigi is walking along with you. You'll be okay. Just play it safe. Okay?" he stressed as we zipped along smoothly through the streets of Santo Domingo.

Feeling unfazed, I nodded my head in appreciation of Enri's thoughtful advice. I checked my phone and noticed that it was almost 5 p.m. Although Enri had repeated several times not to worry, in reality I was worrying because I knew that I was running late. All of a sudden, I began sweating profusely. I was starting to feeling over-heated, so I quickly removed my Panama Jack hat so I could cool down. I also noticed that my shirt was wet from beads of perspiration trickling down my back. I was grateful at that moment that my parents had taught me to always wear a tank top underneath my dress shirt.

The temperature had climbed steadily to more than 107 suffocating degrees of tropical heat—and Enri didn't have his air conditioning on. In an agitated tone of voice I told Enri to turn the air on to full blast so I could get some cool relief. The last thing I wanted to do was to start my evening with Gigi off as a sweaty and stinking mess. As Enri gazed at me through his rearview mirror, he started saying something to me in super-fast Spanish. It was at that moment that I realized, to my surprise, that I was NOT able to decipher anything he was saying to me. I had somehow hit a "wall" and was now experiencing a "foreign language mental block" episode!

You see, when people are learning and communicating in a second language, they can sometimes suffer a mental block. Their brains can literally "shut down" or "crash," causing them to have a mental lapse that may make it impossible for them to assimilate and comprehend the new language for an unspecified period of time. I have learned that these "foreign language mental blocks" can happen to anyone. Many people who travel and speak more than one language have horror stories about how it has affected them at inopportune times. Suddenly, out of the blue, they discovered that they no longer possessed the ability to comprehend what is being said to them! Unfortunately, I'd experienced this scenario several times before while traveling abroad—and it usually struck at the moment when I least expected it. However, I'd learned through bitter experience to fight my way through it by staying calm and asking questions I already knew the answer to, which made it easier to reply at my own pace. This became my personal way of jumpstarting my brain until I was able to work my way through the mental funk.

A few seconds had gone by and Enri continued to stare at me through his rear view mirror. I silently stared back at him baffled. He repeated his comment to me in Spanish once again. But the only response I could give him was a blank stare as I methodically tried to translate what he was saying inside my head. Adding fuel to an already intense situation, my phone started vibrating. It was Gigi calling me because the time was now 4:50 p.m. I say to Enri in the only Spanish I can remember: "Lo siento…un momento, por favor. Gigi Llamándome." (Sorry… one moment, please. Gigi is calling me.) I answer my phone and Gigi instantly started talking to me loud and super-fast. I didn't understand what she was saying to me either. All I could do was to repeat over and over, "Galilea…un momento por favor." But she simply ignored me and kept talking. So I had no choice but to switch over into English. "Just wait a second, Galilea…please! Just wait a second!" Gigi paused for a second, just long enough for me to hear her speaking to someone else in a very defiant and assertive tone.

At this point I knew I was in trouble and needed help. I leaned forward and held out my phone to Enri. "Enri…I'm sorry, but I've lost my train of thought in Spanish, and I don't know what's happening right now!"

Enri replied calmly, "No problem, Tré. When we first met I told you that I can speak English if you want me to. I learned it from my wife who was born in the Washington Heights section of Manhattan. I was only helping you to practice…"

Cutting Enri off, I say urgently, "Can you please help me translate what Gigi is saying right now?"

I handed him my phone and he began speaking to Gigi. All I could hear was Gigi talking super-fast in a very emotional tone of voice. Enri looked at me and said: "Tré…Gigi is telling me that she is waiting outside your secret location all alone, and she doesn't know where she is. And she is also asking me if you gave her the wrong address." Before I could respond, Gigi started talking again. Enri then shoots me a "What the fuuuucccck?" look. "She's really pissed off with you, Tré!" Enri says to me, "because where she is standing right now, there is only a laundry service building, a clinic for low income expecting mothers, and a job center full of "criminal types" who are all trying to be her future husband!"

Enri burst out laughing, but Gigi apparently cut him short with a sharp verbal reminder that he needed to take her situation seriously. Enri immediately apologized as he turned to me for the address of the salon. I explained to Enri that I knew that Gigi was going to show up early and inadvertently ruin her own surprise, so I purposely gave her directions to a building directly across the street from the spa.

Enri's eyes lit up as he replied, "Ahhhh, Tré! That was very smart thinking." I next ask Enri how far away we are from Gigi. "We are pulling up to her right now," he told me. Enri honked his horn and we see Gigi ignoring a couple of guys who are trying to compete for her attention. Still on the phone with Gigi, Enri tells her, "Turn around because we are driving towards you now." Gigi turned and I was instantly mesmerized by her beauty. It was quite obvious to me why these guys were going berserk over her.

Gigi was wearing a silk semi-see through, mid-thigh length teal blouse that was playing racy mind games with the male psyche because it revealed the glowing bare skin of her toned and tanned thighs, the shapely contours of her athletic legs, and her teal-colored manicured toenails which were rocking a pair of stylish high heels. Gigi had also perfectly accessorized herself with teal-green feather earrings accented by teal-green beaded bracelets, small purse, and sun glasses. Gigi looked like a delicious swirl of teal-green eye candy!

As I opened the door of the taxi, Enri and I could instantly smell Gigi's light floral perfume which was very stimulating and pleasurable to the male sense of smell. But Gigi immediately shot me a look that screamed: "Tré, where the hell am I?" as she started speaking to me in rapid-fire Spanish again. Going into damage control mode, I rushed forward to give her a big, warm, soothing hug as I say to her in Spanish: "Gigi…please relax and please trust me right now, okay?"

Immediately, her tensed up body began to mellow out as she wrapped me up with a long and loving hug. I complimented her on how beautiful she looked and she hugged me even tighter. "Gracias," she whispered to me as I feel her nose against my neck as she sniffed the "orange-ginger" scent on my skin. Gigi then grabbed me by the hand and I helped her into the taxi. She and Enri exchanged pleasantries and Enri said to her in English, "Galilea…sit back and get ready because you are really going to appreciate my friend Tré's surprise."

A Sensual Mind-Blowing Full-Body Massage for Two

Gigi responded with a pleasant smile. A few seconds later we arrived at the Day Spa Salon which was located just across the street. Gigi's eyes lit up like the sun hovering over the exotic beaches of Rio de Janeiro. She excitedly shrieked, "Where are we, Tré?" Enri then turned to explains something to Gigi in Spanish. She looked back at me, smiled, and kissed me on both cheeks as she whispered, "Thank you, Tré!" She went on to tell me that she had heard wonderful things about this particular salon, but had never had the chance to indulge herself.

"Gigi…this is only the beginning of our very entertaining evening!" I tell her in a sultry and sexy voice. Gigi winked at me as a smile lit up her irresistible "cherub cheeks."

Enri opened the door for Gigi and me, inquiring if I still wanted him to pick us up at 6:30 p.m. or if he should wait for my call when we were ready to leave for our 7 p.m. dinner reservation. I instructed Enri to please pick us at the scheduled time, paid him for his services, and included a generous tip for all of his invaluable help.

Gigi and I entered the Day Spa Salon at exactly 5 p.m. It was packed with middle class women who were all very well groomed and attractive. While waiting for their appointments, everyone was occupying themselves by reading, relaxing, talking, playing games on their smartphones, and enjoying a complimentary glass of sparkling wine. The salon was luxuriously outfitted with elegant, contemporary furniture. The soothing sound of soft music and the tranquil sound of running water from a marble fountain in the center of the lobby provided a pleasing and relaxing atmosphere. The lobby area featured vibrant lighting, colorful flowers, scented candles, and creative interior design, all of which contributed to a comfortable ambiance.

As we arrived at the receptionist's desk, we were greeted by a very good-looking and fashionably dressed woman in her early fifties. She welcomed us in Spanish ("Bienvenido!") with a warm and friendly smile as she inquired about our appointment time. Meanwhile Gigi's eyes quickly scanned the exquisite décor as a wide-eyed look spread across her face. I was still having some difficulty with my Spanish, so I was speaking extremely "slooooow," much like a robot as I introduced myself and confirmed our appointment.

Even though I felt like the eyes of the world were watching me because of my peculiar manner of speaking, I still displayed a million dollar smile on my face as I continued to fight my way through my language mental block. My foreign language professor had always told me that when I am speaking in Spanish and Portuguese, I have a very charming and comforting presence. So, I immediately addressed everyone in the salon. "Sonríe todos," I said excitedly, "Yo estoy teniendo un mal día de Español…porque yo soy Americano!" (Smile everybody. I am having a bad Spanish day…because I am American!) Then I flashed my winning smile for all the ladies in the lobby to see. The greeter started giggling and gave me a warm hug. The other ladies in the room began giggling also as they commented: "Ohh…how cute!" My humorous little joke had succeeded in breaking the tension in the room and now everyone, including me, could just relax. I happily pronounced myself "cured" of my foreign language mental block!

At this point, our Dominicana greeter apparently got caught up in my bold and flirtatious aura and began smiling uncontrollably. She now responded in English with an alluring Dominican accent: "You are too cute Tré, and yes we all love your accent. Good job with your Spanish because it has gotten better since we began speaking!" By this time, the majority of the women in the lobby were whistling, clapping, and toasting me with their wine glasses, making me feel like a very welcome and special guest. Some of the ladies were even taking photos and video clips of me. The greeter then introduced herself as Yahaira, the owner of the salon, as she graciously volunteered, "We normally don't get many Americans who come here to my wonderful spa. But when we do, we make our American friends feel very special."

Yahaira hugged and kissed me on both my cheeks, then she and Gigi also introduced themselves and exchanged hugs and kisses. Yahaira went on to tell us that every year she visits her family in Orlando, and that she herself used to live in New York City. I tell her I used to live in New York as well, in the Marble Hill section of the Bronx and also in the St. Albans-Queens and Jamaica-Queens areas. "Yes…I know Queens!" Yahaira said effervescently, "I have family living all over that borough. What a small world! Though, I must admit that I love Orlando more because of the warmer weather. I hate the snow!"

Gigi and I laughed. Yahaira smiled and informed us that we were both scheduled for Hot Stone Full Body Massages followed by Soft Tissue Oil Massages. Afterwards, Gigi would receive a manicure and pedicure, while I would receive a complimentary deep tissue foot massage because I am a first time customer. As Yahaira goes on to describe what Gigi's surprise spa treatment will be, Gigi's facial expressions and body language became more and more animated. She turned and hugged me hard as tears glided down her cute perky face.

"Oh my God, Tré! Thank you, dear!" Gigi told me as she went on to express her gratitude. "You don't know how much this means to me. No one has ever taken the time like you to make me feel like a queen!" she said with heartfelt sincerity. "Especially since you know how hard it has been for me these last four months because of my decision to move to South Africa." Yahaira turned to Gigi and said in Spanish, "Yes, sweetheart…Tré specifically told us that he wanted us to really take good care of you. And yes, we have every intention of honoring his wishes." Gigi tightened her grip around my waist and I gently wiped away the tears falling from her eyes.

Yahaira touched my shoulder and asked if I wanted the services of a male masseuse for my massage session. I instantly replied in English so there wouldn't be ANY misunderstanding: "Oh nooo! Only the soft delicate hands of a woman can touch this caramel-brown body!"

Gigi hit me on my arm and yelled, "Tré!" All the women in the lobby who understood English began shouting, "Wahoooo!" Yahaira, trying her best to suppress her laughter, turned to ask Gigi if she too would prefer the services of one of her most talented female masseuses. Gigi smirked, a wicked smile curling her lips as she replied: "No...I think that I would prefer a massage from a man." My sexy and mischievous friend then looked at me with the hope of luring me into an automatic response.

"Ohhhhhh!" I reply in a deep and risqué voice. "Okay Gigi, but you do realize that there is nothing sexier than when a woman gives another woman a soothing and sensual massage." An embarrassed Gigi started blushing as she yelled, "Tré, stop!" All the women in the lobby of the spa who understood my comment exploded with cheers and toasts, raising their wine glasses high in the air.

Then with a devilish smile on my face, I say, "Gigi, if you wanted a massage from a man...all you had to do was ask me! I would have given you all types of Full Frontal Body Massages every night for free—and with a big happy grin on my face!"

"COMOOOO?" All the women sang in unison.

Gigi couldn't help chuckling as she retorted, "Whatever Tré... whatever! This is wishful thinking for you."

Yahaira stared at me, her eyes filled with tears of laughter. "Tré, you are just too much!" she told me. Next, she took me and Gigi by our arms and led us through a private door. We passed through an attractively furnished hallway which led past luxurious rooms specifically designed for private massage sessions. Soft music was playing and the fragrance of fresh flowers filled the air. Yahaira then paused to open the door to a lavish dressing room with a see-through glass shower. The room was also fully stocked with chilled bottles of champagne and bottles of wine maintained at room temperature.

Yahaira turned to us. "You both can get comfortable, undress, and shower before your hot stone massages." She walked us inside the room, grabbed a fuchsia-pink ensemble off the shelf that consisted of a robe, towel set, and shower shoes for Gigi. Next, she presented me with the same items in a lavender ensemble. As she prepared to leave us, Yahaira smiled and instructed us to put our robes on after we finished taking our showers.

I turned to wink at Gigi, beaming with amusement as I say, "Sounds like a plan to us, Yahaira!"

Gigi stared at me with a slight grin on her face as she responded, "No, Tré! That is not going to happen!" She quickly turned to Yahaira. "We are going to need separate rooms to undress and shower, please," she said. Yahaira, however, was immediately taken aback by Gigi's request. She looked at us, puzzled. "Aren't you guys a couple?" she asked.

Gigi and I stare at one another. "We are just really good friends who love to have fun together when we can," I volunteered.

"I'm sorry! I thought you guys were together," she apologized. "You make such a handsome couple, and even I can feel the strong and positive energy between you."

Yahaira took my arm and escorted me to my new private room located directly across from Gigi. She announced that she would be back in fifteen minutes to accompany me to my massage therapy along with Gigi. As I entered the therapy room, escorted by Yahaira as promised, I see two massage tables and a stunningly peaceful view of the city of Santo Domingo with the Caribbean Sea in the distance. Of course I couldn't help but notice Gigi relaxing on a black leather couch, sipping a glass of chilled Chardonnay wine. She was wearing her sexy, tight-fitting fuchsia-pink robe and her hair was Voguish-ly wrapped with a matching towel. Gigi was looking "goooooood!"

She looked across at me with baby doe eyes and smiled. "Tré...come on over and sit next to me please," she said sweetly. I eagerly obliged as Gigi handed me a glass of champagne. Then she readjusted her position for maximum comfort and laid her head on my chest. Easing the door open slightly, Yahaira says: "Just relax and enjoy your drinks. We will begin your massages in the next five minutes."

As soon as Gigi and I finished our drinks, we heard a subtle knock on the door. Then Yahaira entered along with our two masseuses--her daughter, Anatesia, and her top protégé, Ernesto. Anatesia was drop dead gorgeous just like her mother, except she was twenty-five years younger. Anatesia was also taller and possessed a tight, captivating body and exotic facial features. Following our introduction, the attractive young woman walked over to me smiling and shook my hand with a very firm grip. Yahaira next presented Ernesto—early thirties, metro-sexual flair, and the body of an Olympian—to a very pleased Gigi.

Sensing our happiness with our respective masseuses, Yahaira smiled mischievously as she called out: "Have fun everyone and enjoy your massages because everyone in this room is SINGLE!"

Anatesia flashed a look at her mother as if to say: "Mother, will you please shut your mouth!" But in reality, like a true professional, Anatesia addressed her mom respectfully in perfect English. "Mother… will you stop trying to match everyone up. We *are* in the business of sophistication here."

Yahaira muttered something incomprehensible as she quickly left the room.

"Chao, mami!" Anatesia called out coolly.

"Anatesia, I loooooove your mother!" I offered as a light-hearted tension breaker. "She is alright with me!"

Anatesia smiled pleasantly. "Tré, I know that my mother is very unique in her own way," she said, "and yes…I agree that she is a very loveable person."

Anatesia then turned off the lights in the room, leaving only the glow of the scented candles and the last rays of the evening sun still visible through the windows. Ernesto, like a real caballero (gentleman) guided Gigi to her massage table and helped her to position herself comfortably.

In a soft, soothing voice, Anatesia tells me to relax as she turns up the spa relaxation music that now incorporated the tranquil sounds of a waterfall. She then checked the warmer to see if my stones were ready.ABigi and I had an "open range" view of one another from our respective sides of the room, and our combined "synergy" was easing the two of us into a peaceful paradise. "Please loosen your robes," Anatesia said softly as Ernesto proceeded to cover Gigi's upper and lower body with a sheer, almost see-through fuchsia-pink sheet. He removed her bathrobe and gently folded her sheet back to the upper section of Gigi's plump rump area.

Anatesia did exactly the same with me. By this time, my mind and body was going through ecstatic conniptions because I love being thrown into provocatively surrealistic situations. In this case, I was virtually naked, lying face down in a room with scented candles and mood lighting, and an extremely gorgeous masseuse was about to lay her warm and sensual hands on me. I simply can't wait for Anatesia to start touching my body! Even more mind-blowing was the fact that I was privileged to have an unobstructed view of Gigi's nude curvy heart shaped cheeks lying just to the right of me. I admit that I didn't know what Gigi was thinking at that moment, but all types of naughty and risqué thoughts were racing "wild and free" through my mind. And I confess that I liked what I was seeing. And if that was not sufficient to take temptation to its peak, yet to come was a shower of fresh flowers—with Anatesia raining tulip petals all around my body, and Ernesto ringing Gigi's erotic frame all around with pink rose petals!

Anatesia strategically placed flat hot stones in key positions on my upper body. But just then my attention shifted to Gigi's moaning. She was "ooooing" and "ahhhing" and breathing heavy as Ernesto went to work on her entire upper body with a vengeance. He was rubbing her body with two heated stones, and showing her petite and shapely frame no mercy. Gigi looked as if she'd lost her sense of reality, like she'd been swept away into a whole other dimension.

Then suddenly my body shut down, and I was instantly transported to a universe of peace and calmness. Anatesia exhibited the "gifted touch of God's miraculous hand" as she relentlessly attacked my body. She took me on a journey that caused me to slip in and out of consciousness continuously. At one point I felt like I had nothing covering my naked body because I was blanketed with hot stones from my neck all the way down to my feet. Anatesia was creatively massaging every single muscle in my body. I just couldn't understand how she was doing this if I supposedly had a lavender sheet partially covering me. The only thing I was aware of was Anatesia's voice softly whispering in my ear: "What type of American sport do you play, Tré? You have a nice, lean muscle tone that needs to be loosened up." However, I wasn't able to verbally respond to Anatesia because I was lost in my own world.

On a whim I looked over towards Gigi who was currently staring at me with a distinct expression on her face that I had never seen before. It was very clear to me that Gigi was "eyeing me down" without a care in the word. Realistically, I didn't know if I was lying face down fully naked or not because Anatesia had covered my body with hot stones. Everything was open and liberating at this point, so I certainly wasn't shy about it. Gazing at Gigi, I could see the whole of her appetizing bare body, except for her "bubbly plump curvature" which was arched high in the air.

All of a sudden, Ernesto began pulling and folding Gigi's fuchsia-pink sheet into small geometrical rectangles as he continued massaging her body. The smaller the rectangles became, the more I wanted to see. Illumined by the glow of burning candles, Gigi's entire caramel candy physique glistened in a golden haze. It was obvious now that we were both checking each other out as well as expressing a new level of attraction toward one another. Gigi smiled at me, and before I could smile back, Ernesto turned her face in the opposite direction.

Once the massages were over, Ernesto and Anatesia slowly transitioned Gigi and I to our final thirty minutes of Soft Tissue Oil Massages. The lights gradually came back up and I noticed that my body was covered with lavender tulip petals. I also noticed that an artsy wardrobe room divider was separating our two sections of the room, including our see-through shower stalls. The only thing I could see now was Gigi's oiled legs resting on her massage table. I was also pretty sure Gigi was able to see me too.

At that moment Yahaira made her presence known with her sultry voice. "I hope that everyone enjoyed their massages," she said enthusiastically as she rolled a portable clothing rack toward me. Inside, I observed that all my clothes and undergarments had been neatly pressed and placed on wooden hangers. Yahaira had even placed all my personal items in clear plastic bags, including Gigi's surprise gift. The strange thing was that Gigi still had not asked me why I was walking around with a woman's fashion bag swung over my shoulder.

Finally Yahaira opened the door to our room with a warning: "Behave yourselves and I will be back in fifteen minutes." I asked Gigi if she was enjoying herself and she responded emphatically: "Yes Tré! I will always remember this day because of you." I put on my robe, got up from my massage table, and pulled back the wardrobe divider. I walked over to Gigi who was still covered up by her robe. She looked at me in a surprised manner, smiled, and said in a soft and humorous tone, "You know that you are supposed to stay on the other side, Tré!"

With a mischievous grin on my face, I nonchalantly replied, "I know…but I wanted to find out if you needed my personal assistance. I have special expertise when it comes to private one-on-one showers." Gigi started giggling as she shrieked, "Whatever, Tré…and the answer is no! I'm a big girl and I think I can manage to take a shower all by myself. Muchas Gracias, Señor!" Throwing her pink towel at me, Gigi exploded with laughter. "Tré, you are too crazy! Stop!" she said.

"Okay…okay…I'll stop," I said laughing as I pulled the Wardrobe Divider back into place and hopped in the shower.

After my shower, I got dressed. This time Gigi pushed back the Wardrobe Divider so that both of us were able to see the entire room. She was now "decked out" in her teal-green outfit once again as she walked over and hugged me. "Thank you, dear," she said, then asked for my help in putting on her jewelry. She stood facing me as I attempted to latch her sparkling butterfly necklace. Although I was doing my best to assist Gigi, I started losing focus because I was paying more attention to her glistening coconut-brown and perky décolletage. Sensing that I was having issues in getting the job done, Gigi moved in closer to me and pulled her hair up. Then she made what I took to be a flirtatious suggestion. "Tré…how about I turn around so you can see more better," she whispered. As Gigi turned slowly around, I deciphered exactly what she was trying to say to me. She was letting me know in her own feminine way that she wanted me to get a "taste" of her phenomenally contoured body—up close and personal. When she finally turned with her derriere facing me, I realized for the first time the fullness of Gigi's magnificent womanly attributes. "Oh…my…God!" I kept repeating over and over in my mind. As if she had just tuned in on my thoughts, Gigi purposely moved in even closer as her lower body greeted and caressed my taut body parts all in one smooth motion.

We were a perfect match and our intimate connection lasted for about two elongated seconds before Gigi gracefully took a step forward and I finally attached her necklace. Then she turned, caressed both sides of my face, and said: "How about a drink…Tré?" I responded with a yes and we locked arms and walked over to the couch. Gigi sat while I poured each of us a glass of champagne. When I sat down, I was immediately overcome by her aromatic perfume, which was having an arousing effect on me. In order to maintain my self-control, I proposed a champagne toast.

After our toast, I said to Gigi in a playful and teasing manner: "So did your eyes like what they were seeing?"

Gigi leaned back to stare at me with a puzzled look on her face.

"Tré...what do you mean when you say this?" she asked softly.

I gazed at Gigi with a slight smirk. "When Anatesia had me totally NUDE on the massage table, I clearly saw you with my own eyes, smiling and staring me down from head to toe. So once again, did you like what you were seeing?"

Gigi looked at me coyly. "Maybe I should be asking you the same thing, Tré. I too saw you looking over at me in the same passionate way with your naughty eyes. So let me ask you: Did you like what you were seeing?" There was a seductive pause as Gigi and I stared at one another. We were both standing our ground with regard to what was now happening between us.

Suddenly our door opened and Ernesto and Anatesia walked into the room. They thanked Gigi and I for our services as Anatesia handed Gigi a very unique looking key along with a black credit card. Gigi and I inquisitively examined both items, noticing that the black credit card had some form of encrypted lettering on it. "What is this?" Gigi asked. Ernesto and Anatesia looked at each other and began embracing. They looked back at us and smiled as Ernesto started speaking in Spanish. He told us that they were extending us an invitation to an ultra-exclusive club event that happened only once a month. This special event moved each month to different unspecified locations in Santo Domingo, Ernesto told us.

"We like you guys, so Ernesto and I are inviting you out tonight to be our personal guests," Anatesia chimed in.

Gigi thanked them and asked in Spanish, "Why do we need the key and credit card?" Ernesto and Anatesia begin explaining, mainly to Gigi. Their animated Spanish was too fast and too advanced for me to comprehend. However, while the couple was speaking, I noticed how large Gigi's eyes became as she reacted to what they were telling her. She would look at Ernesto, then at Anatesia, and finally at me. Then Gigi pointed at them and shrieked in amazement, "It's true?" Ernesto and Anatesia responded with a definite yes, no hesitation.

Gigi's gaping mouth gradually transitioned into a smile as she shook her head from side to side. Anatesia winked at me as she spoke very freely and directly to Gigi. Meanwhile I was left standing awkwardly on the outside of their non-translated and candid conversation for the most part. The only thing that I could understand was Anatesia's comment that the key club was a "guaranteed ultimate experience," and that she and Ernesto were secretly a couple. Even her mother had no knowledge of their hidden love affair.

Anatesia stopped talking briefly to kiss Ernesto on the lips. Gigi took a deep breath, adjusted her posture on the couch, stared at me, and refocused her attention on the couple. In a heavy Dominican accent, Gigi said in English, "This is unbelievable…I never knew that these types of clubs existed here?" Meanwhile Anatesia openly examined me with her mysterious greenish-blue eyes. "Yes, and we would really like you two to be our personal guests!" Anatesia said enticingly. Gigi took another look at the invitation and thanked the couple once again. Ernesto affectionately kissed Gigi's hands while Anatesia leaned forward to softly blow on my right cheek as she gave me a soft, warm kiss goodbye.

As the couple exited the room I noticed that Gigi was staring at me with a strange look on her face. "What were you guys talking about?" I asked. "I didn't understand."

Gigi confided that we were invited to come out to celebrate at a special club tonight, but it was obvious she was holding something back as I asked if she wanted to go. "I don't know, Tré," she replied calmly as she continued to sip her champagne. "I have never been to this type of club before."

"So let's go and find out why this club is so exclusive!" I say excitedly. "Is it a club exclusively for the rich?"

Gigi shook her head. "No, Tré…you don't understand. It's a club for…" she stammered as she did her best to explain it to me in Spanish. However, I still couldn't grasp exactly what Gigi was trying to tell me. I removed her empty champagne glass from her hand, set it on the table, and asked her to please explain it to me in English. Slightly embarrassed, Gigi replied in a straightforward manner, "Tré…it is a special club where EVERYTHING goes, if you know what I mean. If a man wants to be with multiple women, it's okay. Or if a woman wants to be with more than one man…no problema because no one judges."

Not able to contain my emotions, I roar sarcastically: "Hey, that sounds like our type of club, Gigi!"

Gigi started laughing as she replied, "No, no, no my dear…you still don't understand. It's a club where 'Chaca-Chaca…Boom-Boom' is all out in the open for everyone to see and enjoy." She performed a "Chaca-Chaca…Boom-Boom" sexual gyration using her lower and upper body. This time there was no way I could miss what she was saying. Titillated by Gigi's risqué body movements, my eyes flared like an out of control forest fire. "You mean…we got invited to a hidden sex club for swingers!" I said wide-eyed.

"Sí…a swingers private sex club," she said coolly.

"Gigi…are you serious?"

Gigi took a sip from my champagne glass before responding. "Sí Tré…it's a club for 'Chaca-Chaca…Boom-Boom.'" Then she explained to me how the key and the encrypted black credit card worked.

We both start laughing uncontrollably and talking super loud. "So… you mean…Anatesia likes to 'freaky-freaky' and her mother Yahaira doesn't have a clue about what she is doing behind closed doors?"

Gigi slowly shook her head as we continued laughing. Right on cue, Yahaira walked into the room with a huge smile on her face. Gigi and I suppressed our laughter as Yahaira introduced us to our two new spa technicians. It was so hard not to laugh at Yahaira since she had no idea about her daughter's monthly "freaky-freaky sex-capades." Tears were literally bursting from my eyes; Gigi had to wipe my face with her hands.

Yahaira left shortly to attend to her other clients. As soon as the door closed, our technicians began working on Gigi's manicure and pedicure as well as my foot massage. While we were luxuriating in our treatments and enjoying our complimentary refills of champagne, I looked over at Gigi with a serious expression on my face. "You never answered my question," I said. "Do you want to go to the club tonight?"

Caught off guard, Gigi burst into laughter, accidentally spitting out her champagne. She quickly whispered to me, "No, Tré! I don't think that my father would approve of me going to this type of club!" We then raised our glasses in a toast and immediately exploded with euphoric laughter for almost thirty minutes non-stop. Gigi and I were laughing so hard that I believe our spa techs thought we were both drunk out of our minds!

Following our spa session, Gigi and I returned to the lobby where Enri was talking on his cell phone while waiting for us. Yahaira hugged us. "Did you guys like the services of Ernesto and my daughter Anatesia?"

"We certainly did," I replied, "and they are definitely two very special people."

Gigi giggled and hit me on the arm. Then she pinched me on the sly just below my butt. Facing Yahaira once again, Gigi said: "And Tré was especially fond of Ana-ste-sia!"

I immediately turned towards Gigi with a "Girl, what are you talking about?" look on my face. Yahaira's face lit up like the morning star rising out of the heavens, and her energy level noticeably amped up. She grabbed me excitedly as she responded: "Ohhh really, Tré! Is this true? This is so sweet! Till this very day I have always wondered why my Anatesia is still single…because she is so pretty and intelligent," Yahaira exclaimed as she went on. "I admit that she is shy, but all Anatesia needs is a good man to help her break free from her shyness."

Fighting my urge not to laugh, I smiled and went along with Gigi's little stunt. Yahaira kissed me on the cheek. "I'll make sure to pass on your feelings of interest and contact information to my Anatesia," she assured me.

I stare at Gigi who now had a "Got you!" smirk on her face. But, in my mind, I kept saying to myself: "Yahaira if you only knew about your daughter's closet freaky-freaky side!" That being said, if there was one thing that I enjoyed about Gigi it was the fact that she was wild and crazy just like me, but in a loveable way. While I was willing to admit that Gigi had got me pretty good, she had to know that I was going to reciprocate the love with a vengeance. Embracing Yahaira, I said, "Gigi and I really enjoyed our time today because of YOU…Yahaira! You are a very good person!"

"G-r-a-c-i-a-s, Tré," she replied warmly. I glanced at Gigi for a split second as I went on. "Yahaira…Gigi and I were talking earlier today about you. And we would like to invite you and your husband to a private party tonight." I turned to look at Gigi. "Now, Gigi still has not revealed the location of the party to me because she loves to surprise me, but she has told me that the place is luxurious and fabulous! As a matter of fact, she is not going to release her party's exact location to anybody until 10 p.m." I took a step closer to Gigi as I exclaimed: "I just can't wait anymore!"

Yahaira gave me a peck on my cheek. "That sounds exciting!" she said eagerly. "How ironic that my husband and I were trying to make plans to do something this evening. So, yes, we are coming…and I can't wait to be surprised as well." I glanced over at Gigi who had a shocked look of "Oh, my God!" on her face. I also told Yahaira that Gigi was throwing this private party for her older sister, her favorite uncle, and of course…ME. I paused to look over at Gigi once again and I noticed that she was hanging on every single word I was saying.

Thoroughly enjoying Gigi's shock and embarrassment, I kept the practical joke going. "Yahaira…Gigi is about to give you a unique secret key and an encrypted Invitation that only you and your husband can use. Not even your daughter can have access to the invitation because she will NOT be let in by staff security. Do you understand?" I asked.

Yahaira replied "Sí" to which I exuberantly responded: "I'm 100 percent positive that tonight you will see people at the party you are already acquainted with." Yahaira winked at me. "Yes…I'm sure too because everyone in Santo Domingo knows one another." I looked over at Gigi as I quietly waited for her to give Yahaira the key and black credit card. But she defiantly ignored me. Smirking, I said, "Oh…Galilea! Please don't forget to give Yahaira the key and invitation card to your big party tonight." Doing her best not to laugh, Gigi handed Yahaira her new prized possessions. She then squinted her sexy "baby doe" eyes at me as if she wanted to kill me dead right on the spot!

I went on to give Yahaira the exact instructions needed to be admitted to the club, including the anonymous text to her cell phone which would provide the GPS location to follow. "And then," I said to an innocent and grateful Yahaira, "get ready for an epic night of surprises!" By this time, no longer able to contain herself, Gigi started laughing uncontrollably as I quickly guided her out the front door. Enri helped us into his taxi and we zoomed away to our dinner engagement.

On the way, Gigi and I couldn't stop laughing. We were laughing so hard that we were having a difficult time telling one another how bad each of us had acted. "Poor Yahaira!" Gigi screamed. "She has no clue that her daughter loves a freaky-freaky…boom-boom with Ernesto and other sexual swingers for everyone to see and enjoy!" Gigi made more naughty sexual gyrations with her body as we both screamed with laughter.

"COMOOOO?" Enri blurted out, but Gigi and I couldn't stop laughing long enough to explain. "Qué pasó?" Enri kept on repeating.

Gigi finally managed to check her laughter enough to tell Enri about our incredible adventure at the salon. Enri immediately went berserk. He began driving out of control as he swerved dangerously in and out of the lanes of oncoming traffic.

Finally restraining himself, Enri says passionately, "You should have given me the key and the black credit card." Gigi and I looked at one another and then at Enri. We both asked in unison: "Enri…are you a swinger?"

Enri chuckled. "No…no…but every once in a while, me and my wife will hear about these swinger events hosted in different secret locations. We've always wanted to go because we are free-spirited people and we love to experience new things. But no…we are not swingers."

"It's okay, Enri," Gigi replied.

Enri turned around and said: "Tré…don't you dare tell my daughters that their mother and I want to go to a swinger's club."

"Don't worry, Enri," I replied, "your personal freaky-freaky fantasy is safe with me."

"Stop Tré…just stop!" Gigi said as we all start laughing again.

A Slice of Naples in Santo Domingo

Enri dropped us off at the Italian-Dominican Fusion Restaurant and told me to call him twenty minutes before we were ready to leave. Gigi and I walked into a packed restaurant. As soon as we entered, our noses were immediately "blessed" with the aroma of delicious Italian-Dominican Fusion cuisines. We noticed that everyone was enjoying a band performing Italian love ballads. The candle-lit restaurant was not a place of striking visual opulence, but it was absolutely a hidden gem of comfort, culture, and intimacy! This spot was an identical match of the owner-chef's personality because he had brought a slice of his hometown of Naples, Italy with him to Santo Domingo.

Gigi and I checked in with the hostess who informed us that our table would be ready in ten minutes. In the meantime, we decide to walk over to the bar and have a drink. Gigi tells me that she wants a Vodka Cosmo and I indicate to her that I want one as well. I held up two fingers and asked Gigi to place the order. She smiled as she began talking to the bartender while I checked the missed text messages on my smartphone.

My mother had texted to wish me a "happy vacation." Just then I look up at the bartender, noticing that she is making three Vodka Cosmos. It struck me as a little strange, but I figured that another customer had decided that they wanted one, too. The bartender finished making the drinks and carefully served all three to Gigi and I as she handed me the bill with a smile. I turned to Gigi, shaking my head. "No," I said, "I asked you to order us two Vodka Cosmos, not three." Gigi stared directly into my eyes and I could literally see her switching personalities. She frowned and loudly raised her voice in front of everyone at the bar, yelling in Spanish: "Tré, you said to order three drinks!" Not caring at that particular moment that everyone was now staring at me, I paused in silence with a nonchalant smile on my face. Then I say softly to Gigi in Spanish: "It's okay…no problem," as I wink at her. This defused her anger immediately.

I pay the bartender and include a big tip without blinking an eye. But in my mind I was trying to figure out what just happened because there was no reason for Gigi to freak out on me like that. The whole thing was simply an honest mistake on her part, and mistakes will certainly happen from time to time. I thought to myself that I certainly knew the difference between "dos" (two) and "tres" (three) in Spanish, and besides I was holding up two fingers at the time! I was really caught off guard and couldn't quite let go of this strange incident. I knew that Gigi wasn't drunk, but I thought perhaps the pressure of moving away to a foreign country all alone was starting to take a toll on her psychologically. This type of scenario could cause almost anyone to become "unglued" on occasion, including me.

So I decided to let the incident go so we could spend the rest of our evening sharing warm, positive energy. It was truly a night to celebrate because I honestly didn't know when or if Gigi and I would ever see each other again. I handed the extra Vodka Cosmo to the bartender as I said, "Disfruta" (Enjoy)! I turned toward Gigi with an amorous smile on my face, and we do a Toast. Gigi's smile has come back and she is now enjoying sipping on her Vodka Cosmo while listening to the live Italian band performance.

As our waitress escorted us from the bar to our dining booth, we were both amazed by the fact that our table was illuminated entirely by candle light! Admiring the visual enchantment, I thoroughly appreciated how the use of candle light gave the Illusion that everyone in the restaurant had somehow been transported into their own little private world, a magical world filled with serenity and intimacy, where a couple could relish an excellent meal, converse, and listen to romantic Italian love ballads.

Seizing the moment, Gigi and I decided to share a meal of multiple Italian-Dominican Fusion entrees and desserts. We laugh, drink, feed each other, and enjoy the great music. I tell Gigi how much I respect her and also how extremely proud I am of her for following her passion by starting a new career and daring to move to South Africa. Gigi began to tear up as she said, "Tré…I want you to know that I really appreciate your support, especially since all of my loved ones and friends have turned against me because of my decision to leave my home for a foreign country. All this has been very hurtful to me. You are the only one who has said to me that it is alright to want to have a better future. Thank you, dear."

"Gigi…it is important to be patient with your friends and family because one day they will come around and rejoice in your success in South Africa," I tried to reassure her. "It's just that at this moment they are afraid of what the future may hold for you, and that is why they are all against you!" I wiped the tears from Gigi's eyes. I also smoothly flipped the script and began making jokes about how, right now, Yahaira, our hostess from the spa, was probably going "loco" after seeing her "innocent jewel of a daughter participating—live and in person--in the adult world of sexual swingers!" Gigi and I both exploded with wicked laughter as her sad demeanor morphed into a mischievous grin.

"Ohhhhh, Tré! Our joke on Anatesia and Ernesto is going to be priceless," Gigi squealed. "But it serves them right for coming on to us so bold and aggressively, assuming that we were both swingers." Feeling better about our own lives after enjoying our priceless joke, Gigi and I continued eating, drinking, and talking about our passions, goals, family, and dreams. Moreover, we acknowledged and expressed our appreciation for the many advantages and opportunities being opened up to us by an increasingly diverse global economy. It was so awesome that we could now live and work anywhere in the world! The evening was actually turning out to be one of the best dining experiences I'd ever had.

Relaxing more and more with one another, our pleasant conversation slowly transitioned into a genuine heart-to-heart. "Tré...I feel one hundred percent comfortable expressing myself to you because I know you are always looking out for my best interests," Gigi told me. "That means a lot...and you are truly special to me." Staring into her eyes, I suddenly realized how much she meant to me as well. "Gigi...I just wish that you lived in the States because we have so many things in common." Gigi nodded. "Yes, Tré," she said softly. I felt compelled to express my feelings for her at that moment as I went on. "Galilea, I have to admit that I've always wanted to meet a girl like you back in the States, but now I'm thinking that the actual you would be a real blessing."

Gigi's face flushed like a rose and her eyes glowed in the golden candle light. "Yes, Tré," she responded, "it's a shame that you don't live here. It would be nice for me to have someone to share my time with in Santo Domingo." Gigi paused as she twirled a loose strand of hair. "So I hope that you will find your way to South Africa now," she said.

"I've always wanted to go there," I confided, "because I hear that South Africa is a magnificent country. Maybe now is the time," I said wistfully. And even though we'd never verbally admitted it to one another, I was sensing once again, like earlier at the spa, that Gigi and I were beginning to feel a romantic attraction to each other. In fact, what I was feeling was something "caliente" that boldly breached the boundaries of our long term friendship.

After almost two and a half hours of dinner conversation, I was becoming anxious to get on with Gigi's night of surprises. So I tell her that our night together is not over by far because we are now going to one of the hottest Merengue clubs in the city with a breathtaking view of Santo Domingo and the Caribbean Sea. Sensing her excitement, I now tell her that tonight is the night that she's going to teach me some hot Merengue moves. "I really hope that you are ready," she replied, "because I am going to wear your azz out on the dance floor!" Gigi had already started moving her lower body to the rhythm of the Merengue. Looking at me seductively, she whispered in a sexy voice, "I'm ready, Tré!" Not to be outdone, I hit back with "I'm ready, too!"

Whipping out her smartphone, she challenged me, "Let's go! Do I need to call a taxi?" I politely tell her no and that I will call Enri. But once on the phone with Enri, he indicated that he couldn't come now because he was just leaving the airport with a family of four Germans heading directly to their hotel. He then told me not to worry because his Cousin Mauricio was going to pick us up, and that he was already on his way. I thanked Enri who added that his cousin did not speak English, but that I shouldn't have any problem communicating with him. "If you have any problems Tré, just let Gigi talk to him. He is a very good man that I trust," Enri assured me. Enri then told me to be on the lookout for a blue and red taxi with a green top because Mauricio should be arriving in about fifteen minutes.

Enri had obviously thought of everything as he went on to tell me that he had already told Mauricio what Gigi and I looked like and what we were wearing. "He also knows all about the Merengue Dance Club too Tré, because he and his girlfriend go there at least two or three times a month," Enri said finally.

Meanwhile I ordered two small neat glasses of chilled Italian Dessert Moscato to help pass the time. Gigi had never had an Italian Moscato before and she loved it. I look at my smartphone and I tell Gigi that it's time to go. As we exit out of the restaurant, we see waves of people getting in and out of taxis of all sizes and colors: yellow taxis, white taxis, red taxis, brand new blue and red taxis, all eagerly awaiting their next customer. Both Gigi and I looked around for a blue and red taxi with a green top but came up empty. Gigi next suggested that she could call a taxi driver that she knew personally and trusted. Sensing that Gigi was ready to go, I calmly asked her to be a little patient because Mauricio would surely arrive soon.

Honestly, I knew exactly why Gigi was ready to leave. It was the suffocating 105 degree Santo Domingo heat bearing down on us, aggravated by a soggy humidity that was starting to make us both feel sweaty and dirty. The thought of arriving at an upscale club, dressed in our best evening attire, while broadcasting a plethora of funky body odors was definitely NOT COOL. So Gigi and I were both anxious and uncomfortable as we continued to scan the streets for our taxi.

The Taxi from Hell

Five minutes later we heard a honk and looked up to see a driver waving at us from a red-and-blue taxi with a green top. I asked Gigi to please wait for me by the restaurant's front entrance as I walked over to greet the taxi driver. In Spanish I asked him if he was Enri's cousin Mauricio. The driver replied, "Sí," at which point I cordially introduced myself and explained that he would be transporting me and my friend Galilea. Mauricio smiled and nodded his head. I then verified that he was going to be taking us to the Merengue Dance Club with the most scenic view of the Caribbean Sea. Even though Enri had told me that Mauricio frequented this particular Merengue club with his girlfriend, I still showed him a club flier which displayed the address. Mauricio excitedly replied, "Sí…Sí…Sí…I know this place!" I walked back over to Gigi, and taking her by the hand, I escorted her to Mauricio's taxi. Next, I hopped in beside her and purposely moved in close, our bodies touching.

Mauricio took off and we rode away into the Santo Domingo night. During the ride, Mauricio turned on some hard hitting classic American Hip-Hop jams! My head and body immediately started pulsating to the "sick" beats. Mauricio turned around briefly and gave me a thumbs up. Gigi started grooving too as she re-positioned her surprise going away gift so she could sit even closer to me. It was still unbelievably "mind blowing" as to why she still had not asked me, "Tré…why are you walking around with a woman's fuchsia-pink-and-black travel bag?"

Who knows why she hadn't, but as we were sitting there body to body, mentally I was getting ready to surprise her within the next couple of minutes. As we cruised by the beautiful scenery, enjoying the enchanting night view of Santo Domingo, Gigi and I reignited our heart to heart conversation that we'd begun earlier in the restaurant. All of a sudden, I noticed Gigi's head turn from left to right and back again as she began looking at our surroundings in an unusually attentive way. Then she said something in Spanish to Mauricio. He looked at us through his rear view mirror and answered back, but I didn't understand what they had said to each other. Going into Instant alert mode, I recalled my father's timely words of wisdom: "Tré, pay attention to your surroundings, no matter where you are in this world—and always look for landmarks!"

Following my father's good advice, I promptly began looking around the area with more scrutiny. I realized immediately that I didn't recognize this section of Santo Domingo that Mauricio was driving us through. Gigi continued talking to me, but her mind was obviously distracted. It was very apparent that she was more interested in where we were going. Gigi took another look around and loudly protested, "AY…AY…AY…AY!" She then began talking more aggressively to Mauricio as she pointed directly at him with her right index finger. Mauricio looked directly at us through his rear view mirror but responded in a peaceful manner. Whatever was going on between them, I still couldn't make out, but judging by Gigi's frantic body language, there was obviously something very wrong. I was now scoping every detail of the area we were driving through, but unfortunately, everything I could see was foreign to me—and especially so at night time!

I tell Gigi to lean back and she does. I next ask her, "What's going on…are we lost?" With a fiery look in her eyes, Gigi points at Mauricio and vents to me in English. "Your friend's cousin is either lost and not saying he's lost or he is taking us the long way round to charge us more money…because this is NOT the correct route to the club!" Just then Mauricio said something and Gigi loudly and viciously attacked him while pointing her finger at him once again. Losing his self-control, Mauricio fired back. A full-fledged volley of insults in Spanish erupted at super-sonic speed. But miraculously, I was comprehending everything at a 100 percent level of accuracy. The insults between Mauricio and Gigi got so nasty that I began unloosening my belt buckle in order to make a noose because at that point I thought I might have to choke Mauricio in order to maintain control of the situation. I could literally see by the way Gigi was "punking" his manhood that Mauricio was ready to fight both of us!

Driving well past the legal speed limit, he began relentlessly accelerating his taxi, darting in and out of traffic. We were still driving through an isolated area of Santo Domingo that appeared totally unfamiliar to me. As I have learned over the years, despite how a city may look during the day, it will look totally different at night! I continued looking around for a busy area, but there were no bars, no restaurants, no hotels, no local businesses and no pedestrians in this part of the city. Many times in my mind I wanted to tell Mauricio to stop the taxi and let us out, but my street smarts kept telling me that it was better and safer not to get dropped off in an isolated and unpopulated area of the city. Gigi said something to Mauricio and he made a sudden right turn. We were now driving in a different direction. The change in direction seemed to have appeased Gigi's pistol-hot emotions. But then she leaned back in her seat and immediately started "popping off" at me in English. She yelled, "Our driver is a LIAR and he lied to you! He's not Enri's cousin Mauricio, and he now admits that he is lost." I looked at the driver as he stared defiantly back at me. I'm thinking like, "What the shit?" I turned to Gigi. "Who is he?" I asked.

"I don't know! He is a LIAR!" She yelled back at me as if her statement explained everything.

Gigi paused just long enough for her frustration to swell like a tsunami. "I should have called my taxi service, Tré!" she lashed out at me. "And…you never should have communicated to him in English because it is estúpidos idiotas (stupid idiots) like this who will always take advantage of foreign gringos like you!"

Interrupting Gigi, I tell her, "Hold it, Galilea…now you listen to me!" Gigi stopped talking but continued to accuse me with her seething eyes. I pointed at the taxi driver. "The man honked at us…and he was the ONLY taxi driver in a blue-and-red licensed taxi with a green top. I walked over and spoke to him in SPANISH…to ask if he was Enri's cousin Mauricio, to which he answered yes. THEN…I explained to him who we were and he said okay. Finally, I showed him the address of the club and he told me that he knew how to get there! So Gigi…why are you so angry with me when you know this taxi driver boldly lied to my face!? I'm not from Santo Domingo…so how was I supposed to know that this maldito cabrón (fucking asshole) was lost?" I paused and my tone softened. "But I'm very happy that you were here with me to set him straight."

Gigi's eyes flashed as if to say, "Whatever, Tré!" I ignored her as I stared down the taxi driver who was now looking at us with a pair of agitated eyes. But Gigi refused to back down as she started mouthing off at him again while pointing her finger in his face. Still on high-alert, I noticed that our driver was now taking us through a different section of the city filled with vacant street corners and dimly lit streets. Meanwhile I was trying to scope out any signs of an area with normal traffic or pedestrians. Then I was going to order the driver to stop so Gigi and I could quickly get out and find another taxi—an honest and reliable one this time!

I conveyed this to Gigi in an attempt to calm her down, but she only responded with sarcasm. "I know where we are going now!" She snapped.

Maintaining her aggressive attitude, Gigi popped off once again at the driver as she yelled, "Just drop us off at any busy intersection in the Santo Domingo East Section!" Looking around me, I begin noticing that we were indeed driving down streets leading into the Santo Domingo East Section. From time to time, the taxi driver would mumble things to himself, but every time he mumbled, Gigi would yell, "Shut up, you liar!" I always knew Gigi had a fiery edge to her personality, but this hot-tempered and vicious side of her was something I had never seen before. It was as if she had suddenly become a different person. After a few peaceful moments passed with no further outbursts from Gigi, I decided that now was the time to give Gigi her surprise gift. More importantly, I was also hoping to keep her raging emotions sedated.

"What is this?" Gigi reacted as she gently stroked the soft material of her new designer travel bag.

"Congratulations on your move to South Africa, Gigi!" I said with a wide grin. "This is my going away gift to you. I wish you much success and many blessings because your exciting new adventure is just about to begin."

Surprisingly unfazed by my sincere words, Gigi proceeded to clinically analyze her new travel bag as she replied nonchalantly, "Tré…I was wondering why you were carrying a woman's bag."

I chuckled as Gigi began fondling and squeezing the travel bag's finely woven material. Then she looked at me with an air of indifference as she said in English, "But Tré…you shouldn't have done this. Coming to Santo Domingo to see me was enough."

I was a little caught off guard by her comment as I observed how meticulously she once again examined the gift bag, checking out its quality and style.

"Well…it's the most unique gift I could think of with regard to you, Gigi," I said with perfect composure. "Every time you use this bag you will always remember me and the good memories we shared together… which is extremely important to me."

"But you did not have to do this for me. I was not expecting this," Gigi said in a flat and unemotional tone, her manner unusually frigid. I was still a little baffled as to what her point was, so I decided to take a detour around her attitude by explaining some of the travel bag's unique features. I indicated to Gigi that her travel bag was especially designed to operate on solar power.

"How does it work?" she asked.

I showed her where the solar power bars were on the bag's top and also its electric input plugs. Next, I carefully explained to Gigi in Spanish that her bag would enable her to recharge her smartphone, computer lap top, MP3 player, radio, her tablet, and all forms of electronic devices. I finally told her that no matter where she was in the world, as long as she had access to the sun's rays, she would always be able to "handle her business."

However, Gigi remained dispassionate as she continued to scrutinize the unique features of her new travel bag. Without looking at me, she kept repeating over and over in English, "No! No! No…Tré! You should not have done this."

Ignoring Gigi's last comment, I asked her to please open the bag. She opened it and pulled out three perfectly rolled chic shirts that were going to look sensational on her. I grinned broadly at her surprise as she carefully perused her new clothing. But my adoring smile quickly changed into a steel-jawed frown as Gigi started shaking her head once again. Without looking me in the eyes, she kept repeating: "No, Tré! No…No…No…you should not have done this…no!" But strangely, she continued scavenging through her new clothing until she came upon her stylish fuchsia-pink flip-flops. This time I felt a million percent certain that I was going to get a positive response out of her because I knew for a fact that no other woman on the entire island of the Dominican Republic was going to have a pair of flip-flops like hers!

I was wrong. Gigi resumed shaking her head. "No!" she asserted emphatically. "No! No! No! No! Why did you do these things, Tré?" At this point, her lack of graciousness slashed through my exposed feelings like a straight razor. I heard no expression of warmth, no gratitude, no respect, and no consideration for my emotions! I was both hurt and confused by her raw and callous actions. I just could not understand where she was coming from, and more importantly, how blatantly unappreciative she was acting!

As we sped through the streets of Santo Domingo, Gigi would still verbally attack our taxi driver from time to time. Fortunately, he now realized that it was best for him to keep his mouth shut in order to avoid another scathing attack. All he could do was to look at me through his rear view mirror. I could see him shaking his head with a disgusted look on his face. It was his hang-dog look that was sending me a strong subliminal message that I was receiving loud and clear: "What the fuck! You poor bastard! You miserable son-of-a-bitch! You hopeless, godforsaken motherfucker! What the hell did you do to deserve her wicked, triflin' azz? H-O-L-Y....F-U-C-K!!"

But his telepathic messages to me didn't stop there. The sorrowful eyes in the rear view mirror went on to say: "I acknowledge that I started a shit storm by lying to you! And because of my lie, your night and your relationship with this ungrateful bitch is totally fucked! OH GOD… from the looks of you, you are about to beat my azz down as soon as I stop this taxi! But my brother…I AM SOOOO SORRY! I didn't mean for any of this shit to happen!"

The taxi driver was absolutely correct with regard to what he had just communicated to me as I sat there quietly fuming. Gigi finally pulled out the last articles of clothing from her new travel bag: three posh designer hats. Unsatisfied once again, she shook her head and repeated her previous statements. By this time I'd had enough. I was feeling very angry and hurt because I don't like being taken for granted. When a person acts in an ungrateful manner towards me, and very selfish and mean-spirited to boot, their relationship with me is automatically canceled. I am NOT one to be shy about making it known that they simply do not exist for me anymore. In other words, I invoke a total ban on their presence in my life that is like a death sentence. Just move the hell on out of my way and leave me alone is my motto! If Gigi didn't like my gifts, then at least she should have respectfully kept her comments to herself.

The more I thought about it, the more I was convinced that most girls would have LOVED my surprise package. In fact, before I left the States for Santo Domingo, I showed Gigi's gift bag to some very special female friends because I wanted their honest opinion. They all adored it without hesitation! Now, as I sat in the back of the taxi pondering the situation, my seething emotions felt like they were about to erupt like a volcano. It was time for me to "check" Gigi to her face and let her know how her ignorant and mindless behavior infuriated me!

Suddenly our taxi came to a stop in a busy section of East Santo Domingo. This part of the city was thriving, with local people walking all over the place, with traffic congestion, hotels, bars, restaurants, clubs, and various neighborhood businesses still open for the benefit of the late night crowd. Gigi quickly stuffed all of my gifts "that she didn't like" back into her new travel bag. She then quickly exited the taxi yelling, "Tré…I am not paying this liar NOTHING!" I looked over at the driver who was busy printing out his bill, then I hopped out of the cab filled with pure rage. I was sick of both Gigi and this lying-azz muthafuckiń taxi driver!

I quickly glanced over at Gigi who was now on her phone calling her Preferred Choice Car Service. Ignoring her for the moment, I walked deliberately toward our imposter of a taxi driver with the malicious intention of beating the shit out of him as he patiently waited to be paid. The thought that I couldn't get out of my head was that in less than forty-five minutes, this man's bold-faced lie had single-handedly poisoned a great friendship and blown into oblivion any possibility for Gigi and I to ever retrieve the unforgettable parting night that we'd both looked forward to as the high point of our cherished friendship.

The imposter looked up to find me standing next to him. I had a blank expression on my face, and I made sure that he couldn't see my balled-up fists strategically placed in the front pockets of my dress shorts. In an innocent and sorrowful way, he mouthed very slowly in English: "I am sorry…that I lied to you!" Glancing up at me, he went on. "I was not purposely trying to ruin your evening and cause problems between you and your girlfriend," he confessed. "And…I feel terrible right now."

Although I stood there patiently listening to him, I didn't really give a fuck at this point. So I remained silent as his English faltered and he switched over to Spanish. "Sir…I urgently need to make as much money as I can," he pleaded, "because my wife is having our fourth baby. We are on hard times and struggling right now. My previous job has gone out of business, and my wife is a stay-at-home mother. Last month we lost our house and we are currently living with my sister. So now…I must drive a taxi to support my family because we are poor. This is the reason why I lied to you."

All the while he was speaking I didn't say a word. I just stood there staring at him. Finally, he sighed and pointed to a photo of his pregnant wife and three kids taped to his steering wheel. "Please forgive me, sir!"

he said pitifully in English. "I know that I was wrong to lie, but I am desperate to make money for my family." I looked closely at his overall appearance, now observing that his clothing were wrinkled and frayed. He was also wearing a pair of mismatched dress shoes: his left shoe was brown and the right shoe was yellow. Also, his botched shave and haircut looked like a homemade job.

Little by little I felt my anger and desire for revenge draining out of me as I became more aware of his situation. After all, in my own short lifetime I had seen people do all types of desperate things while just trying to survive. The thick cloud of rage that had previously blanketed my mind began to evaporate and I discovered that I could think clearly once again. It was only at that point that I concluded it was NOT a good idea to beat the shit out of this guy! To be honest, my decision wasn't based on what the taxi driver had said to me, but rather on something far more important. Being a foreigner or "gringo" in this country with no immediate access to my family and friends back in the States was not an ideal situation to be in if I were sent to jail for assault and destruction of property. My support system here was in fact a big fat zero! Thinking rationally now, I was not going to allow myself to get caught up in the trap that I had seen other foreigners fall prey to while traveling abroad.

No matter how minor a situation may appear to us Americans, I've discovered that it's always a major issue in the eyes of local officials in a foreign country. So let the traveler beware! Interpretations of laws and regulations on foreign soil are a different animal altogether which, in the blink of an eye, can result in a devastating impact that may change your life forever. So I took a long, deep breath and remained calm as the driver politely informed me that my fare came to $2,000 Dominican dollars ($42 U.S.). But since he felt bad about lying to me, he told me he only wanted $20 U.S. in cash. I remained silent the entire time. He apologized once again, this time telling me that $20 U.S. was the minimum he could accept because he needed to buy groceries for his family tonight. Meanwhile I continued to stare at him unmoved.

After an awkward moment or two, I slowly un-balled my fists. Then I reached into my pocket, pulled out what the taxi driver wanted, and placed it in his front shirt pocket. But before I could say anything to him, the man suddenly pointed to Gigi who was now standing on the corner talking on her smartphone, her travel bag hanging comfortably from her shoulder. The driver turned to me, shaking his head as he said: "Amargo Corazón! Cuidate!" I took a hard look at Gigi. She was in her own little selfish world, leaving me all alone to deal with the messed up situation at hand. Disgusted, I stepped away from the taxi driver as he warned me once again: "Ten Cuidado de que Amargo Corazón!" Then he started up his engine and sped away into the busy traffic. I watched him disappear around the corner, wondering what the hell he was trying to say to me!

Little did the deceitful imposter know, but I can play the game with the best of them! But he was going to find out quickly enough once he decided to reach into his shirt pocket to claim his money. What he didn't know was that he was about to be the recipient of a big surprise! Courtesy of me! That American $20 bill he thought I had given him was actually just the folded up flier advertising the Merengue club that I'd showed to him earlier—the one he was supposed to be taking us to!

Surprise!! Do you honestly think I was going to pay this man? This perpetrator who LIED to my face, drove around lost and confused, and who was the "trigger man" in offing my cherished friendship with Gigi. HELL NOOO!! Although the American $20 bill the taxi driver was banking on may not sound like a big deal to you, if efficiently allocated, it could have bought his family several days' worth of healthy and wholesome food. But this was NOT going to happen with my hard-earned money!

A Bitter Heart

I turned and started walking towards Gigi, now focusing my attention on her stylish pose in sporting her chic new travel bag. Judging by the way she was posing with the bag on the busy sidewalk, it was obvious to me that she was unquestionably LOVING my special gift! I deliberately positioned myself right in front of Gigi, who was no longer talking on her smartphone, but waiting for our car service to arrive. Still she refused to look me in the face or even acknowledge my presence. I was so pissed with her at that moment that I did the same. The situation grew very intense as we stood there in silence, neither one of us really knowing what to say. But more to the point, neither one of us knew how to say it because of what had just happened between us. What I did know was that both of us were operating on a very short fuse and that one careless word could cause our raw emotions to explode.

I took several deep breaths to help maintain my cool because I knew that if Gigi "popped off" at me just one more time, I was going to unleash on her a relentless fury that she'd never experienced before in her sheltered young life. Yes, I know we were both acting like adolescents, standing there sulking in silence, but I really didn't care. The way I saw it, Gigi owed me an apology and she needed to make the first move if she truly wanted to mend our fractured friendship. Precious moments passed as Gigi and I continued to stand there on the busy corner staring each other down. Although we were not communicating verbally, our hostile stares and body language was saying it all—and not in a good way. I was utterly clueless regarding Gigi's wacked out behavior. What the hell could be going on inside her head right now? During this whole trip—since I first landed in Santo Domingo—her mood swings had been totally unpredictable and erratic. I had honestly never seen her act like this before!

My thoughts turned suddenly inward as I reflected on our friendship and the genuine sense of caring that had blossomed between us over the past five years. I also realized that in my heart I really DID want to take the high ground because I didn't want to say anything that I might later regret with regard to confronting Gigi. I particularly didn't want to say anything vile or upsetting to her in view of the mutual respect and affection that had been extended to me by her family. They had always treated me like I was one of them, and I didn't want to disappoint them. If I had not stopped to consider all this, I probably would have lost my cool with Gigi. However, given the deep personal relationships we shared and the fact that Gigi and I had always had each other's backs during tough times, made me think twice about anything I might say to her now as we stood rudely ignoring each other. How twisted is this? I thought to myself.

Our icy silence was finally broken when the car service arrived, pulled alongside us, and honked. Without hesitation I opened the left passenger side door for Gigi, and she got in. I casually picked up Gigi's travel bag from the seat. Taking the hint, she moved closer to the center of the seat to make room for me to sit next to her. But as she turned toward me expectantly, what she witnessed instead was the car door slamming in her face! I watched as Gigi's eyes widened in sheer shock! My emotions were so out of control that I slammed the door so hard that the entire service car shook, rocking like it was caught in an earthquake. Everyone passing by in close proximity to us were startled and instantly began looking around to see where the explosive noise was coming from. I turned and quietly walked away unnoticed, with my new designer travel bag slung over my arm. But that didn't stop the service car driver from screaming at me. "What did you just do!" he called out angrily. "What did you just do to my car door!!!"

I never looked back as I continued strolling along as if nothing had happened. Suddenly, I heard the driver yelling at Gigi in Spanish: "If he broke my door woman, you are going to pay for the damages!" Meanwhile I disappeared inconspicuously into a sea of human traffic as I made a quick right turn onto an adjacent street full of lively people all enjoying the Santo Domingo night life. As I made my way down the block, I felt my smartphone vibrating. As I removed it from my pocket, I saw that it was Enri calling. I also noticed his multiple missed calls, voicemails, and text messages. I stopped to sit down on a nearby bench to answer his call. Enri was obviously concerned as he yelled, "Tré…Tré…are you okay?" I assured him that I was okay as he went on. "My cousin Mauricio told me that he waited for you and Gigi outside the restaurant for over twenty minutes, but you guys never came out. So he went inside to look, but even the restaurant staff couldn't find either of you. Mauricio called me and I became worried and started calling you and leaving messages for the past hour." I apologized to Enri and told him that I was having a bad night. "What happened Tré?" he asked promptly. I then told Enri the whole bizarre story in full detail. Enri listened patiently with concern before asking, "Where are you right now, Tré?" After describing my location, he told me to sit tight and he would be there in less than ten minutes.

I relaxed on the bench and cleared my mind of all of the negative thoughts that had taken me over in the last hour. Enri arrived in less than eight minutes along with his cousin Mauricio. He introduced me and we all shook hands. "Finally…I'm very happy to meet the real Mauricio," I smiled. Mauricio smiled back and expressed his solemn regrets about what had happened to me. They both took a seat on the bench beside me.

With a calm demeanor, I said to them in Spanish: "Don't worry about what just happened to me, my friends, because that's all in the past now, thank God! I simply refuse to let one person ruin the marvelous experience I've had here in Santo Domingo. That would be a shame and I'm NOT going to let it happen. And with regard to Gigi's irrational behavior, let's just say that I'm glad I finally saw her for who she really is sooner rather than later. I'm just not going to allow her foul and disrespectful attitude to destroy my last two and a half days here in this paradise!"

Mauricio patted me on the back and said, "You have a good attitude Tré, and I want you to know that we Dominicanos are not all bad people." I assured Mauricio that I had many good friends in Santo Domingo and that every place in the world had dishonest people, including every city in the United States. Mauricio and Enri both laughed at my remark. But then the conversation took a surprising turn. Enri remarked that he wanted me to take a look at a picture on Mauricio's smartphone. I stared at the all-too-familiar face with surprise.

"Is this the man who lied to you?" Enri asked.

"Yes," I said, unable to believe my eyes.

Mauricio shook his head in disgust as he began speaking to Enri in an agitated manner. I didn't understand what Mauricio was saying, but it was very clear to me that he was infuriated.

"We know this guy, Tré," Enri told me. "For the last six months or more he has been working as an unlicensed taxi driver so he can make money without the city of Santo Domingo knowing about it. Which is illegal…because he is not paying union dues and city taxes like the rest of us! To make matters worse, this guy purposely steals everybody's best customers by listening to phone scanners and taxi transmitters. Once he learns about a high-paying opportunity, he goes out and deceitfully solicits an Innocent customer's business by pretending to be their designated taxi driver. Tonight Tré…you were his latest victim and it cost you Gigi's friendship!"

Mauricio immediately chimed in with Enri translating. "Four times this month already, this asshole has stolen big paying jobs away from me! On two of those occasions, I was instructed by my dispatcher to pick up loyal customers who needed a ride from the Santo Domingo Airport to their vacation condos located in the city of Juan Dolio, about an hour's drive. To make a long story short, both times I immediately rushed out to the airport only to find out that my customers were already gone! I could have made a lot of money for my family!" Mauricio grimaced as he looked me in the face. Enri also had a few horror stories of his own about this rogue of a taxi driver, including one in which he had stolen a loyal customer by lying to her face that Enri was at home sick! Enri suddenly pounded his fists as he continued. "Tré…this greedy liar has caused nothing but confusion among us taxi drivers by destroying relationships with our personal customers and stealing our money."

Mauricio checked his text messages and turned to Enri. "We need to go now!" he said emphatically. Enri looked at me. "Come on Tré," he said, "I'm going to take you back to your hotel free of charge." We all got into Enri's taxi as he sped off into the night. Mauricio then told Enri that their friend Rocco had just sent a text message indicating that the imposter had been spotted placing an order for hot coffee and a baked turkey dinner at Manny's Restaurant. "As soon as we drop you off Tré," Enri looked at me through the rear view mirror, "Mauricio and I will head over to meet with the taxi driver who lied to you tonight. We are going to show up unannounced with a total of fifteen other co-workers that this man has screwed over. After our little chat with him…I promise you that this greedy, lying son-of-a-bitch will NEVER interfere with our livelihood again!" Mauricio laughed as he chimed in, "Amen to that cousin!"

That being said, Enri changed the subject. "Tré…I know that you didn't intend for your night to end up like this," he said with concern, "but I believe that things happen for the best." I nodded my head in agreement as he continued. "The other night I was having dinner with my daughters Maria and Tatiana, and we were talking about your friend Gigi."

"What did you guys honestly think about her?" I asked.

Enri sighed. "Honestly Tré, we got some weird vibes from her. It was very evident to all of us that Gigi is dealing with some dark side issues. Maria and Tatiana kept stressing that to me, and I trust their judgement. Gigi is not a very affectionate and social person. It just didn't make any sense to us why your so-called friend didn't want to have dinner with us the other night. Especially when you two had not seen each other for over a year. That's just not normal. Someone who truly cares about you doesn't act that way." Enri paused for a moment as if to make sure that my feelings weren't hurt by his remarks. "Tré, I believe that girl has an 'Amargo Corazón'…so it's best to leave her alone and let her deal with her craziness by herself. In my opinion, she really doesn't deserve your friendship. And especially not now, after the way she acted tonight. No way, my brother!"

Suddenly, I realized that the immaculate light of God's knowledge was speaking to me through Enri's inspired words because he had sincerely confirmed for me the ONE thing that the lying taxi driver had actually told the truth about. And that one truth was that Gigi had an "Amargo Corazón" or "Bitter Heart." This fact was obvious to me now as I nodded my head in agreement. Somebody really must have hurt Gigi in the past. Unfortunately, the damage to her heart now made her prone to destroy precious friendships by lashing out at innocent people who sincerely wanted to be part of her life. I told Enri that I agreed with him one hundred percent, but more importantly, I still had two and a half more days to live life to the fullest during the remainder of my stay in Santo Domingo. "Cool!" Enri replied calmly. "The night is still young and I really would like for you to go to the live Merengue concert that I was telling you about earlier today. Tati and Maria are there now and they will be thrilled to see you again, Tré."

"Hey Enri, I'm ready to celebrate and have a good time tonight!" I said enthusiastically. "Maria and Tati can finally teach you how to dance the Merengue like a true Dominican tonight," Enri responded.

I was already super-hyped about tonight's concert as I roared back in Spanish, "I'm looking forward to everything tonight…with much pleasure, my brothá!"

Enri took a deep breath and sighed. "I wish I could go, but Mauricio and I need to deal with our situation tonight. I want you to make sure that no man gets too macho with my baby girls, Tati and Maria! Okay, Tré?"

"First of all Enri…Tati and Maria are in their mid-twenties," I told him. "So I'm pretty sure they can thoroughly handle themselves. But, mi mano, I will make sure that no one gets out of line with either of them." Enri nodded as he paused to make a phone call. He then began speaking into the phone in rapid Spanish. "Tati…Tré is coming and I want you and your sister to look after him. He will be there in twenty minutes. I love you and have fun tonight!"

We arrived back at my hotel, which was so close to the concert that we could hear the Merengue band playing nearby. I quickly darted through the busy hotel lobby filled with animated customers. I didn't see Serena at the front desk, so I took the elevator directly up to the executive suites. Arriving at my floor, I noticed immediately that new guests were now occupying three other executive suites. I noticed that my friends Sofia and Oscar were enjoying their evening as well. Entering my room, I noticed that the clock in the kitchen read 10:17 p.m. I knew that I needed to hurry because Tati and Maria would be heading to the bodega to meet me very soon. So I quickly undressed, freshened up, and changed into casual attire which consisted of a nice pair of jean shorts, a short sleeved shirt and my athletic sneakers. I next deposited my wallet, all the jewelry I was wearing, my smartphone and camera in the room safe. Following Enri's instructions to the letter, I was only going to carry a small amount of cash on me to the concert. Next, I opened up the designer travel bag that I had retrieved from Gigi and dumped all of its contents on my bed. Then I grabbed two plastic clothing bags from my suitcase and put two designer shirts in one bag and a designer hat and shirt in the second bag.

I walked over to the dining room table and began taste-testing my four Strawberry Fusion masterpieces. Wow! I was totally blown away by what Serena, Yoly, Jessy, and I had accomplished in a major way! I went to the kitchen and filled a small Ziploc bag full of Sparkling Strawberry Cider-Apple Fun Cubes. Next, I sat down at the dining room table and set aside one of my Strawberry-Coconut flavored fusion drink jars. Overcome with positive energy, I began writing a note to the newlyweds, Sofia and Oscar. I congratulated them on their happy marriage and told them to enjoy my personal wedding gift. I also included instructions on how best to serve and enjoy their Strawberry-Coconut Fusion cocktails together with the Fun Cubes.

Running out of time, I exited my suite and pushed the down button on the elevator. Meanwhile I rushed over to Oscar and Sofia's front door to neatly place their exotic cocktail, Ziploc bag full of Sparkling Strawberry Cider-Apple Fun Cubes, the clothing bag with Sofia's new designer gifts tucked inside, and my note. Just as I hear the elevator arriving, I knock loudly on the door until I hear Sofia's voice saying, "I'm coming…I'm coming." I suddenly dart back to my waiting elevator.

Just as I get in, I hear Sofia opening her front door. The elevator doors close abruptly and I ride down to the hotel lobby.

Following Enri's instructions as I exit the hotel, I begin walking down the street that will lead me directly to the Merengue concert. Enri was right on target in advising me to be extremely careful because the hovering street lamps were all but dysfunctional. The entire block was engulfed in dark shadows for as far as I could see. Only the center of the street had any illumination at all. All of the run-down businesses along the street were closed. Looking around me, I didn't see anybody. The only thing I could hear was the surging cheers of passionate people enjoying the concert performances. I decided to play it safe by walking in the shadows instead of the street where I would be plainly visible to any predator. Being all alone, I reasoned that concealing myself might prove to be my best protection. It would also put me in a dominant position in case of a surprise attack, especially if it came down to me having to take somebody out before they could get to me. Employing this strategy—and with the blessings of God above—I walked the five-and-a-half short blocks untouched and unbothered!

Finally, I found myself standing at the edge of a huge public park. I still couldn't see the cheering crowds or the live band, but I knew that I was extremely close. As instructed by Enri, I looked to my right and instantly spotted the Bodega store. The store was lit only by a dingy green florescent light and stood tall among the other antiquated businesses already closed for the evening. I quickly began walking towards the Bodega when I spotted Tatiana and Maria waving at me. As I came closer, I could hear Maria telling Enri over the phone, "Tré is safe with us now." They both rushed over to greet me with big, warm hugs and kisses to my cheeks. I was happy to see them too, especially after having survived my messed up adventures with Gigi just an hour or so ago!

"Ohhhh Tré…you poor baby!" Maria gushed sympathetically. "Enri just told us everything that happened to you! Are you okay?"

Before I could respond, Tati interrupted. "Of course he's fine!" she quipped. "Otherwise, he wouldn't be here with us right now, Mari!" Tatiana paused for a second to look me over before she went on. "I can't believe that ungrateful, mentally deranged girl snapped on you Tré, when it was clear that the taxi driver lied and pretended to be our Uncle Mauricio."

"I know…how insane is that, Tati?" Maria chimed in.

After listening to the two of them going on about my misadventure for about five minutes, I can honestly say that I felt fully vindicated. I was my normal, laid-back self again. These two stylish young girls were so energized and full of life that I was truly grateful that Enri had insisted that I hang out with them tonight. "Ladies…yes the beginning of my evening was really unfortunate, but that's all in the past now…I'd much rather be here with the two of you anyway!" I said, politely interrupting them. "It's really okay…now give me a hug!" I said enthusiastically, opening my arms as both of them rushed to embrace me.

"Okay…okay…anything for you, Handsome," Mari purred in Spanish.

Meanwhile Tati softly squeezed my chin and said, "Good answer, Tré! Because you should know right now that you are out on the town with the two hottest girls in the entire Caribbean! And best of all, we will always have your back. Understand me?"

Together they assured me they were going to personally teach me how to Merengue dance, introduce me to all of their favorite Dominican dishes, and that we were going to party out under the stars to the sounds of the most talented Merengue bands in the Dominican Republic. "Does that sound good to you, Tré?" Maria asked. With a big grin on my face, I emphatically responded, "Sí". Then I took a moment to present both of them with a gift as I thanked them for sharing their time with me. The look on their faces said they couldn't believe what I'd just done as they opened the bag and pulled out two designer shirts. Overjoyed, they showered me with more hugs and kisses.

They also started flirting me. "Don't you want to marry a nice Dominican girl, Tré? Well…don't you? Tréeeeé…we're trying to tell you that marrying a good Dominicana will be the best thing to ever happen to you in your LIFE!"

Tati and Mari then began high-fiving each other as I stood by silently enjoying their little game, a broad smile on my face. As a duo, they were "off the chain" in my book, and I loved their free-spirited charm. Never one to be shy, I couldn't resist doing a little flirting myself. "Don't hug and kiss on me too much with marriage proposals on your lips," I fired back, "because I hope you realize that I'm single and very available! And besides, we don't want to upset your father, do we? I know how possessive and overprotective fathers can be when it comes to defending their precious but very naughty baby girls."

Both girls burst into laughter as Mari responded in a sexy voice, "Oh…Enri won't care, Tré. He only wants the best for us…and he knows that whatever we choose to do, we know how to handle ourselves."

"That's right, Tré," Tati chimed in. "And furthermore, we're the ones who boss Enri around and tell him exactly what we want him to do for us." They giggled and high-fived each other. I couldn't help laughing at their crazy, fun-loving antics myself. Tati then says in Spanish, "You see, Tré…Enri and our mother had me when they were 15 years old and they had Mari when they were 17 years old. Realistically, Enri is like our overprotective big brother. But he really is an excellent father, and we are his little princesses, because he does everything for us," Tati said as she amped up the sexiness of her soothing, sultry voice. "Tréeeeé…Enri likes you a lot and he especially loves it when you are spending time with us…his two naughty baby girls!" Maria, who rarely failed to support her big sister, winked and flashed a pretty smile at me. Suddenly, we were interrupted by a loud roar stemming from a pumped-up crowd of music lovers. We all stopped talking as we listened to a highly energetic hostess introducing a very famous Merengue band. The band started playing and it seemed like the whole island erupted. Everyone inside the Bodega hurried out of the store and sprinted toward the concert stage, screaming with excitement.

"That's one of my favorite bands! Let's go!" Tati yelled.

"Come on, Tré! It's time to go dancing!" Mari joined in as I locked arms with the two of them.

We hurried up a hill that led to another section of the park. With a clear view from the top, what I saw was unreal. Every square inch of the park's concert area was jammed-packed with over six thousand Dominicanos partying like there was no tomorrow! People were dancing in the concert area and in the surrounding streets. I even saw Dominicanos drinking, celebrating, and barbecuing on the roof tops of local businesses! The thing I liked the most about the crowd was that it had a definite blue collar vibe about it. Everybody was so down-to-earth.

The only light in the park stemmed from the poorly lit street lamps which gave off a dim yellow haze; the make-shift lighting rigged up around the concert stage; and the full moon shining down from the heavens above. Nonetheless, the entire entourage of stage performers were NOT deterred in the least. Instead, they seemed even more inspired to demonstrate their personal best—and perform they did as they fired up the crowd into an uncontrollable frenzy! Tati turned to me and said, "We all need to go get a drink first…It'll help us to loosen up." I was certainly "down" with the idea, so Maria and Tati carefully guided me through a gigantic maze of people and over to a street vendor. Mari and Tati both knew the vendor and asked him to make his famous "Brugal Rum Punch."

Feeling ecstatic to be spending this time together, the three of us shout out a group cheer before consuming our delicious drinks. The potent "kick" of the Brugal Rum Punch was instantaneous. I was loving the new "heady" sensations I was experiencing. I started smiling as I began to feel the polyrhythmic Merengue beats pulsating through my body. Maria and Tati noticed the change too and started grinning at me. Mari said to Tati, "I believe Tré is ready to dance the Merengue with us now." My two beautiful dates did their usual high-fives as they escorted me to the stage area. We got as close as we could since there were already thousands of happy Dominicanos eating, drinking, and partying near the stage. Visually, the scene was utterly mind-blowing and surreal, because from a certain distance, the thick crowd looked like three-dimensional silhouettes all jammed together in the obscure lighting.

Meanwhile Mari and Tati began showing me some basic Merengue dance steps, though real conversation was impossible because of the loud music. At times I can be a slow learner when it comes to getting into new dance moves, but Tati and Mari were both very patient with me. To my surprise, after about fifteen minutes of hard work, I was ready to showcase my new talents. Satisfied at what she was seeing, Mari quickly grabbed me and tried to annihilate me, showing no mercy! And…YES! She was destroying me with a whole new series of exotic moves that she had evidently kept to herself because she certainly hadn't taught them to me! Still, I managed to stay in the moment. I was recalculating, working it, and hanging tough with Mari.

I then look over my shoulder and see Tati dancing up close and personal with some guy. She was obviously out maneuvering and dominating him as well. So it didn't take long to figure out that both Mari and Tati were exceptional dancers. Miraculously, I was holding my own with Mari, even though she was still sliding in some exotic Merengue moves every chance she got. Ain't no need of me lying, I enjoyed every second of our dance as the hard-hitting live band performed hot Merengue hits back-to-back for a roaring and adoring crowd of fanatics. Soon I began letting loose a roar or two myself because this was my type of party!

While staying in rhythm with the song being performed, Mari smoothly passed me off to Tati. Once again I was introduced to a totally new series of smooth dance moves stamped with Tati's own alluring signature. Her sensual, contoured movements were especially expressive of the slower Merengue beats. I wasn't the perfect partner, but I still managed to hang with Tati, who coincidently opted for the role of lead dancer. I glanced over at Mari and saw her dancing with another guy. Their steps were beautifully synchronized, but throughout the dance Mari had to keep reminding her partner to keep his hands above her waistline.

Tati, Mari, and I must have danced for almost ninety minutes straight as the performers on the bandstand kept changing. Deciding to take a much needed break, we walked over to the street vendors to buy food, beer, and a bottled water for me. True to their word, Mari and Tati introduced me to their favorite Dominican foods, which consisted of Pica Pollo (fried chicken pieces seasoned with lemon, garlic, and Dominican oregano); Croquetas de Camarón (fried shrimp croquettes); and Memelos (tiny candy suckers with a coconut cream center). I treated Mari and Tati to their favorite dishes and they bought the drinks. Afterwards, we found a comfortable spot to sit, chat, and just enjoy the concert.

"Dios mío...la comida es tannnnnnnn deliciosa!" I exclaimed as I tasted the delicious food. Mari and Tati both nodded as they flashed knowing grins at me. As we were finishing up our meal, our dynamic hostess announced that the last Merengue band of the evening would only be performing for one hour. The humongous crowd groaned in unison because everyone was having a fantastic time. I looked up to see a cute little girl selling candy, gum, miniature scented oil sprays and travel-sized bottles of mouthwash. I called her over and made several purchases. Maria gazed at me with a smile. "Tati…It looks like Tré is trying to freshen us up for another dance," she teased.

"Well…you ladies do owe me one last dance!" I responded.

"Then let's go!" Tati shot back, almost daring me. "I want to see if you can handle both of us Tré before Enri arrives! He will be here in twenty minutes."

"I'm ready," I yell. Mari stood up immediately in response to my challenge. We all refreshed ourselves with mouthwash, scented oils, and chewing gum before heading for the stage area.

The band kicked off their performance at a feverish pace, and everyone exploded into a frenzy! The girls and I somehow managed to claim a small area for ourselves, although we were surrounded by an endless sea of people all dancing like it was "No Tomorrow!" For real, the park was packed to optimum capacity. By now, Mari, Tati and I were all dancing together. The dynamic duo was now boldly exhibiting their sexy, dare-devil moves right in front of my face. With a "take no prisoners" attitude, they were challenging me to "bring it on!"

After a minute or two, I felt like I was being hypnotized. The way they were able to gracefully manipulate the delicate contours of their bodies to the high-tempo Merengue beats, without even a hint of fatigue, was almost spellbinding. I no longer had any doubt that these sexy and fun-loving girls were members of an exclusive elite when it came to dancing. Before long, other people nearby starting noticing them as well. Just watching Mari and Tati's two gyrating and appetizing young bodies in non-stop, fluent motion was forcing everybody to up their dance game.

Without breaking her stride, Maria grabbed me by my waist and we started dancing together. I noticed that Mari always slipped into the role as lead dancer. This time was no exception as she smoothly guided me through a series of intricate Merengue steps. All I could do was follow her lead because she made it easy for me. As I looked into her confident eyes, she gradually began to increase the pace until we were in perfect unison with the relentless tempo of the band. All of a sudden, not to be outdone, Tati stole me away from her sister as she began to match her unique and sensual body movements to the beats, which kept getting faster and faster.

Tati loved to play and tease as she danced. She could also be very aggressive when you least expected it as she began spinning me around at arm's length, then quickly pulling me back into playful contact with her upper and lower body. Checking out her skill set, the people around us began chanting and yelling, "Va! Va! Va!" (Go! Go! Go!). In the meantime, I was just doing my best not to embarrass myself.

But to tell the truth, my confidence level was off the charts because I knew I was in good hands with Tati. Wanting back in on the action, Mari intervened and all three of us started dancing together. I purposely placed myself between Mari and Tati. Then we all "attacked" one another with frenetic Merengue moves. Suddenly, Tati checked her text messages and grabbed me and Mari by the hands. Enri had arrived. So as we headed back up the hill, he began signaling us by flashing his lights and honking his horn. Within minutes we were all inside the taxi.

The thorough "debriefing" that Enri's "two little princesses" gave him about the concert during our ride back to my hotel, was like a rollicking after party with Mari and Tati going tit for tat as they filled Enri in on the highlights. All too soon we were pulling up to the front entrance of the hotel. After wishing everyone a good night I walked over to Enri to offer my sincere thanks. I also handed him a $20 bill in American cash. Enri stared at me with a perplexed look on his face. "What is this for?" he gave me the third degree. "You don't have to pay me, Tré!" he said emphatically.

I stood there smiling at him for a suspense-filled moment before I replied, "That $20 bill you're holding is the money that I owed to the dishonest taxi driver who lied to me. He didn't deserve it, but you do, mi mano!" I extended my hand as Tati and Mari both exhaled in unison. As I walked toward the hotel, Enri yelled out: "In two days' time, your ride to the airport will be free of charge, Tré. My daughters are also going to make you a special going away breakfast for all of us to eat on the way!"

I thanked Enri, blew Tati and Mari a goodbye kiss, and went inside. As I strolled around the empty lobby, I saw Serena hard at work at the front desk computer. I walked over to her and shouted, "Hola…Hola…Hola…y buenas noches, Serena!" Serena immediately stopped what she was doing to interrogate me. She wanted to know if I had just come back from the Merengue concert. I nodded yes and went on to tell her all about it. "Yes, I heard that the performances were all spectacular," she said regretfully. "I hate that once again I missed out on another fantastic concert in the past two days!"

"Did you go with your friend Gigi?" she asked smiling.

"NO WAY!" I roared back, without stopping to think how this might come across to Serena. "I ended up going with two other friends," I confided to her.

Noticing my aggressive body language, Serena leaned towards me inquisitively. "Did something happen between you and Gigi, Tré... because I am sensing some very bad feelings?"

I shook my head in disgust. Then I flash a grin as I look into Serena's puzzled face. "Yes! Something did happen earlier this evening and it's a very long and crazy story." Serena's hazel eyes widened in disbelief. She patted my hand. "Don't move!" she said abruptly as she walked over to her coworker and told him she was going to lunch. She quickly returned to the front desk, grabbed her lunch container, and told me to follow her.

We sat down at a vacant table in the fine dining area, and Serena began assembling her five-star gourmet lunch, lovingly prepared by her husband, Chef Rafael. She looked up and said, "Tré...I have a one hour lunch. So I want to hear all about this crazy situation that happened between you and Gigi this evening. I'm not trying to know all of your personal business, but I am a little concerned that you might be in some sort of trouble. Are you in trouble with Gigi, Tré?"

"No...no I'm not in any trouble with Gigi or anybody else!" I said emphatically.

Serena closed her eyes, took a deep breath, and made the sign of the cross. "Thank God, Tré!" she said. "I got so nervous and scared for you."

I apologized for my careless manner and told Serena that I didn't mean to scare her. After offering me half her lunch, which I graciously declined, Serena's curiosity got the best of her. "So...what happened to you, Tré? I want to know," she said impatiently.

Without hesitation, I rehashed the whole sordid story for her, live and in color. It was like I was a sidewalk artist painting vivid action scenes in her mind, complete with all of its twists and turns, right up to my explosive climax of an ending. But since I always like to accentuate the positive, I went on to tell her about the happy epilogue from my "night from hell" when I was gallantly rescued by Enri's two beautiful daughters, Mari and Tati, and whisked off to an extraordinary evening of dance, food, and fun at the live Merengue concert. Serena sat there captivated the whole time. All she did was to eat her lunch and listen without even one interruption!

Only after I'd finished my story did Serena break her silence. "Tré...I have NEVER heard of all these things happening to a person in less than five hours! You've certainly experienced quite a day, my friend!" she said, exhaling with relief. "Are you okay?" she gazed at me with sympathetic eyes.

"Despite everything that has happened to me...I honestly feel GREAT!" I said calmly.

Serena smiled at me as she began packing up her lunch dishes. "Tré...I feel like I have just watched a good movie filled with exciting drama because I am exhausted right now," she confessed. We both had a good laugh as I walked Serena back over to the front desk.

I had a sudden feeling that I should do something different the following day. So I asked her if there were any interesting tours still available. Checking her computer, she indicated that my choices were a sight-seeing tour of Santo Domingo's most famous historical landmarks or a cocoa plantation tour. Neither appealed to me, so I said no to both options as I told Serena that I simply wanted to relax under the open sky in some place with a great scenic view. Serena continued checking until she stumbled upon something off the beaten path. "Hey! Tomorrow we are doing a multi-hotel all day excursion tour to the beaches of Juan Dolio," she said, excited. "There you can relax all day or go swimming in the crystal clear waters of the Caribbean Sea," she told me. Serena seemed to be on a roll as she went on. "You can also choose to either stay to yourself or mingle with Dominicans and other tourists from all over the world. And by the way, Tré...the tour also offers a late afternoon luncheon on the beach, an evening barbecue dinner, and a champagne toast as the finale!"

Now I was excited, too. I told Serena to please pencil me in for the tour, but she was obviously distracted by something she saw on her computer screen. "Tré...look...we had a cancellation from a family of three...they evidently had to take an emergency flight back home to Germany this afternoon. And since their tour was non-refundable, they decided to donate their reservations to anyone who wants them," Serena said, her voice rising with excitement.

"So does that mean I can go for free?" I whisper as I lean across the counter.

Serena nodded enthusiastically, then asked if my friends Jessyca and Yolanda would like to accompany me!

"I know I want to go," I replied, "but let me call Yoly and Jessy to see if they are available. What time do they need to be here in the morning?"

Serena tells me that the tour bus for Juan Dolio will be leaving from the hotel at 8 a.m. I thanked her for her generous hospitality and told her I would be back in ten minutes with the word on Jessy and Yoly.

Approaching my suite, I see a card with my name on it taped to my door handle. I grab it as I enter the room, turn on the lights, and sit down at the dining room table. It was a wonderful thank you card from Sofia and Oscar which read: "Tré…we are so grateful for your kindness, friendship, and well wishes. Please give us a call when you have some free time." I paused to enjoy my moment of appreciation before deciding to keep it moving despite the fact that it was almost 2 o'clock in the morning. I picked up the bedside phone and dialed Jessy's cell number. She answered on the second ring as she moaned "Buenas noches" in a tired and sleepy voice.

"Hello Jessy…it's Tré," I say softly.

"Is anything wrong, Tré?" she queried.

"No…and please forgive me for calling so late. But, I would like to know if you and Yoly would like to travel with me to the beaches of Juan Dolio tomorrow?"

Jessy's voice starts to come alive as she tells me to stay on the phone because she needs to ask Yoly. A couple of minutes passed before Jessy switched over to the speaker phone. "Buenas noches, my love!" Yoly purrs into the phone before quickly adding, "We would love to accompany you, Tré!"

"Excellent!" I responded. "So please meet me in the Hotel Lobby at 7:30 a.m. sharp!" I say as I wished them both a good night.

Hanging up the phone, I began stuffing all of my beach clothing and other paraphernalia into my backpack, including the two remaining designer hats that were originally intended for Gigi. These were now going to be my personal gifts to Jessy and Yoly. I knew that they would "rock" these hats out with style and "mucho" sex appeal! My free-spirited and giving personality was now in overdrive as I grabbed Gigi's remaining gifts off my bed—a fabulous boutique travel bag and a chic pair of fuchsia-pink flip-flops which I happily placed inside my bag.

I exited my room and headed down to the front desk to meet Serena. I stood in front of her smiling face as I gave her a thumbs up on the tour. She nodded and quickly entered our names onto the travel list for tomorrow's excursion. I thanked Serena for all her kindness and presented her with my surprise gift.

"What's this?" she asked with a bright smile on her face.

"It's a solar powered travel bag!" I announced.

Serena couldn't resist examining and stroking the softness of her new gift as I explained to her how the solar power bars were specially designed to power up and operate all of her portable electronic devices on demand.

By now Serena was literally swooning with excitement as a girly shriek escaped her lips. Hotel staff and customers alike looked over in our direction. Suddenly aware of the commotion she'd caused, Serena quickly put everyone at ease. "Everything is okay everybody…I am just experiencing an incredible moment of happiness!" Then she hugged me firmly. "Gracias, Tré!" she said. I have to admit that I was touched by her happiness and how much my gift obviously meant to her.

As I prepared to return to my room, I told Serena that her Strawberry Fusion cocktails and her Sparkling Strawberry Cider-Apple Fun Cubes were all ready for her guests, and that she and her husband could pick them up from my suite anytime.

"Rafa and I will come by early tomorrow morning before you leave for Juan Dolio," she assured me.

But before I could walk away, Serena indicated that she wanted to tell me something. My curiosity was piqued as I turned toward her.

"Tré…promise me that you will NOT allow anything that has happened to you this evening rob you of the pleasurable time you will spend with your good friends….okay?" Serena's expression was caring and sincere. "Make sure that you take the time to really embrace the elegance of Juan Dolio," she went on, "because it is our tropical paradise to the world outside, and it deserves to be cherished."

I promised her that I was going to enjoy my trip, and more importantly, that I was no longer upset. Wishing her a good night, I headed back upstairs to my suite. Once inside, I ironed my clothes for tomorrow's trip and then took a long hot shower. Afterwards, I set the alarm on my smartphone AND on the bedside radio clock to wake me up at 6 a.m. sharp!

DÍA CUATRO
(DAY FOUR)

It is 7:15 a.m. the next morning, and I'm in Serena's office talking with both her and Chef Rafael. The Chef has a small food cart stacked with two different versions of the Strawberry Fusion Drink and a medium-sized cooler containing sixteen Ziploc plastic bags filled with my Sparkling Strawberry Cider-Apple Fun Cubes. Everything is ready for their annual summer party. I was confident that by the end of the party, Chef Rafael and Serena were going to be super stars in the eyes of their colleagues and bosses!

Serena and I next begin wrapping a protective plastic covering around her and Chef Rafael's personal Fusion Drink Jar. For concealment purposes, we put it into a brown cardboard box along with the bags of Fun Cubes. We'd all previously agreed that it was best to keep the couple's co-workers out of their personal business. Chef Rafael thanked me and left with his prize food cart full of alcoholic goodies so he could get started on a very long day of prep work.

Now it's time for me to embark on my all day beach adventure to Juan Dolio! So I put on my sun glasses and strap on my backpack. Seeing that I was ready to go, Serena quickly grabbed her personal belongings, including her new solar-powered travel bag. I carefully pick up the concealed box of goodies, and we walk outside the hotel where Serena hails a taxi to take her home.

Meanwhile Jessy and Yoly arrived at 7:30 a.m. sharp by local car service just in time to wave goodbye to Serena and thank her for our complimentary trip to Juan Dolio. Jessy, Yoly and I all greet each other with warm hugs as our luxury bus pulls up in front of us. Hotel tourists immediately began forming a long line behind us. Fabio, a tour guide and chaperone, escorts Yoly, Jessy, and me to the upper deck which was already filled to about seventy-five percent capacity. However, I knew that within the next few seconds the whole bus was going to be jammed-packed with super-hyped tourists from at least five different European countries.

 A good friend of Serena's, Fabio then led us to a private area where the three of us could sit together. Tapping me on the shoulder, he confided: "Tré…Serena tells me that you enjoy taking photos. Well if you sit here by this double window, you will have the opportunity to get some really cool pictures on the way to Juan Dolio. On the way back, you can shoot some extraordinary night photos as well." I couldn't help thinking at this point that Serena had gone all out to make sure our tour was special. "Wow…that's great Fabio! Thank you so much!" I reply as I shake his hand. Fabio was obviously giving us the five-star treatment as he handed us bottled water, fresh fruit, and chips. We settled in for the hour and a half ride, grinning at each other in anticipation of our fabulous day on the most beautiful beaches in Santo Domingo.

 Yoly immediately began reading computer trade magazines and glamor fashion blogs on her smartphone, but fell asleep just twenty minutes into the bus ride. Meanwhile I spent my time showing Jessy how to take photos with my 35mm camera. She had often expressed to me how she wanted to evolve into a visionary artist by learning how to take high-quality photos for professional purposes. You see, Jessy and Yoly weren't just two pretty faces. They were highly intelligent and motivated professionals who wouldn't hesitate to tackle all obstacles in order to achieve their dreams. Yoly and Jessy both worked as Creative Web Designers for an established company based in Santo Domingo. However, I knew that their ultimate goal was to launch their own web design company on the international stage. I began showing Jessy the different shooting modes available on my camera, and within minutes I had her photographing abstracts of the sunny shoreline of the Caribbean Sea. Just then my body started to remind me that I'd only gotten three hours of sleep last night, so I decided to take a nap and allow Jessy to practice with my camera on her own.

 The time flies by quickly and the next thing we hear is a booming voice over the bus's intercom system. "Welcome To Juan Dolio!" Fabio calls out enthusiastically, waking everyone up from their morning nap. Fabio next instructs us to exit the bus and to gather around Daniela,

You Don't Have to Be a Mixologist to Party and have a Good Time!

our female tour guide and chaperone, for an important ten minute briefing. Approximately 150 people congregate around Daniela as she communicates to us in Spanish, English, Italian, and French using a bull horn. Daniela is full of energy as she roars exuberantly, "Welcome to the Dominican Republic's lost paradise of Juan Dolio!" to which we all responded by clapping, cheering, and whistling!

Speaking in four languages, Daniela says: "As you can see, we are Isolated from all commercial areas for our own privacy. The only thing located here is a Beach Bar-Rental Shop, where you can have a drink if you wish and also rent whatever equipment you would like for the day." She then pointed in the direction of the Beach Bar-Rental-Shop, and informed us that we would be here for the entire day. An Italian woman in her 60's asks: "Where do we go to use the bathroom and to wash off all the salt?" With a straight face Daniela translated the question for everyone as she pointed to the Caribbean Sea. "You have more than half a mile of open sea at your private disposal for all your bathroom breaks and cleansing purposes," she said. "You can be liberated and free with Mother Nature."

"Scusi" (Excuse me)!? The shocked woman responded, overcome with embarrassment. Daniela started laughing as she quickly told the group, "I'm joking…I'm joking!" We all laugh hesitantly at Daniela's humorous little joke as she proceeds to point out the impressive bathroom facilities. Daniela then paused to stare at all of us as she asserted, "Don't look so serious everyone! You are here to have FUN!"

Not to be outdone, I yell back flirtatiously in Spanish, "Daniela… does it look like I'm serious! I'm here to party with you, Baby Girl!" All who understood Spanish and Italian erupted in laughter! Translations of what I'd just said were quickly communicated to the rest of the tourists who began laughing and cheering. Suddenly Yoly hit me on my arm. "Tré…stop playing so much," she scolded me, then she turned to the group and said loudly in English: "Don't mind my crazy American friend Daniela…he was only joking." Daniela smiled, walked over to me and said, "I like you, American! And thank you for your offer…Baby Boy!"

After a little more group bonding, Daniela offered us some words of advice. She told us that it was extremely important to make friends and to watch out for each other, especially while swimming in the sea.

"If you cannot swim…stay close to the beach and relax!" she said in a serious tone. "And if you DO decide to go for a swim, do not swim past the buoys and nets placed there for your safety!" She went on to tell us that if we wanted to venture out in open waters, it would be wise to rent a water raft because the sea currents are very strong. An Englishman raised his hand and asked a sobering question: "What about the sharks? Are they swimming around in this section of Juan Dolio?" he said with no hint of humor.

Daniela smirked slightly, then chuckled. "No sir…this entire beach section is protected by both the local fishermen and by the Juan Dolio Police Water Patrol. But once again…do not swim past the buoys and nets!" she said. At this point an unknown Dominican woman hidden in the crowd said loudly in Spanish, "Those silly damn Englishmen are always paranoid about something! They really know how to kill a good mood!" Everyone who spoke Spanish and Italian began laughing hysterically, including Daniela.

As for me, I turned and instantly fell in love with the sparkling turquoise waters of the Caribbean Sea! The water was so clear and calm that I could literally see the astonishing multi-colored rock formations resting on the sea floor. The temperature was like a tropical inferno, so it was a perfect day to go swimming. Blankets of puffy white clouds were scattered across deep aqua-blue skies while the sun's rays gave off a golden shimmer. However, I was caught off guard by the baby-powder soft sands of Juan Dolio—which appeared to be angelic to the naked eye—but that burned your feet with almost malicious intent!

As Yoly, Jessy, and I were walking along the shoreline, I started snapping photos of our scenic surroundings while Jessy and Yoly struck sexy poses just for me and the camera. Nearing the Beach-Bar Rental Shop, our threesome decided NOT to do the shot of liquor enthusiastically offered to us by our fifty-five new friends. Instead, we decided to rent beach chairs, umbrellas, and a water raft for Jessy. Then we proceeded further down the beach to set up our own little private retreat. Immediately afterwards, we all began to strip down to our sexy and eye-catching swimwear. As usual, Jessy and Yoly looked stunning. Never one to waste an opportunity, I let them know just how great they were looking by flirting and attacking them with hugs. They returned the favor by letting me know that I too was looking spectacular in my

Quiksilver Boardshorts.

It was time to soak it up and just enjoy ourselves, so by this time people had fanned out all over the beach. Everyone appeared to be in their own world. They were buzzing the Beach-Bar Rental Shop, drinking beer and cocktails, tanning, swimming, or just floating on top of water rafts, determined to catch their fair share of Caribbean sun rays. I looked over and noticed a handsome British couple in their 60's setting up near us. I approached them and politely asked if they could watch over our personal items because Yoly, Jessy, and I all wanted to cool off in the sea. They quickly agreed, indicating to me that they were also watching over other people's personal belongings as well. Nonetheless, the elderly couple was definitely doing their own thing because they were listening to symphonic music, sipping on a bottle of wine, and devouring an appetizing tray of fresh fruit.

All at once Jessy and Yoly grab me by my arms and we stroll down to the Caribbean Sea. On the count of three we all dived in, but instantly popped back up screaming because the cold water gave our bodies a shock. Although it took us a minute to adjust to the chilly waters, soon the sea waters actually began to feel therapeutic because the hovering Caribbean sun was biting.

I looked over at a group of people swimming towards the water buoys and asked the girls did they want to swim along with them. Yoly's crazed eyes suddenly assaulted me as she shook her head vehemently.

"Ohhh no, Tré! I'm scared!" she said.

I was really caught off guard. "Scared of what, Yolanda?" I asked.

"I can't swim and I am afraid to venture out into water that rises above my shoulders!" Yoly confessed.

I started laughing. "Girl, stop playing," I told her.

But Jessy quickly corrected me. "Nooooo, Tré! Don't laugh! It's true…It's true! Yoly has a fear of the water!"

I fell silent for a moment before innocently replying, "I've never heard of a Dominican not being able to swim. It doesn't make any sense to me how a person can live on an island their whole life…and never learn to swim!"

Jessy and Yoly both started giggling. Then Jessy looked at Yoly and chimed in, "Girl…you know that does sound CRAZY! For eleven years I've been trying to teach you…our friends have tried to teach you…

AND even your own family members have tried to teach you!"

Yoly took a deep breath. "I know…I know…" she said. "It's time for me to conquer my fear of the water."

I suddenly focus all of my attention on Yoly with a comforting smile on my face. "After lunch I'm going to teach you how to swim. Okay?" I look directly at her. "And my specialty is the breast stroke," I laugh as I picked up an unsuspecting Yoly, cradling her against my body. Instantly, she began shrieking "Stop Tré!" "Don't you dare say NO to this sexy, caramel-brown-skinned American!" I say in a commanding masculine voice.

Yoly batted her eyes, purred, and smiled. "Alright…sounds like we have a date Tré," she said sweetly. "But can you also teach me how to doggie paddle? I'm a fast learner."

Jessy burst out laughing as she asserted, "You guys really need to get a room right now! And Yolanda…Indianara…Raquela…Pereira! You are such a big flirt, mama!"

I gently put Yoly back down.

Jessy, Yoly and I resume walking and amusing ourselves in the tranquil waters of Juan Dolio. Eventually we find a nice spot that we all like. Stretching out in the friendly water, we allow the free-flowing waves to massage and cool down our roasting bodies. I put my arms around my two lovely "partners in crime" and thank them for making this such a special day for me. I also tell them how much I am going to miss them when I return home to the States. At that precise moment I was interrupted by an Italian guy who introduced himself as Dario. Speaking to us in both English and Spanish, Dario invited us to join his group in a game of water volleyball. I look over in his direction and I see a massive ensemble of about seventy people playing with five multi-colored volleyballs! I also noticed that there were five volleyball nets attached to one another in a single file. It was absolutely "jaw-dropping" to see seventy people splashing around in the turquoise waters of the Caribbean Sea. Jessy turned to Yoly and me and says in Spanish, "Let's go…I want to play!"

We all stand up and tell Dario that we're ready to play! After snapping a couple of photos with my point-and-shoot camera, Dario insisted on taking a photo of the three of us with the volleyball game in the background. Returning the favor, I ask Dario if he wanted to pose for a photo with Yoly and Jessy. Without a word, Dario aggressively pulled both of them in close. But I could see that he was obviously attracted to Jessy as one hand rested on her shapely derriere while the other was wrapped circumspectly around Yoly's waist. Dario began posing and smiling as if he was "El Rey" (The King) of Juan Dolio, and I was doing my best not to burst out laughing!

Seeing that Jessy was uncomfortable, I purposely took my time in snapping the photo as she gave me that "hurry up and take the damn picture" look. But I continued to dawdle. Meanwhile Dario couldn't stop grinning because he understood exactly what I was doing. Unable to restrain herself any longer, Jessy took action by giving Dario a quick, sharp elbow jab to the ribs. "OOOOUCH!" Dario shouted, obviously exaggerating, as he moved his hand upwards to Jessy's well-defined waistline. At that precise moment I say, "Sonríe" (Smile)! and take the photo. Dario gave me a thumbs up while Jessy was looking away. He then explained that he would meet us over at the volleyball nets in fifteen minutes because he still needed to recruit ten more players. He winked at Jessy and jogged off smiling.

"Tré…! I am going to kill you!" Jessy yelled, turning sharply toward me. "Especially when you knew that Dario was massaging my BUTT!"

"COMOOOO" (WHAAAAT)? Yoly and I yell in unison. Attempting to defuse an embarrassing moment, I say, "Jessy…I honestly didn't know that Dario was *massaging* your butt! I only saw him touching it!"

But Jessy wasn't having it. "Yes you did, Tré," she shouted as she charged at me. I quickly grab and throw her over my shoulder. But Jessy starts shrieking, "Put me down, Tré!" at the top of her lungs, which prompted an immediate halt to the volleyball game because everyone was now staring at us! I tried to play the whole thing off by strutting smoothly toward the volleyball players, but all of a sudden I lost my balance causing both Jessy and I to topple over as we made a hard splash into the water. We both regained our bearings quickly and sat upright. At the same time we looked over to see Yoly laughing at us.

"Sorry…I couldn't resist," Yoly zipped it up as we stared at her. She nonchalantly raised her hands above her head and walked toward the cheering and invigorated group of volleyball players who began to "high-five" Yoly as they welcomed her into the game. I stood up, helped Jessy back onto her feet, and we walked towards the group who also greeted us with a lively cheer as we approached. Jessy, Yoly, and I were all welcomed by high-fives from our new teammates. We learned soon after that there were only two teams, and in order to win the game, one team had to relentlessly smack the five colorful volleyballs over the nets until the other team as a whole decided to quit.

I also learned that the losing team had to pay the entire bar tab at the end of the game! Every fifteen minutes, the owner of the bar was going to bring us trays filled with his famous homemade Mango-Raspberry Mojito mini-shots. Upon the owner's arrival, everyone had to stop playing, do a group shot cheer, then resume playing under the merciless tropical sun. This was actually my first time playing water volleyball, and I was ecstatic to be playing in this tropical paradise with people from all over the world. I kept saying to myself: "How many people can say they had the opportunity to do what I am doing right now!" I also loved our unique variation on the rules: popping down delicious-tasting cocktail shots every fifteen minutes and trying to beat the other team into sheer exhaustion so they would get stuck with the bar tab. The idea was as bold as it was ingenious, and was making the game even more memorable.

As the contest began, both teams were trying to win at all cost. But honestly, we all just wanted to have some fun together. Once things heated up, everyone tenaciously hit or kicked the balls over the nets. The congratulatory high-fives, fist pounds, and cheers of excitement duly accompanied by groans of frustration, were practically non-stop. Also, frequent exchanges of soft kisses and hugs amongst new friends and romantic lovers were in evidence everywhere. And of course there were lots of overzealous, out-of-control tumbles into the Caribbean Sea followed immediately by comical taunts and jeers in Spanish, English, and Italian that kept all of us in stitches. Just when we thought our game couldn't be anymore insanely exhilarating, two free-spirited married couples from Germany and Argentina bumped up the excitement by several notches. These two wild couples thought it was a hilarious idea to go around pulling down the swim trunks or bikini bottoms of innocent and unsuspecting volleyball players. The "naked" embarrassment of falling victim to this naughty prank goes without saying.

You see, it went like this. Once a player began looking up into the air with the intention of hitting the ball across the net, they automatically became an easy target. Before they could react, their shorts had already been pulled down and they stood there exposed for the world to see. Every time the pranksters struck a surprised victim, we would all explode into cheers and laughter. Some people even snapped photos of the red-faced victim as he or she scrambled frantically to pull up their trunks, wanting desperately to put an end to the "freaky-deaky" peep show! But when someone was too quick on the draw, and the German and Argentinian couples failed to accomplish their mission, we all booed loudly to show our disappointment!

Personally, I made sure that I tied the draw strings on my swim trunks extra tight because I wanted to play the game worry free of being embarrassed. Anyway…no one really seemed to mind what the mischievous couples were doing. So everyone continued playing as if the situation was normal. Though, from time to time during the game, we would hear someone screaming, "Stop…Stop! Don't do it!!" on cue. The volleyball game would suddenly come to a halt as we all gawked at the latest victim struggling to hide the crown jewels. After the live show was over, we sometimes took a break and downed another shot before resuming the competition.

I have to admit that playing on a bed of soft, sinking sand in mid-thigh water for a couple of hours was starting to feel a little taxing on my body. The glorious noonday sun was also roasting us alive as the temperature climbed to over 105 degrees Fahrenheit. Miraculously, no one complained and no one passed out! We were having way too much FUN to stop!

Eventually we did have to end the game because Fabio, our chaperone, indicated to us that it was time for lunch. Minutes later, as we arrived at the bar, the Americans (including me), British and Italian volleyball players decided to pool their money and pay the bar tab. However, after lunch, it was made clear that the South Americans and Dominicans would have to step up and buy the next round of drinks. Meanwhile, Jessy, Yoly, and I decided to head over to the underground unisex bathroom facilities to take a cool, refreshing shower. Let's just say that none of us were disappointed, and we all had a fantastic experience!

By the time we finished our shower, the food was smelling delicious, and long lines of hungry tourists were already forming. As we were waiting, I encouraged the girls to eat lots of fresh fruits and to drink plenty of water because it was important to rehydrate their bodies.

Then turning my attention to the lunch offerings, I noticed that we were being served grilled Red Snapper cooked over flaming charcoals; slow-roasted pulled pork; and a mouthwatering chicken dish with black beans and brown rice stewed together in a fire pit black kettle. There was also an abundance of fresh raw vegetables, tropical fruits, and several Dominican dessert dishes that made me close my eyes and shake my head. There were just so many appetizing foods! Nonetheless, Yoly, Jessy, and I decided to maintain our decision to eat a light lunch because the mid-day temperature was steadily rising!

After retreating to our own little area to enjoy our lunch, Jessy noticed a guy sitting by himself. The guy immediately detected Jessy staring at him and smiled at her. Jessy quickly turned her head bashfully as she said, "God! He is so cute!"

Observing Jessy's blushing cheeks, Yoly said, "Why don't you invite him over to have lunch with us, girl! He *is* cute…and maybe he's single!"

"I don't know, Yoly? Oh God…what would I say to him!" Jessy responded nervously. "And besides…I'm not trying to lead anybody on because I just got over a really hurtful relationship."

I suddenly interrupt Jessy. "Listen…you are not trying to *marry* the guy," I chided her. "Now…I want you to go over there and talk to him. And furthermore…it will be good for you to start mingling again. It's been almost a year since you broke it off with your ex!"

Yoly agrees with me and orders Jessy to go over and introduce herself. Feeling flustered, Jessy whines, "I can't…I can't…I'm so nervous!"

Yoly shakes her head and taps me on the shoulder. "Come on, Tré," she says, "let's go find out if he's single because I really want to know if he has any interest in my girl Jessy!" Yoly and I stood up. Jessy tried to stop us, but she couldn't. As we were walking over towards the guy, I could hear Jessy pleading softly, "Please don't embarrass me!"

A moment later, as we stand in front of Jessy's new crush, Yoly and I introduce ourselves to Yannick who cordially shakes our hands. Yannick next asks if we would like to join him, and we take him up on his offer and sit. Without hesitation, Yoly fires from the hip. "Yannick…where are you from and are you here by yourself?"

"I am from Toronto, Canada and I am currently traveling around the Caribbean region on my own," Yannick replied. While we are conversing, I notice that Yannick is still glancing over to where Jessy is sitting. Jessy immediately reciprocates by shyly smiling back. Yannick becomes bolder and blows Jessy a kiss.

He then slowly refocused his attention on Yoly and me. "Who is your friend?" he asked.

"That's our dear friend Jessyca and I see that you have interest in her!" Yoly said.

Yannick peers over at Jessy once again as he says calmly, "Yes! I do... and she is beautiful."

Yoly reached over to gently redirect Yannick's chin, forcing him to look her in the eye. "Are you single with no kids? Do you have a good job? Do you have a college education AND know how to treat women well and with respect?" Yoly fires several volleys at Yannick who is totally thrown off by her unaccustomed bluntness. Over the years I had witnessed Yoly's unexpected feistiness on a number of occasions, but always with other people. I'd actually come to love this side of her personality, which, for me, added yet another dimension to her overall sex appeal.

Collecting himself, Yannick smiled. "Yes...to all of your extremely curious questions. Yes, I am single, I have no kids, and I own a small business. And furthermore, I know how to adore women very passionately."

Yoly's serious demeanor evaporated into a smile. Yannick turned to me next and was immediately met by a "death stare!" His smile vanished as he quickly leaned back in his chair. I looked him dead in the eyes. "Good...because if you are lying to us...you and I are going to have some serious problems!"

Yoly pinched my arm as she scolded me. "Don't scare him away, Tré!"

Maintaining my evil-eyed stare, I reply: "I'm not trying to scare him...I'm just telling him what's going to happen!"

Yannick sat back up. "It's okay, Yolanda," he said. "I will respect your friend Jessyca like a true Canadian gentleman."

That being said, I nod my head and reply, "My man! That's all we wanted to hear." I shake Yannick's hand and wave for Jessy to come on over. Meanwhile I excused myself so I could meet her halfway. A wide-eyed Jessy kissed me on the cheek. "Gracias, Tré," she whispered. Yoly formally introduced everyone as Jessy and Yannick greeted each other with smiles and kisses to the cheek. Then Yoly inconspicuously rejoined me back at our table. From time to time we would both look over at the new love birds. It looked like Yannick and Jessy were really hitting it off. They were laughing and being a little "touchy-feely" with each other.

The time is now 3:45 p.m. Lunch is over and people are heading back to the beach. I look at Yoly and I say, "It's time, Baby Girl!"

Yoly replied excitedly, "It's time to go play volleyball?"

"No!" I told her.

Yoly looked at me slightly perplexed. "It's time for what Tré?" she queried.

Beaming with confidence, I say, "It's time for me to finally teach you how to swim."

Yoly took a deep breath as she stared at me intently. "I'm ready to learn Tré," she said calmly. "I know that you want to help me overcome my fear of the water." Surprised, I give Yoly a big hug and tell her that I am very proud of her. As we stand up, Jessy asks us if we are going to play volleyball again.

"No…Tré is going to teach me how to swim," Yoly volunteered.

Jessy suddenly became animated. "Oh my God!" she exclaimed, "who would have thought that after all these years of you saying NO to thousands of people who were desperately trying to teach you how to swim, that Tré would be the Special One that you finally say YES to!" She smiled impishly as she added, "This is very interesting, chica!"

Meanwhile Yannick walked over to us wearing his backpack. Jessy rested a hand on his shoulder. "Yannick…Let's go hang out at the beach and talk some more," she said familiarly. A moment later we all began walking back toward our beach retreat from this morning. As we were strolling along, we got caught up in a mass exodus of highly energetic tourists all rushing back to their favorite spots on the beach. When we arrived back at our own spot I noticed that my new British friends were packing up their stuff. I jokingly asked if they were leaving us, to which they cheerfully replied that they wanted to experience a new scenic area of Juan Dolio. Then they graciously invited us to join them. It sounded like an excellent idea, so Jessy, Yannick, Yoly and I all decided to follow them. We relocated to an entirely different section of the beach, this time where the majority of tourists were either swimming or floating on top of their water rafts.

The British couple proceeded to set up their private relaxation haven. Not wanting to intrude, Yoly, Jessy, Yannick and I respect their intimate space by setting up our area ten yards away. Next, Yoly and I strip down to our swimwear. I look at her and say, "Let's explore this beautiful Caribbean Sea so I can teach you how to swim, Amor!"

On cue, Yoly turned to Yannick and Jessy and said brightly, "See you guys!" They tell us goodbye and quickly refocus their attention on one another, clearly caught up in the getting to know you process.

As soon as we step into the water, Yoly and I hear Jessy yelling, "Do you guys need my water raft?" She lifts the raft into the air, waving it at us.

Yoly looks at me and I yell, "No!"

"Okay, be safe!" Jessy yells back.

In a slightly subdued and anxious voice, Yoly asks, "Tré, are you sure that we don't need Jessy's water raft?"

"We're going to be okay, don't worry," I casually reassure Yoly as I flirt with her a little. I give her a kiss on her forehead and slowly begin guiding her out into the waist-high water. We were in a new section of Juan Dolio that was very peaceful and not overcrowded with tourists, which was perfect for Yoly's introduction to the water. Sensing that she was battling with her nerves, I quickly devise a strategy to ease her mind. Flirting shamelessly now, I tell her how gorgeous and irresistible she is. Almost immediately, her body language signals the shift in her focus; I could literally feel her muscle-tension easing.

Continuing my diversionary tactics, I tell her that I love her body, and that she is built like a heavenly, heart-stopping, Dominican princess! My words were clearly having their desired effect. Yoly seemed to be feeling more than a little enamored with me. Dialing the heat up a notch, I tell her that I'm having a difficult time controlling myself because she is looking so incredibly sexy, and that it is getting harder for me to be on my best behavior. Which was the absolute truth. Yoly is a natural beauty, and just the thought of me teaching her how to swim on a one-on-one basis was entrancing.

Blushing like a bright red tomato at the boldness of my words, Yoly began to avoid direct eye contact with me. Overcoming her initial shyness, she says, "Gracias, Tré. You're looking rather handsome, too—especially your exotic eyes." As she began flirting with me, I was one hundred percent sure that she was finally starting to relax. Taking hold of her hands, I asked her to please look at me. As we lock eyes, I say, "Yoly, I want you to trust me…because I swear to God and even on my own life that I will not let anything happen to you. So do you trust me?"

Briefly hesitating, she answers, "Yes, I trust you—but I'm scared, Tré!"

"I know," I say, squeezing her hands reassuringly. "But just relax and stay focused on me. By the way, Yoly, thank you for allowing me to teach you how to swim…I'm very happy to be able to help," I tell her, smiling into her captivating eyes. Wanting to build her confidence, I add, "I'm also really proud of you for showing a lot of heart and courage."

Never letting go of her hands, I began leading her farther into the open water. After following me nervously for about ten seconds, she stops abruptly when she registers the water swirling just below her neck. We both become aware that the rhythmic push and pull of the Caribbean Sea undercurrents is growing stronger, moving us effortlessly into the waves. I tell Yoly that this is the perfect place to teach her the correct breathing techniques for swimming. One of my primary goals was to help her feel completely comfortable while underwater, but even more importantly, I wanted to teach her not to panic during a potentially serious situation.

I also wanted to make it abundantly clear that executing improper breathing techniques and succumbing to nervous energy would most likely result in physical exhaustion, which could place her in serious danger. That being said, I finally explain that it is "muy importante" (very important) to try to maintain mental and physical relaxation while in the water, which will enable her to respond calmly when faced with unexpected difficulties.

After sharing a few "words of wisdom" based on my own experience as a swimmer, I began the lesson by teaching Yoly how to breathe correctly while she is submerged in the water. I also cautioned her that proper breathing was absolutely necessary in order to maintain optimum lung and brain function while swimming. Always a quick study, Yoly rapidly mastered the correct techniques. In fact, her initial fear seemed to evaporate right before my eyes as she reported to me how much more comfortable she was feeling in the water. Case in point, in five minutes or less she had mastered the art of floating by using her upper and lower limbs. Yoly was actually starting to enjoy her introduction to swimming.

Moving past the basics, I began teaching Yoly how to float and conserve energy by remaining motionless. Getting her to relax and just have fun was definitely paying off because I could literally see her bursting with self-confidence! Yoly was feeling so super relaxed with me that she didn't even realize I had intentionally led her into the deep waters of the Caribbean Sea. We were now mid-way between the beach and the buoys area where a multitude of tourists were resting on top of their water rafts.

Trying not to frighten Yoly half to death, I calmly asked her to face me, to wrap her hands around my shoulders, and allow her lower body to float on top of the water. She did everything I told her to do. Now I stare into her eyes and I say, "Yoly…I want you to continue taking deep breaths as you relax your body and look all around you." Yoly's eyes suddenly opened wide as her fear of the deep water surrounding us unmercifully assassinated her new-found confidence. She immediately clenched her athletic arms tight around my neck and shoulders. At the same time she was kicking relentlessly as she tried to wrap her legs around my waist while screaming in sheer terror.

"Oh, my God! Oh my God, Tré…! Please don't let me drown! Please don't let me drown!" she yelled. "I don't understand how we got all the way out here!" she screamed, still gripping my neck hard. Doing my best to stay calm, I tell her: "Yoly…look at me and focus." But instead Yoly continues to panic. I then soften my tone and attempt to pacify her. "Yoly…calm down…" I say gently, "and remember your breathing techniques." Even I could see the unwavering fear swirling in Yoly's eyes as she looked at me. Fighting to regain her self-control, she slowly stopped panicking and began taking long, deep breaths. I next instructed her to wrap her legs around my waist and to release her grip on my neck. I silently lifted my eyes to heaven in gratitude as she followed my instructions without hesitation!

Now I was able to freely paddle with my arms and kick my legs at the same time so we could both stay afloat. Looking around frantically, a horrified Yoly now shouts out in hyper-speed Spanish, "Tré…how are we going to get back to the shore? We're so far out! I can't believe that you did this to me when you know that I can't swim!" I gently shush her, telling her to relax. I ask her, "Yoly…what was the most important thing

I told you when we first came out into the water?" Fighting back tears, Yoly took a deep breath. "That you SWEAR to God that you will not let anything happen to me…AND to trust you," she said passionately.

"Correct!" I reply. "And to be honest it was you who swam us out here, but you were having so much fun till you just weren't paying attention." Yoly's fear of the water seemed suddenly to evaporate as we both started laughing at one another. Sensing that I had regained her trust, I tell her, "It's time to show you how to doggie paddle! Are you ready?"

"Yessssss!" Yoly responded exuberantly.

"Okay…grab my shoulders and release your legs from around my waist," I tell her in a self-assured manner.

Yoly follows my directions precisely, so I now instruct her to start "flutter kicking" her long legs like a pair of scissors, which she does perfectly. At first Yoly's legs were fluttering like a hydro-powered whirlpool, so I tell her to slow down. I didn't want Yoly to deplete all of her energy because we were going to have to take one of two options: a five-minute leisurely swim back to the beach shoreline or a two-minute exhausting swim to the group of tourists resting on top of their water rafts near the buoys and nets!

Breathing in a relaxed manner, Yoly slowed down her flutter kicks which were (unknown to her) now propelling both of us because I had intentionally stopped treading water in order to give my arms and legs a brief rest. Then to my surprise, Yoly broke away from me and instinctively began mini-stroking toward the shoreline, shouting: "I can swim! I can swim, Tré!"

Her excitement was so infectious till I immediately started cheering her on. "Yes you can! Yes you can!" I shouted.

By now we were making such a commotion that the tourists floating on their water rafts near the buoys immediately thought that something was seriously wrong! They all started yelling in several different languages: "Are you in distress? Do you need our assistance?"

Yoly and I quickly yell out, "We're okay!" Content that we are safe, our new friends go back to enjoying themselves in their own private worlds. Moments later, Yoly and I hear a man with a distinctly British accent say: "They're fine, darling. It's just an Italian couple engaging in a little horseplay."

I roar back, "We're NOT Italian!"

I was really proud of Yoly and it was a pleasure to see her actually swimming and accomplishing one her life's most elusive dreams. So observing her frolicking about in the Caribbean Sea with a joyful smile on her face made me feel very happy! I signaled Yoly to swim over to me because I wanted to chat with her. She complied with strong, confident strokes, grabbing me by my shoulders because she wanted to relax while listening to what I had to say. I tell Yoly that if she ever gets tired, remember to always stay loose and don't panic, to continue taking deep breaths of fresh air and to float on her back for a couple of minutes to help recharge her energy.

"I also want you to remember that I'm here with you, and that you can always hold onto me to relax just like you are doing now," I said.

Yoly smiled and blew me a kiss. Then she unexpectedly splashed water in my face and gave my forehead a playful push. "Tag…you're it, Tré! Come catch me if you can, Papi!" Yoly shouted as she broke away from me! I was left alone choking on salty sea water that I had accidentally inhaled into my lungs. Once I was able to get control of my breathing, I saw Yoly sprinting towards the buoys and netting area. I chased after her, almost closing the gap between us. Then suddenly I reached down and grabbed hold of my right leg as I responded to the sharp pains shooting up through my leg and thigh. "OHHHHHHHH-AAAHHHH!" I groaned as I instantly stopped swimming. Fortunately, Yoly heard me, stopped racing toward the water buoys, and turned around.

As she approaches me I try to maintain my composure by treading water to stay afloat, and the sea waves make it possible for me to bob up and down with ease. Yoly has a look of serious concern on her face as she nears me. "Tré, are you okay? What happened?" she yelled frantically.

"Yes…I'm okay…but my right leg has locked up on me," I tell her as I continue bobbing up and down. "So right now I'm having some bad muscle spasms and I can't make them stop!" I was actually thinking that I was probably dehydrated from playing two and a half hours of water volleyball in the hot sun, and then giving Yoly swimming lessons.

"Can you still swim?" Yoly asked with growing concern.

Pausing to take a deep breath, I begin swimming towards her, but my leg muscles literally scream with pain as I make the attempt.

"Awwwhhh…Ooooh!" I groaned as Yoly tries to reassure me.

"Stay calm, Tré…I'm coming," she said as she raced over to me. Although I am finding it more difficult to stay afloat, I don't panic, which allows my body to relax and conserve energy. Seconds later my "heroine" arrives and instructs me to hold on to her for support. Next, she tells me to extend my right leg. I follow her instructions and she begins massaging my tight leg muscles. "Wow, Tré!" Yoly looked at me surprised, "Your thigh muscle does feel unusually hard."

Grimacing in pain, I reply, "Yoly…I don't think I can make it. You are going to have to help me swim back to the beach." Scanning the area, I point in the direction of our friends over by the water buoys. "Better yet," I tell Yoly, "help me to swim over there by the buoys! Those people are closer and they can escort me back to shore using their water rafts."

Yoly began to tear up as she looked at me. "But I asked you, Tré. I asked you if we needed to bring Jessy's water raft and you said no!" she said, her nerves on the verge of unraveling. Maintaining my composure, I hugged Yoly and attempted to calm her down. She took in a deep breath and tried to relax, but I could see that her mind was still desperately calculating what to do as she continued to massage my upper thigh. But the pain in my leg wasn't getting any better, so I began transferring more and more of my weight to Yoly. Making things even more difficult was the fact that the sea waves were constantly pushing us towards the shore and then quickly pulling us back. I turned to Yoly and told her to look at me. I take a deep breath and say to her in a low voice, "I'm sorry…but I want you to save yourself now. Go for help over by the buoys!" Yoly's face now mirrors a barely controlled hysteria as she looks at me. But once again the waves force us away from the buoys and towards the shoreline.

It was time to take decisive action, so I pushed myself away from Yoly who desperately tried to grab me, but the currents rapidly propelled my body five yards away from her in a split second! I suddenly felt myself gliding across the water with Yoly screaming, "Tré…Tré…Tré!" as I sank beneath the waves.

The world beneath the Caribbean Sea appears to be bottomless as I slowly descend downward. Gradually, I begin to see hundreds of colorful tropical fish maneuvering their way through the water surrounding me. As I descend closer to the sea floor, I begin noticing how the color of the water transitions from a jeweled turquoise to an aqua-blue hue. Looking up, all of a sudden, I see Yoly shooting toward me like a torpedo, with the intention of snatching me from the jaws of death. As she grabs hold of me, we both catapult upward toward the sea's surface!

Exploding into the open air, Yoly started coughing up salty sea water while still attempting to see if I'm okay. Pausing for a second to allow her to catch her breath, I say "GOTCHA! TAG…YOU'RE IT!" I then tap Yoly on her forehead and start laughing. Yoly's eyes open wide in shock because only now does she realize that I've been playing a rather cruel joke on her all along!

But Yoly instantly goes berserk and starts biting me on the arm because she is infuriated! I push her off me and she began screaming in Spanish: "You mean that you were deceiving me, Tré? How could you do this to me!!!" I didn't have time to respond because Yoly grabbed me by the arm and started swinging at my face. I blocked her punches and got away by splashing water in her eyes. But that only slowed her down as she charged me again. However, I was too elusive for her, which only made her more enraged. Then she began yelling at me in a very sexy Dominican accent. "I am very upset with you right now!" she screamed. "And Tré…I'm going to get you back for scaring me like that!"

Laughing even harder, I reached out and embraced Yoly with the intention of pacifying her wicked temper. Then I say to her, "It was just a joke Yoly…I'm sorry!"

"Nooooo!" she snapped back. "What you did to me was not a joking matter, and now I am about to make you feel very sorry!" Yoly then grabbed hold of the big muscle on the left side of my chest and started twisting it, forcing me to loosen my grip. Suddenly we were water wrestling non-stop to the point where we were both breathing extremely hard. In fact, we were quickly becoming fatigued, which is not a good thing to do in the sea. That being said, I knew that I had to calm Yoly down. Otherwise, we were both going to be in serious trouble with regard to swimming back to shore against the strong undercurrent of sea waves.

I promptly explained to Yoly why it was so important for us to STOP and CONSERVE our energy. Yoly responded by yelling angrily at me. "I'm not playing with you no more, Tré! Don't ever scare me like that again! Do you understand me?"

I reply contritely, "Yes, I understand!" and we let each other go. But because of our boisterous commotion, the tourists floating on their rafts near the buoys thought that something was seriously wrong again. They all called out to us, "ARE YOU IN DISTRESS AND DO YOU NEED OUR ASSISTANCE?"

Yoly and I quickly yell back, "We're okay! Sorry to have alarmed everyone…thank you!" A lively chatter takes place among the group of tourists. Then we heard a woman giggling, "They're fine…It's just those crazy Germans up to their wicked pranks again!" Then they all erupted in hearty laughter.

This time Yoly yells out, "We're NOT German!"

Then Yoly looks at me, hits me on my shoulder and says, "You see how you are embarrassing me in front of all these strangers from all over the world!"

Shaking my head with a mischievous smile on my face, I reply, "Come on Yoly! Let's go meet our new friends."

We slowly begin mini-stroking our way towards the buoys area. For some odd reason I began looking all around us. Yoly noticed and started looking around as well. "What's going on Tré? Why are you looking around?" she queried.

"Ahhh…nothing…no reason," I reply nonchalantly.

Not satisfied with my response, Yoly stops swimming and repeats her question. "What's wrong, Tré?"

I then swim over to Yoly with a sober look on my face. "Remember when we first arrived at the beach and we all laughed at the Englishman?"

Trying to comprehend my ambiguous question, Yoly asks cautiously, "Yes…you mean when that paranoid old man from England asked Daniela if there were sharks in this region of Juan Dolio?"

"Yesss…" I reply slowly.

"So what about the Englishman?" Yoly now asked with concern.

I slowly began scanning the area around us once again without saying a word.

Yoly suddenly placed her hands on both sides of my face, forcing me to look her in the eyes. "Tré…what are you trying to say to me about the Englishman?"

Focusing all of my attention on Yoly, I reply: "We had no right to laugh at him."

With a look of bewilderment in her eyes, Yoly tightened her grip on my face. "I'm still not understanding you, Tré? What exactly are you trying to say about the Englishman?" Yoly asserted, doing her best to control her emotions. Releasing me abruptly, Yoly's head jerked awkwardly, attempting to follow my every move as I gazed solemnly out over the water, my finger tracing a 360 degree angle. "Yoly…if you look at where we are…realistically, if a shark would ever happen to infiltrate our area because of faulty netting, you and I would be the perfect shark bait!"

Yoly grabbed me by both my shoulders and started shaking me, all the while yelling out a warning. "Shut up, Tré! I am NOT going to listen to you trying to scare me again!"

I look her directly in the eyes and respond, "I'm not trying to scare you, Yoly. But think about it! We are all alone out here in open water and no one is anywhere near us!"

"Shut up, Tré…just shut up!" Yoly was nervously repeating over and over.

I interrupted Yoly by splashing salty sea water in her face and softly "shuuussshing" her into complete silence. Now that I had her full attention, I indicated to her that while in the sea, we needed to be part of a big group of people because that would lower our chances of being attacked.

At this point it was obvious that Yoly was completely unnerved by my reasoning. She took a deep breath before trying to shut me down. "Okay…okay…okay! Tré, will you please STOP talking about sharks! Let's hurry up and swim over to the tourists hanging out by the water buoys. I'm ready…so let's go!"

But just as we were about to leave, my body was slammed by a sudden jolt. Wincing in pain, I yell, "Ooouch, Yoly! Watch it! You've got some super hard kicks. That's the third time you've kicked me in my thigh." I paused to stare at Yoly in amazement. "And stop trying to pull down my board shorts. I'm having a hard enough time keeping them tied."

"COMOOOO, Tré!!!" Yoly retorted. "How can I kick you in the thigh when I am floating on my stomach and my legs are behind me?"

I quickly focused my attention on Yoly's long athletic legs splashing in the water behind her.

Yoly quickly adds, "You only *wish* that I was pulling on your board shorts! But as you can see, my hands are still holding onto your shoulders."

Without warning, I am hit with another hard jolt as I begin frantically looking all around me. Suddenly I am twisting about at super speed and splashing water everywhere! Suddenly my eyes become fixated on SOMETHING in the water! I yell out, "Yoly look! Do you see it? Do you see it?"

Looking around frantically, Yoly screams, "No Tré...I don't see it! I don't see it...where?"

I point to a specific area in the open water as Yoly and I focus all of our attention on a menacing looking splash that is being trailed by a smooth slipstream of water zeroing in on us! "I see something coming toward us!" I yelled out.

Suddenly, Yoly broke free from me and started wildly kicking and punching the water and yelling at the same time: "What do you see? What do you see, Tré?"

"Shark!" I roar back without hesitation as I began swimming toward her.

Yoly started shrieking in terror, her body shaking all over.

Then, out of the blue, I found myself being manhandled and dragged underneath the waves. "HEEELLLLP MEEEEEE!!" I holler out at the top of my lungs just before I go under.

Fascinated by Yoly's psychological delirium at this point, I propelled myself upward from beneath the water. Swiftly closing in on her, I see Yoly's entire body ferociously twisting and turning while her arms and legs are flailing wildly. I firmly grabbed onto Yoly's ankles and aggressively yanked her underwater as she desperately tried to break free from my grip because she thinks I am an attacking shark! Yoly's legs were so strong and forceful that I accidentally lost my grip on her!

Still fearing for her life, Yoly quickly recollects herself, causing her to make the shocking discovery that I was the "Big Bad Scary Shark" pawing at her ankles! EXPLODING in rage, Yoly now goes on the attack as she tries to grab me by my waist with both hands, but misses. Nonetheless, she is able to latch onto my extra-long board shorts and starts pulling hard! I tried to break free, but Yoly is unrelenting and is able to maneuver herself close enough to the trunk of my body to grab onto my waist. Instantly, we both spiral upwards towards the top of the water because we were badly in need of air to breathe.

Once in the open, the wrestling contest got even tougher. The next thing I knew I was lying flat on my stomach sucking for air and Yoly was riding my back like I was a wild mustang. I could feel her strong athletic legs tightening around my waist even while I was expending a ton of energy trying to keep us both afloat! Shocked by this switch, I heard Yoly slyly saying, "Look what I have, Tré!!" I turned my head as far as I could only to see Yoly's pouty, kissable lips smiling at me as she proudly twirls my board shorts. Without me even knowing, Yoly had somehow managed to pull my swimming trunks off while we were water wrestling!

"What…? What the hell, Yoly!!" I gasped as I ran my hands over my body to feel nothing but wet, smooth skin. Yoly now slowly leaned in close to me and seductively said in Spanglish: "Tré…you play with me entirely too much, and because you play too much, I'm going to ride you rodeo style all the way back to the beach NAKED because I'm a cowgirl!"

I made a manly attempt to grab my board shorts, but she was too quick. "YIPPPEEE….LET'S GO…VÁMONOS…VÁMONOS…MI CARAMELO CABALLO…LET'S GO!" Yoly started shouting like a cowgirl on steroids. As if that wasn't outrageous enough, Yoly then began slapping me hard on both my buck cheeks with loud, stinging blows! But by now I'd had enough. Bucking like a wild bronco, I tried to catapult Yoly off my back, but I couldn't because she methodically began clenching her legs tight around my waist.

Laughing loudly, Yoly began shouting at the top of her lungs: "YIPPPEEE….VÁMONOS…VÁMONOS…VÁMONOS…MY CARAMEL HORSE…LET'S GO!"

Attempting once more to put an end to Yoly's little "victory lap" at my expense, I abruptly started "crocodile rolling" through the water, non-stop, for as long as I could, in a desperate effort to shake her off me! Unfortunately my all-out effort didn't work because I now found myself on my back with Yoly straddling my stomach, her legs locked tightly around my waist! By now, I was feeling extremely fatigued. I knew that I had been exerting a lot of unnecessary energy and now I was paying the price for it. With my head drooping slightly underwater, it was becoming increasingly harder for me to breathe. So with extreme effort, I stare up into the heavens, but all I can see are golden sun rays illuminating Yoly's mischievous smile. As my eyes come into focus, I notice that Yoly is still proudly twirling my board shorts. She is also saying something to me, but I am unable to understand because my ears are submerged in the water. Realizing that I am unable to hear her, Yoly grabs my head from behind and raises it up out of the water. As soon as my ears drain, I hear Yoly breathing hard and trying to communicate with me.

"Tré…if you don't STOP having fun with me, we are not going to be able to safely swim back to the beach…we are going to drown! I'm tired and I know that you are, too. I don't want to die, so PLEASE let's swim back now and I promise you that I will give you back your board shorts after we make it back to the beach shoreline! Okay?"

Of course she was one hundred percent correct! If Yoly and I kept playing around in the water, we were going to have a super-difficult time swimming back to the beach. Finally catching my breath, I defiantly roar, "Hell no, Yoly! You're NOT going to embarrass me in front of all those people hanging out on the beach by having me swim ashore completely naked! I'm sorry Love, but that is not going to happen…I need you to give me back my board shorts now!"

Yoly's look of concern suddenly dissolved into a devilish stare of pure naughtiness. Then she said in English with a very alluring Dominican accent, "Listen Tré…I've just seen everything you have to offer." Quickly turning her head towards my lower body she quipped, "I am currently looking at all you are working with right now!" That being said, she turned back to face me, smiled, and leaned in very close as she spoke. "And I'm telling you that you don't have nothing to be ashamed of! Okay, Papi?" Yoly gently caressed my face while whispering, "It's time to GO, Kat Daddy…VÁMONOS!"

"Okay!" I said with a sincere look on my face. However, once I had uttered the magic word, Yoly's body started to relax. As soon as I felt her legs loosening their grip around my waist, I abruptly began thrusting my hips in a powerful upward motion while grabbing hold to Yoly's shoulders and pulling her downward toward me. Her out-of-control body flipped over and crashed into the water with a gigantic splash. I then immediately maneuvered my way directly behind her. While Yoly was trying to regain her bearings, I didn't hesitate to return the favor of removing her bikini bottom shorts. The tables had turned suddenly and I flirtatiously called out, "OH...Y-O-L-Y...." That's when she jerked around to find me proudly twirling my new prized possession! Wide-eyed, Yoly looked down and quickly discovered the embarrassing fact that she was no longer wearing her bikini bottoms.

"I can't believe that you did this to me, Tré!" Yoly shrieked in amazement. "For once...will you please be SERIOUS! Now give me back my bottom shorts! I'm not joking around with you anymore because I'm feeling really tired right now!" Yoly yelled, breathing harder than ever.

For real, after all of our horseplay in the Caribbean Sea for what seemed like an eternity, we were both obviously depleted of essential energy. I finally acknowledged to myself that we were currently in a dangerous situation. "Yoly...I'm tired too," I say sincerely, "and we can't afford to waste any more valuable energy playing around...so let's just trade." Yoly agreed and we gladly exchanged our prizes with no issues. Meanwhile, I was finding it very challenging to put my shorts back on because my legs were completely "shot." I also couldn't hold onto Yoly for support while attempting to get dressed because she was already worn down from exhaustion. That being said, I had to put my board shorts back on underwater because it was the easiest way for me to get dressed.

But Yoly was in even worse shape than I was and she now indicated to me that she needed my assistance. Handing me her bikini bottom shorts, she said to me, "Be a gentleman and don't look!"

I wink at Yoly and suavely reply, "With you I will always be a gentleman."

Yoly giggled and replied, "Whatever, Tré!"

Moving behind her, I go underwater and help her to put her shorts back on. Afterwards, I confessed to her that we were going to have to help each other because my legs are shot, and I have no more energy left. Yoly took a deep breath, nodded her head in acknowledgement, and said okay. I next instructed Yoly to get behind me and wrap her arm around my neck. She followed my directions and I began towing her back to shore using my arms, while she made use of her strong, athletic legs. As I guided us along the shortest path to the beach, I could sense that Yoly was exhausted. She was resting her chin on my shoulder so she could comfortably float on her stomach while conserving as much energy as possible. Swimming in silence, we were surprised to hear a man near the buoys, with a high pitched voice, yelling in Spanish: "There go those two crazy Costa Ricans who half scared us to death with their foolish pranks!" The group burst into laughter as they began pointing out which person was scared the most.

Yoly and I roar back, "We are NOT Costa Ricans!"

"Won't they ever get our nationalities correct?" Yoly asked with a puzzled look on her face.

"I guess not!" I replied nonchalantly as we mustered all our strength in maneuvering our way past the rushing waves, our eyes focused on the shoreline. After about five minutes of concentrated effort, Yoly and I arrived back on land. Immediately, we both began shouting, "Thank God! Thank God we made it back safely!" I had to admit that with all of the horseplay going on out in the open sea—without even the precaution of a water raft—we'd definitely taken some wild and dangerous risks! As Yoly and I trudged out of the water and back onto the beach sands, we looked at each another and started laughing. Then we started hugging each other as Yoly vehemently told me, "Tré…you are by far the craziest person that I have ever met! But thank you "Kat Daddy" for teaching me how to swim!"

Out of nowhere, Jessy popped up with my 35mm camera hanging from her neck. Yoly & I were definitely SURPRISED and I didn't know if she had overheard Yoly's "Kat Daddy" comment or not. Jessy stared at us with a curious smirk on her face. "You two have got a lot of explaining to do!" she said, as if she knew something that she shouldn't. Yoly and I looked at each other puzzled, while Jessy silently awaited our response.

"Girl…I'm so happy! Tré taught me how to swim," Yoly erupted with excitement. "And then…would you believe…Tré tried to drown me because he was playing around with me entirely too much!" Yoly and I make eye contact once again as we start to giggle.

Nonetheless, Jessy maintains her knowing demeanor. "Really…so it sounds like to me that you two had a blast…interacting in pleasurable activities all alone in the middle of the beautiful Caribbean Sea," Jessy said as she clicked the photo shoot button on my camera.

"Yes, we did!" I reply and immediately began looking around for Yannick, who was nowhere to be found. "Where's Yannick?" I ask, looking into Jessy's sparking eyes.

Jessy sighed. Her demeanor changed abruptly, now mirroring a dark, angry shadow. "Tré…I had to put Yannick in his place…in other words, I had to check him!"

A concerned Yoly stepped up immediately. "Jessy…what do you mean? Are you okay?"

Jessy rolled her eyes and shook her head angrily. "Girl…Yannick is a straight up fucking asshole!"

"WHAT?!" Yoly and I shout at the same time.

Jessy quickly fires back in Spanish, "Yes! Would you believe this freaky motherfucker tried to "do" me in the women's bathroom shower!!"

"Are you SERIOUS!" Yoly responded. "What did you do, girl?"

Jessy's face tightened up, and it was obvious that she was furious. "I told him that I am NOT that type of girl…and that he would have to respect me! Then I told him to get the hell out of the women's bathroom or else!"

Seething with anger, I try to maintain my composure. "Jessy…while you were in the bathroom…did this 'MO-FO' touch or hurt you in any way?"

"No…thank God!" Jessy told me. "I just grabbed my towel and forced my way past him out of the bathroom!"

My mind began to flood with crazy, vengeful thoughts…so I took a deep breath to help keep myself in check.

But Jessy went on as she looked at Yoly. "Girl, would you believe that as I exited the bathroom, Yannick kept stalking me even outside… AND THEN…had the nerve to corner me when I walked back into the water!"

Yoly yells, "Stop playing!"

"I'm dead serious!" Jessy said vehemently. "I kept telling him to leave me alone because I don't get down with nasty men, but he kept saying he was in love with me, and he ALWAYS wanted to make love to a Dominican woman because he heard from his European friends that Dominican women are incredible lovers. BUT….his ultimate insult was when this piece of shit said how I had him SOOO sexually turned on that he needed to FUCK me right there in the water!"

I hugged Jessy. "Did you tell Fabio or Daniela what happened?"

"No! I handled the situation myself."

I scanned the beach, wishing I had telescopic eyes. "Jessy, where is Yannick? I need to find his ass and go in on him. I don't play when it comes to you and Yoly!" I started to make a mad dash looking for Yannick but Jessy grabbed my arm.

"No, Tré, PLEASE! I already took care of it."

"What do you mean you 'took care of it?'"

Jessy smirked. "Yannick made the wrong move and touched me where he shouldn't have, so I kneed him HARD, twice with both knees, in his tiny little baby bulge sticking out of his girly-cut swim trunks." To demonstrate his "tiny little baby-bulge," she held up a finger and ticked off about two inches.

Yoly shrieked, "Stop, girl stop!" They high fived each other and exploded in laughter.

"Jessy, what happened after you kneed him?" I asked.

Yoly said, "He grabbed his pelotas and fell to his knees, paralyzed."

"Yeah, just like my Cousin Kiko said would happen," Jessy said. "All he could do was squeal like a freaking bitch gasping for air. I left him hunched over in the water."

Yoly waved her finger at me. "Don't mess with Jessy 'cause she's a bad-ass with a brown belt in karate. We take karate and Jiu Jitsu lessons at Cousin Kiko's gym every weekend!"

Jessy chimed in, "Yeah, and Yoly IS the QUEEN of Jiu Jitsu with a purple belt!"

"No wonder I couldn't untangle your legs wrapped around my waist when we were water wrestling!" Yoly winked at me and flexed her long, sexy legs.

"And what is that supposed to mean, Tré?" Jessy asked as we headed toward our set-up on the beach. She was obviously hoping to find out what I inferred had happened between Yoly and me. "You need to finish telling me all about your exciting adventure out there in the waters of the El Caribe," she said slyly.

Skirting Jessy's nosy request, I replied, "Honestly Jessy, I had an UNBELIEVABLE time teaching Yoly how to swim. I am SOOOO grateful that you lovely ladies wanted to spend your day with me. That really means a lot to me because it's hard seeing you only once a year."

Yoly said, "Oh, that's so sweet, Tré" and hugged me.

Jessy hugged me and said, "Hmmm….OKAYYY! It's really great

that you two had such an UNBELIEVABLE time together. We miss you a ton too, Tré, and would love to see you more often! Thank you for your friendship and all you have done for us!"

By now the couple next to us from England was already packed. I thanked them for watching our things. They reminded us we had thirty minutes to wash up and change into our clothes before the BBQ on the beach began. We quickly packed our things, rushed over to the Beach-Bar Rental Shop to return their merchandise, and walked towards the glowing candle-lit canopy tent.

It was a beautiful evening. Juan Dolio beach looked like a dreamy tropical paradise with the sunset illuminating the heavens in a wavy, violet-orange hue. God had painted a glorious masterpiece in our part of the world just for us to enjoy. *Praise Jesus!*

The band was playing soothing yet invigorating music after a day under the tropical sun. Multi-colored flames from the BBQ pits painted the horizon. Enticing platters of assorted meat beckoned us to come and eat. Tourists steadily filled up the tent. Yoly and Jessy quickly found a table close to the band with a view of the sunset hovering over the water as I headed for the shower.

The cold water massaged my tired, sore muscles as I scrubbed away the sea salt with my orange-ginger-scented shampoo and soap gel that re-energized my body, leaving a light, zesty fragrance tailor-made for tropical temperatures. So you never "reek" even when it is SOOO hot. I put on my Sean Jean shorts and Ralph Lauren polo shirt. Yoly and Jessy raved about how delicious I smelled! They could NOT get enough of my zesty orange-ginger scent. They soon returned all beautified, manicured, and decked out in their fashion-trendy summer dresses. I snapped a couple photos of them posing with our new tourist friends sitting at our table.

After seeing what people were eating, we decided to share each other's food. We filled our plates with garlic-grilled crab, blackened lobster, smoked beef and chicken, as well as plates of brightly colored vegetables, mango, pineapple slices, and scrumptious-looking caramelized passion fruit tarts.

As the sun set, it felt dream-like that I was here enjoying some of the most delicious food I had ever tasted, all while sharing this blissful experience with Yoly and Jessy and my new tourist friends from places where I could only aspire to go. It was absolutely magical! Celebrating and being in the presence of God's Utopia was unbelievably humbling. As long as I live, I will ALWAYS remember this special moment.

After mingling with the other guests, Fabio came over to our table with four glasses of Strawberry Mojitos that smelled and looked like strawberry candy. When he sat down, I offered to get the next round of drinks. He said not to worry since I was a friend of Serena and Rafael. He made a toast and asked, "How was everyone's trip to Juan Dolio?"

Yoly took a sip of her drink and said, "I'll never forget this day for the rest of my life. Juan Dolio is unimaginably beautiful." Jessy and I concurred with her sentiments as we clinked our glasses together in unison.

Fabio smiled and proposed another toast. "Remember to make the time to enjoy life with the people you love because life is too short and tomorrow is never guaranteed," he said dreamily. "Did you guys hear what happened to your friend Yannick?" he added abruptly.

I glanced over at Jessy and Yoly who were caught off guard. "No, we didn't hear anything," I said.

Yoly recovered first. "What happened to him? Is he okay?"

"No!" Fabio responded. "He sustained some sort of serious injury."

"Oh…that sounds terrible!" I said.

"It was. He was horsing around in the water with another tourist from Germany and was accidentally kicked in the testicles!"

"OUCH!" I grimaced. "That does NOT feel good. But really Fabio, the Germans are known for their rough housing."

Jessy, obviously mellowed from the effects of her Strawberry Mojito, was all ears but trying hard not to show her delight in hearing about "poor, suffering Yannick."

Fabio, also buzzed, said, "He was in so much pain he swore something was ruptured. So Daniela called for an ambulance and he was rushed to the nearest hospital in Juan Dolio."

I feigned sympathy. "Getting kicked in the cojones HARD by another man is no joke! Yannick is fortunate he wasn't permanently injured."

"I know…and I hope that he'll be fine. He's such a nice kid," Fabio replied.

Jessy took a long sip from her drink. "Did you find out what his injuries were?"

"We were told nothing was ruptured, but he has severely bruised testicles with no major internal damage. He was released from the hospital about thirty minutes ago and took a car service back to his hotel in Santo Domingo," Fabio replied, excusing himself to help Daniela prepare for the farewell champagne toast.

As soon as Fabio was gone, we busted out laughing. I said to Jessy in Spanish, "God damn, Baby Girl! You weren't joking around when you said you FUCKED UP Yannick!"

She smirked. "What can I say? He messed with the wrong little bad bitch." The girls high-fived each other.

Yoly looked at me, "Hey Tré, my girl Jessy can handle herself with anybody."

"I'll say she can! She sent the man to the hospital! But wow…that was close. At first I thought Fabio was saying that he knew that Jessy was the one who had actually injured Yannick."

Jessy playfully punched Yoly and me in our arms. "I know. And you guys were NOT helping me out by asking Fabio all those questions."

We continued laughing and talking until Daniela and her team began handing out glasses of champagne. She asked everyone to join her by the water. I grabbed my camera and we headed for the beach.

Daniela faced us with a lovely smile. "Look around at all your new friends that you've met today and then raise your glasses high with a smile on your face," she said. With our glasses held up, she reminded us to embrace people from all over the world and appreciate the different cultures with love, respect, and harmony. And to always remember that life is meant to be enjoyed with people we care about. We all gave an energetic cheer. She concluded her beautiful speech with, "Cool music, enjoyable foods, and a group of awesome people are all you need in this world to be happy and free." At that point we all did a group toast to an EPIC day that nobody wanted to come to an end, but finally it was time to go back to Santo Domingo.

As people were leaving the beach, I took a series of photos of Jessy, Yoly, and our new friends. Jessy told me she'd enjoyed playing around with my 35mm camera, and as soon as I return to my hotel room, to please send her copies of the photos she had taken. She paused, and with a nonchalant smile, told me she had taken some VERY INTERESTING photos that she was sure I was going to love. I promised her that after I'd edited the photos on my computer, I would send the two of them copies of my entire trip to the D.R. by the end of next week.

I started packing up my camera and suddenly realized I had forgotten to give Yoly and Jessy their gifts! I took the gift bag out of my backpack and presented it to them. They quickly opened it and pulled out the two designer hats.

"That's my special gift to you both so you will ALWAYS remember me with happy thoughts on this very wonderful day that we shared together." They thanked me and tried on their hats, praising each other on how GOOOOOD they looked, while suffocating me half to death with hugs of appreciation.

Fabio made a final "last call" for everyone to get on the bus. We sat in our original seats for the return trip, and our friends from England sat across from us. After all this time, we finally introduced ourselves to Chauncey and Violet. They said they were web designers and in the process of building a new condo in Santo Domingo as a home away from home. They also confided that they were going to start up their own web-design company in Santo Domingo since it was an untapped market.

Being the networker I am, I told them that Jessy and Yoly were innovative web designers who had helped me in the past with advice and creative web designs. And more importantly, they knew the Santo Domingo market. Violet and Chauncey's eyes lit up as they began talking with Yoly and Jessy about business and their personal lives that lasted for the next two hours!

We arrived at my hotel at midnight. I exchanged information with Chauncey and Violet and told them goodbye. Jessy gave me a super-hug and tears welled up in her eyes as she said, "Hopefully, Yoly and I can finally make it over to the States to visit you, Tré…once we get our U.S. permits. So take care of yourself and I'll see you next year, Bebé." She kissed me on my cheek and whispered, "Listen…I will call you in two days to make sure you arrived home safely." Then she slyly said to Yoly, "Take Tré inside the hotel to say your personal goodbyes. I'm calling a taxi so we can ride together with Chauncey and Violet. We need to finish talking business with them and their hotel is on the way to our apartment."

Yoly locked arms with me and walked me through the crowded

lobby. At the elevator I pushed the executive suites floor. We embraced. The doors opened and people exited. Yoly looked into my eyes and said, "Tré…this afternoon when you took me out in the middle of the Caribbean Sea to teach me how to swim…NEVER…EVER in my whole life have I been soooo thrilled….soooo terrified, and soooo turned on all at once!" Then she gently pushed me into the empty elevator and kissed me in a long, fiery, badly needed kiss! Her soft lips were so addictive I didn't want to stop. After kissing for a long time, we broke apart. Without warning she slapped me HARD on my cheek and said, "That's for being a real gentleman and making me wait to kiss you all day long! But…you were worth the wait. Thank you, Tré!"

Yoly walked confidently out of the elevator, stood in front of the curious crowd waiting to get on, turned around smiling and said in Spanish, "What a shame you don't live here in Santo Domingo Tré," eyeing me up and down.

"I know Yolanda…it is a shame!"

Yoly sighed seductively. "Take care Kat Daddy," she purred and waved a cat-claw goodbye. The elevator doors started to close just as Yoly walked on, disappointing the curious crowd waiting to hear more of our tantalizing conversation. As I rode the elevator to my floor I rubbed my cheek where Yoly had slapped me. When I got to my door, there were several messages taped to the door knob. I grabbed the cards, turned on the lights, and tuned into some mellow, tropical jazz playing on the radio. The note on one of the cards said I should contact Sofia and Oscar immediately! It was 1:38 in the morning, so I decided to call them in a couple of hours, after I'd had a chance to get some sleep. I walked out on the balcony to admire the moon illuminating the sparkling waves of the Caribbean Sea, thanking the heavens above for this moment.

Exhausted, I promptly fell asleep in a soothing hot tub of water. I awakened suddenly with my smartphone chirping with text messages. Yoly sent me a message saying that she and Jessy had made it home safely and wished me a "good night." I wished her "Buenas noches!" as well. Jessy sent me a "sweet dreams" text reminding me to email her all the photos of my trip by the end of next week. I replied: "Sweet dreams, also. Don't worry…I won't forget."

Making sure my two cameras were dust free, I scrolled through all the photos Jessy and I had taken. A big smile crossed my face thinking about all the fun and excitement I'd had today. There were photos I had taken early in the day of Jessy, Yoly, and Fabio posing in front of the bus. There were photos Jessy had taken of me smiling and sticking out my tongue, as well as photos of me "knocked out" sleeping, allowing Jessy to "photo-bomb" me with all kinds of silly and crazy faces. I laughed so hard tears ran down my cheeks.

I was very impressed with how Jessy had taken some artistically surreal photos of Yoly and me sleeping, with Yoly resting her head on my shoulder. She'd somehow managed to capture a dreamy, hazy effect by utilizing the golden rays of the sun. Jessy was a natural in the art of photography. I was further impressed by her creative eye after viewing the photos she had taken during our bus ride to Juan Dolio. Her breath-taking abstract photos of the gorgeous landscape between Santo Domingo and the beaches of Juan Dolio were stunning. The next series of photos I scrolled through were ones I took throughout the tropical paradise of Juan Dolio that I wanted to showcase for my friends and family back home in the States. I was so happy and relieved that I hadn't messed up this once-in-a-lifetime opportunity by taking bad photographs!

By this time it was 2:30 a.m. My heart raced when I discovered the photos of Yoly and me in the Caribbean Sea that Jessy had taken with my telephoto lens. She had managed to change lenses, which resulted in pristine, picturesque photos. When a person first learns how to use a telephoto lens, it can be very challenging. That was NOT the case with Jessy! Her photos were crystal-clear. There were photos of me teaching Yoly how to breathe underwater. Photos showing Yoly how to float on her stomach, using the turquoise-blue water as the ultimate backdrop. Photos that captured an intimate moment with Yoly about to cry when I told her I made a horrible mistake by not bringing Jessy's water raft, as well as photos of her trying to save me when she thought I was drowning.

I was already beginning to anticipate what was about to come next because Jessy had captured "live" and "in living color" photos of Yoly sitting on my back with a gigantic smile on her face, proudly waving my board shorts high in the air while slapping my bare caramel-brown butt. Next came a photo of Yoly sitting on my stomach looking affectionately into my eyes and twirling my shorts in the air. The photo spread continued non-stop with one of Yoly still sitting on my stomach while gazing at the lower-half of my naked body with a wicked smile on her face. Luckily, my frantically kicking legs caused a water splash that concealed my private parts! Following that was a photo of Yoly and me proudly holding each other's swim shorts and flirting with each other.

The final photo was SOOO romantic with us swimming back to shore smiling, with Yoly resting her chin on my shoulder and her arm wrapped around my neck. What came next was a video of Jessy smiling and giving Yoly and me a thumbs up! Now I understood why Jessy kept asking what we were doing in the water!

After the photo review I needed a drink to relax me. A miniature bottle of Absolut Vodka on the rocks did the trick. Before dozing off I thought about how the photos would forever enshrine wonderful memories of an exciting and special day that I'd shared with two very special friends!

DÍA CINCO
(DAY FIVE)

FEELING REVITALIZED, I wash up and get dressed to go out for a morning jog through the Malecón section of Santo Domingo. Before I leave, I impulsively decide to snap a few photos of the sparkling sunburst hovering just above the Caribbean Sea. I was just packing up my camera when I heard several soft knocks at my front door. I ask who is it, and a warm friendly voice answered back. "It's me…Sofia and Oscar, Tré."

I opened my door to find Sofia and Oscar wrapped in puffy white hotel bath robes and wearing big smiles. I invite them in and tell them to please make themselves comfortable, but Sofia suddenly hugs me. "Thank you so much my dear Tré for our special gift," she said enthusiastically. "Oscar and I truly appreciate our friendship with you." I smiled back at them with genuine gratitude as I said in Spanish: "No problem. I feel just as grateful for meeting you guys as well."

Oscar looks directly at me as he says, "Tré…you are not understanding what your special gift did for us and how much we *really* appreciated it."

Taken aback slightly, I was puzzled as to what the couple was trying to say to me. "Well…I really felt like you guys deserved it," I said, somehow sensing that I was still missing the point.

"TRÉ…I can see that you are still not understanding us!" Sofia burst out. "It was your Homemade Strawberry Coconut Tequila gift that helped bring PEACE between our parents!"

Oscar chimed in immediately. "Because of your magical drink creation, our parents have now come together as ONE, and everyone has committed to put an end to all of their senseless arguments and accusations against one another."

I was suddenly overcome with positive energy and feelings. "That's wonderful to hear," I exclaim, "but tell me how did my Strawberry-Coconut Fusion Drink managed to accomplish all that?"

"Well Tré…two days ago we were having a family dinner over at Oscar's parents' house," Sofia sighed. "Everyone was having an enjoyable meal until once again our parents started the same argument. My parents believe that I am too good for Oscar to have as a wife and his parents believe that Oscar is too good for me!" Sofia paused in sheer exasperation. "Oscar and I tried our best to defuse the situation by telling our parents that we are perfect for each other…and more importantly, how much we love each other…but nobody would listen to us!"

Sofia went on to relate how the situation got so totally out of control that she and Oscar had stormed out of the dinner party. Next, they drove around the city for about forty minutes until they finally came to the conclusion that if their parents did not stop disrespecting one another, they were prepared to tell them all to stay out of their lives. Of course, she explained, this was something very difficult to do, but that she and Oscar had absolutely had enough.

Meanwhile, I was waiting as patiently as I could for the climax to this confusing story, but truth be told I was dying of curiosity. "But…I still don't understand how my gift…?"

Sofia shushed me as she and Oscar looked at one another with radiant smiles on their faces. They shared a kiss before saying anything more. "Tré…when Sofia and I drove back to my parents' house," Oscar continued with the story, "we were expecting the worse. But to our surprise, our parents were laughing, dancing, and having a good time. Sofia and I automatically became very puzzled about what had happened to them while we were gone because our parents were acting like totally different people!" Oscar exclaimed in amazement. He then went on to explain that was when he and Sofia realized that their parents' had drunk over half of the fusion jar of Homemade Strawberry-Coconut Tequila!

Sofia eagerly interrupted Oscar. "Evidently, after we left, Oscar's father was so angry that he decided to have a cool, refreshing drink to help calm his nerves. So he excused himself from the dining table, looked in the refrigerator, and saw this delicious looking drink full of bright red strawberries. Thinking that his wife had concocted some sort of homemade strawberry fruit punch, Oscar's father drank a glass.

He loved it so much that he decided to share it with everyone! Tré... incredibly, they all thought that they were drinking a Strawberry-Coconut Fruit Juice! But they were WRONG! So because of your special gift, everyone mellowed out to the point where they were ready to listen to Oscar and me. But more importantly...they were now ready to listen to each other!"

"Tré...you are the man! Your drink creation put our parents in such a harmonious space that they were able to put aside their silly differences!"

"Finally, we are a united family again," Sophia joined in. "So thank you, Tré, from the bottom of our hearts!"

Shaking my head in astonishment, I reply, "Guys...I am truly ecstatic to hear that I was able to help out in my own way. My family and friends have always told me that I have a special talent when it comes to creating exotic drinks that bring people together. Would you believe that it was my father who taught me how to make my first Strawberry Tequila drink? All I did was add my own unique touch to it."

"Your father sounds like a good man who really knows how to enjoy life!" Sofia says.

"Yes...that would be him," I say with a broad grin on my face.

Oscar patted me on the shoulder and asked, "Tré...when are you leaving?"

"Unfortunately, I leave tomorrow. I have an early flight back to the States because I have to get back to work."

"So what are you doing this evening around 5:30 p.m.?"

"Nothing...except maybe packing."

Oscar looked at Sofia, then back at me. "Well tonight, Tré...Sofia and I want to take you to what we believe is the best Dominican Restaurant in all of the Caribbean!"

"Yes...it will be our pleasure!" Sofia added.

"That sounds good to me...thank you," I grinned.

"Excellent...because we really want you to join us!" Oscar reiterated.

"Time to go, Honey...so Tré can begin his morning jog," Sofia said as she gave me a goodbye hug.

"Let's meet in the hotel lobby at 5 p.m. and we'll take a taxi over to the restaurant," Oscar said.

"Tré..." Sofia said smiling, "we recommend that you dress stylishly and look really hot for this evening…because where we're going, everyone wants to be seen and noticed."

"Don't worry," I say with confidence, "I'll be at my BEST!"

Right away I begin assembling my outfit. My mother had always taught me to be prepared at all times when traveling or on vacation. She lovingly instilled in me the importance of packing a suave "power suit" for unexpected business encounters. She also stressed bringing along an exceptional suit for evening wear, attire that would guarantee my star power. So whenever I travel the world, I wholeheartedly follow my mother's advice "to never let nobody out shine you when it comes to style!" That being said, I reached for my medium dark-blue pin-striped Euro-cut suit! This was one of my favorite suits to wear because its dark-blue hue had a slight sheen to it. But since it was always over 100 degrees Fahrenheit in Santo Domingo at night, I was only going to wear my suit vest and slacks with a short-sleeved tapered pink shirt with a pink tie. Finally, I decided to finish off the outfit with a pair of polished black dress shoes for that "Euro-Gangster" flair. More importantly, my outfit was battle tested for the steamy tropical heat because the quality of the fabric allowed my body to breathe! I quickly ironed and inspected my attire for the evening and left for my morning jog.

A Heavenly Surprise

I grabbed my pink rose, plucked fresh from the hotel lobby, and cut the entire stem off. I next walked over to the standing mirror in my bedroom and pinned it to my vest. It was the final eloquent touch that expressed my own personal style. It was now 4:50 p.m., time to go meet Oscar and Sofia in the hotel lobby. As I exited the room, I grabbed my point-and-shoot camera, a pack of mint-flavored gum, and my stick of orange-ginger scented oil to insure that I would remain fresh throughout a hot and humid evening!

I get off the elevator and walk through a super-busy lobby. Looking around, I see a sensationally "decked out" Sofia sitting in a lounge chair. Sofia immediately stands up and starts waving at me. She greets me with a warm hug and I compliment her on how gorgeous she looks. She is dressed in a chic baby powder blue one-piece mid-thigh dress that hugs all of her sculptured body curves. Sofia's dress exquisitely wraps around her right shoulder which chicly leaves her tanned left shoulder bare. It is obvious to me that Sofia is also a trend setter on the fashion scene. I nodded my head with approval and awe. I was loving the fact that Sofia had modishly accessorized herself with tiny golden bracelets that accented her wrists, a slim gold belt, and a pair of gold open-toed mid-high heels.

I also couldn't help appreciating how she had creatively manicured her nails (hands and feet) with different shades of blue, while wearing a sky-blue lip gloss that perfectly matched the color of her gemstone earrings. As she checked me out, Sofia was obviously impressed by my impeccable attire as well. "Tré…you dress like a European fashion model," she said exuberantly. "You look so cool and confident…I love it, Bebé….I love it!"

I thank Sofia for her positive feedback and told her that some of my major fashion influences are from Italy. Sofia then began touching my pink short-sleeved shirt and my pink tie as she took a pleasant whiff of the pink rose attached to my vest.

"Is pink your favorite color, Tré?" she asked.

"No, green is my favorite color, but I chose pink because it really makes my dark blue suit pop!"

Sofia nodded her head in agreement. "Yes…it really does, Tré!" she said approvingly. "And where we're going for dinner, I can guarantee that at least one person is going to give you a really nice compliment and all the attention you deserve."

"Well…I'm certainly ready!" I said excitedly.

As we exit the hotel, I see Oscar standing beside a waiting taxi waving at us. As Sofia and I walked toward him, I noticed that Oscar was also very fashionably dressed in a metro-sexual baby powder blue slim suit. He was also sporting a lavender dress shirt with a gold tie, a black belt, and a pair of lavender shoes. Sofia and Oscar's outfits fashionably complemented one another, and they made a handsome couple.

"What's up, Tré!" Oscar greeted me. "Are you ready for tonight?"

"Yes I am!" I said with a grin.

"By the way, the pink is an excellent choice, mi mano!" he observed, giving me two thumbs up.

"That's what I've been telling him, Oscar!" Sofia chimed in as she and Oscar give each other a "pound" and abruptly start giggling. We all climb into the taxi, with Sofia sitting in the center between Oscar and me. Oscar tells the taxi driver where to go and we dart off into the early evening traffic.

We'd been cruising through the streets of Santo Domingo for several minutes, with Oscar and Sofia pointing out key landmarks, when Sofia politely asked the driver to pull over to the side of the street.

As the car came to a complete stop, Sofia removed a rosy-colored floral chiffon scarf from her purse. "Tré…do you trust us?" she asked with an innocent smile on her face. Slightly taken aback by her odd question, I gazed at Sofia for an instant before I confidently replied, "Seguro" (Sure)!

"Good!" Sofia responded. "Because we are only five minutes away from the restaurant and we would like to blindfold you for the rest of the way so you can't see where the restaurant is until we arrive. Está bien" (Okay)?

I reply, "Está bien…No problema!"

"Tré…If you see where we are about to take you…it will ruin our very big surprise for you," Oscar said soberly.

"Yes, I understand and I love surprises!" I responded enthusiastically. Sofia then gently wrapped the scarf around my eyes.

"Tré…you are going to LOVE what we have planned for you!" Oscar tells me.

I nod my head eagerly. "I'm ready to go…let's DO this!" I roar as the taxi eased back into the traffic. Having lost my sense of vision, my ears were now hyper-sensitive. Several minutes later the taxi came to a smooth stop and I heard Oscar paying and thanking our driver as he opened the car door.

Sofia's fragrance became suddenly more intense as she moved in closer to me. "We're here, Tré!!" she shouts gleefully. Sofia helped me get out and I heard the car door slam shut. There was a brief moment of silence before our taxi slowly drove away. Next I sensed Oscar close to me. "Alright Tré…we are almost there," he confided. "We just have to walk a short distance from here. But first I want you to wrap your left arm around Sofia's shoulders and your right arm around mine so you don't accidentally stumble."

I follow Oscar's instructions as he and Sofia slowly guide me up a flight of concrete steps. All of a sudden, I stop walking to sniff the aromas surrounding me. A big smile spread over my face as I whisper: "Ohhh, my God! That smells so good!"

The couple started giggling as Sofia quickly replied, "We told you, Tré! You are about to experience delicious foods from the world's greatest Dominican chefs!"

If there is one thing I relish in this world it is the smell of scrumptious, mouth-watering food that I am just about to devour! I was totally engulfed in the delectable ambrosia of fresh garlic, onions, exotic spices, grilled meat and some sort of fruity dessert that was making my stomach roar like a hungry lion. My sense of smell was becoming stronger as we passed through some kind of entrance, and I knew that I was getting closer to the food. I could also detect that I was now indoors as Sofia and Oscar led me through a maze of narrow walls.

For a minute or so we were clanging and banging against the walls, and the only thing I could do was concentrate on our echoing footsteps against the hardwood floors. However, I was starting to sense odd presences in my vicinity, but I didn't know what they were. Then we passed into an open area and the temperature rose instantly by thirty degrees! Food was directly in my pathway because the aroma was overpowering. I could also hear the delightful sounds of frying, grilling, baking, and broiling, all of which was sweet music to my ears!

Suddenly, Oscar and Sofia disappear and I am standing all alone—and yet I was sensing a warm, comfortable presence all around me. Then I felt the soft, gentle strokes of a woman's hand caressing my cheek, followed by two soft kisses to both sides of my face. "Queee lindooo" (How handsome)! The rich, velvety voice of my Mystery Admirer gushed with excitement. Not knowing exactly what was going on, I smiled and replied, "Gracias!" Seconds later, I felt a different pair of feminine hands caressing my face, followed by a second unfamiliar voice complimenting me. This was followed by two warm kisses to both cheeks and a quick peck on my lips. Immediately, I hear an instantaneous explosion of laughter and giggles.

"Mami…will you stop flirting! You always like to flirt all of the time!" I hear Oscar shouting as someone steps up and removes the scarf from my eyes. At that moment I am blown away with gratitude and amazement!! I realize that I am standing in the middle of a large kitchen in someone's home, surrounded by a charming and attractive family of perhaps twenty people, all smiling and extremely happy to see me! This was Oscar and Sofia's beautiful and fashionable family; they were all dressed up and looked sensational for this special occasion.

Just then I began focusing my attention on a lovely middle-aged woman with hazel eyes standing next to me. She was outfitted in a summer dress and wearing an apron. She smiled at me and said, "Buenas Noches, Tré!" Then in unison everyone in the room recited in perfect harmony: "Welcome to our family!" Looking to my left, I saw another adorable woman in her early 60's, with sparkling gray eyes. She is standing right next to me. Without hesitation she gives me another quick peck on the lips and tells me how handsome I am. The entire room goes: "AHHHHH!"

A slightly embarrassed Oscar mouthed off at his mother once again, "Mother…please stop flirting with Tré!" But she quickly shushed him as she retorted in high-speed Spanish: "If your father isn't jealous, you shouldn't be jealous either!" She then pointed to Oscar's father who was busy concocting some sort of fruity cocktail. He halted suddenly, smiled at me, and waved. Everyone burst into laughter once again. Meanwhile Oscar's mother sashayed over to the kitchen table—which was chock full with appetizers, entrees, and desserts—to resume prepping our dinner offerings for the evening.

Speaking Spanish, I turned to address the entire room. "I would like to personally thank everybody for welcoming me into your beautiful home and family. This really means a lot to me. I'm truly touched right now…so thank you all once again." Everyone cheered and shouted in Spanish: "With much pleasure, Tré!" Overcome with emotion, I hugged Sofia who confided to me that she and Oscar had invited only their favorite family members to come celebrate the evening with a special home style Dominican dinner. Sofia proudly introduced me to her mother who caressed my face again (the first time while I was blindfolded) and complimented me. "You have such beautiful skin—like a sweet caramel chocolate—I just can't believe you are not Dominican."

I laughingly reply, "I am Afro-American mixed with Native American." Just then, out of the blue, I heard a voice yell out in English: "Shit Papi…you look more Dominican than half the people in this room!" I couldn't help laughing at the sound of the boisterous and hilarious voice as Oscar's first cousin, Javier, walked over and introduced himself.

Gradually, I made my way round the room meeting and greeting one relative after another. Then Oscar patted me on the shoulder as he gestured toward the entire room. "Everyone in this kitchen can cook, Tré. And honestly, mi mano...Sofia's and my mother, back in their younger days, could easily have been successful chefs and owners of their own restaurants. I say this because they both learned and mastered, over many years, all of our secret family recipes going all the way back to the late 1800's." Oscar pointed to Sofia's father who was cooking on an open pit grill outside. "Sofia's father is a Pit Master!" he said enthusiastically. "He can grill, smoke, and roast on an open flame— goat, lamb, fish, chicken, pork and beef, you name it! And his meats are always succulent and flavorful."

That being said, Sofia and Oscar guided me in the direction of Oscar's father. "As you can see...Oscar's father loves to create innovative new drinks like yourself, Tré! Papa Oscar was sooooo inspired by your Strawberry-Coconut Fusion Tequila drink that he is now in the process of creating a Mango Fusion Vodka and a Pineapple-Watermelon Tequila drink for all of us to enjoy later this evening!" Sofia went on excitedly. "And Tré...you will be happy to know that Oscar and I are also celebrating the good news that I am now having a baby!"

My eyes widen as I shout: "FELICITACIONES! Does your family know?"

Oscar rubs Sofia's stomach. "Yes...we told everyone early this morning," he says.

"So you can see Tré..." Sofia joins in, "we have many reasons to celebrate today, and we're going to live it up by eating all of our homemade dishes, like Dominican Cod Salad, Breaded Stuffed Chicken Fritters, Breaded Stuff Beef Fritters, Smoked & Grilled Blackened Pulled Pork, Pulled Beef, Garlic Flavored Grilled-Fried Chicken, Fried Fish Fritters, and Seafood-Vegetable Dominican Stew that has been slow cooking all day in an open flame black kettle. Tré...Dominican Stew is my all-time favorite because it's made from corn, potatoes, beef, chicken, pork, garlic, onions, carrots, fish, shrimp, crab, lobster, octopus, black and red beans, green jalapenos, peas, bell peppers, black rice and tomatoes!" Sofia was so excited that she just couldn't stop herself.

"And for dessert we are going to have homemade Mango Torta Cake, Pineapple Dominican Cake and Strawberry Dulce de Leche Cake. And finally…we are going to toast the evening away by drinking Papa Oscar's special dessert drinks." Just then Sofia's mother whispered something that captured Sofia's and Oscar's attention. However, I wasn't close enough to understand what she'd said. But whatever it was, it was apparently super important because everyone in the kitchen immediately stopped what they were doing and began staring at me with beaming smiles on their faces. Sofia turned to me mysteriously. "Tré…It is now time for your big surprise…but I must blindfold you once again," she said giggling.

"Another surprise!?" I reacted, slightly overwhelmed. "Oh my God! How can this get any better!?"

"You will just have to wait and see," Sofia quipped as she carefully covered my eyes with her scarf. Now all I can see is pitch blackness. Next, I begin to hear family members all saying kind words of affirmation to me. By then my anticipation was building up to a super-charged state where I could hardly contain my emotions! Sofia took my hand as if I were a small child and began leading me around the kitchen. As we passed out of the kitchen area, people began clapping and cheering me on. Then, all of a sudden, everything went quiet. I now had the sense that we were outside. Sofia says, "Be careful, Tré!" as she escorts me down a slightly uneven cobblestone walkway. As we're walking, I am gradually being captivated by a floral, jasmine-like fragrance. Sofia then tells me to stop just at the point where the enchanting jasmine fragrance is most intense. She slowly removes her scarf from my eyes—and standing less than ten feet away from me—I see the girl of my dreams smiling at me. It was Sofia's strikingly gorgeous younger sister, ISABELLA!

Without a doubt, Isabella in person was "hands down" the most beautiful woman I'd ever seen! Her beauty shone so brilliantly that it took everything inside of me to maintain my cool and suave manner. Eyeing her down from head to toe, I was loving the Voguish way she had put herself together for our very special encounter. Stunning in her pink Boho-Chic one piece mid-thigh summer dress that was accentuating her sexy, athletic curves and long sun-kissed legs, Isabella was a six-foot tall heavenly goddess with auburn hair. An aficionado of fashion, even I had never seen a dress like this before, and I appreciated how Isabella's style was so very "Da Jour" and classy with an edge.

Her dress was so sheer that someone like myself with a naughty mind might easily think they would be able to see through the material.

But in reality, you couldn't because the dress was made from high quality chiffon fabric. Isabella's little pink chiffon dress was therefore a perfectly tailored illusion, designed to stimulate the male libido while maintaining her self-assured elegance.

Sofia, observing the broad grin on my face, said to me, "You see, Tré…if you truly believe, dreams do come true!"

I turned to her with a look of "I can't believe that this is really happening" as I whisper, "Thank you so much, Sofia."

Sofia then looked directly into my eyes as she spoke with strong emotion. "You know Tré…Oscar and I were very touched by your poetic expressions a few days ago when we had breakfast together. Your words were very strong and heartfelt to us. Especially when you declared that you would be willing to do everything in your power for the opportunity to have an enjoyable private dinner with my sister Isabella after seeing only a few photos of her."

"Yes…and I meant every single word that I said, Sofia," I said as I embraced her.

"I know that now Tré, and that means a lot to both Oscar and me… and also to the rest of our family because we all want to see Isabella back to her carefree, energetic self again." Sofia teared up as she went on. "After telling Isabella about your very strong desire to meet her, she was moved to tears because I sincerely expressed to her that after eight long years, someone finally had the honest intention of wanting to make her feel happy and full of life again. For the first time in a very long time… Isabella let her guards down, and she was very receptive to me. And let me tell you Tré, when she saw those photos of you—Ohhh boy!—her desire to meet you was just as strong. She just had to have dinner with her 'Sexy Caramelo Bebé Beso' (Sexy Caramel Baby Kiss)!"

Sofia and I both started laughing as I flirtatiously reply, "Tonight I will be anything your sister Isabella wants me to be!" Sofia gently pinched my cheek and whispered, "Thank you for making Isabella believe that she deserves to have someone special in her life. So on behalf of Oscar, my parents, and me, we all hope that perhaps that special someone is you, Tré."

"It's like you said, Sofia," I responded, "if you truly believe, dreams do come true. And tonight I have every intention of winning your sister Isabella's heart."

"Okay then…Sexy Caramelo Bebé Beso! You have my blessings to show my little sister what you are really made of."

Sofia and I resumed walking towards Isabella, who is smiling, waving, and patiently waiting to be introduced to me personally by her big sister. Suddenly, I felt an unshakable calm as I embraced the desire to live fully and exuberantly in this euphoric moment with Isabella. I softly utter the words: "Thank you God for this unbelievable…miraculous blessing…because I'm ready!"

Then, quite unexpectedly, someone hidden inside Oscar's parents' home, put on some slow romantic tropical music with the calculated intention of setting an amorous mood for our first encounter. Isabella immediately caught the vibe and did a graceful five-step dance move with a quick twirl that accented her rose-pink high-heeled shoes. Then she started strutting towards Sofia and me with a sexy and fearless flair. Feeling the vibe as well, I accelerated my pace as I moved towards Isabella. Contact. Isabella and I were finally hugging each other. At that moment I looked deep into her almond eyes as I whispered in Spanish, "My beautiful angel…I am so happy to finally meet you in person."

As I drew Isabella's "caliente" body closer to me, I began gently massaging her erogenous zones (located all over her upper and lower torso) as her soft, full lips parted in an alluring and welcoming smile. "Yes…my Sexy Caramelo Bebé Beso," she whispered. "Your Isabella is here and it is such a pleasure to make your acquaintance." Not knowing if our first encounter might possibly be our last since I was flying home to the States tomorrow, I decided to give my heart free rein when it came to expressing my true feelings to Isabella. Meanwhile, it was apparent to me that Isabella was feeling my ferocious energy too because she just stood there with her arms wrapped tightly around me with no intention of letting go. I loved the way her warm, passionate lips were nuzzling my neck and face; it was as if my orange-ginger fragrance had become an addictive candy to her. As we released each other, I couldn't help observing Isabella up close and personal, realizing instantly how flawlessly sophisticated she was, how impeccably she had accessorized herself by wearing rosy-pink jewelry that beautifully complimented her reddish-pink manicure and pedicure.

Once again the Mystery DJ turned up the volume on our mellow and romantic serenade. Isabella and I wasted no time in seizing the moment as we break out into a flirtatious Merengue dance. Impressed with my moves, Isabella says, "Very nice, Tré! I love it…I love it Caramel Baby Kiss!" Immediately after our dance we start hugging each other once again. Isabella's curious and adventuresome hands were now caressing my face and stroking my shadow beard as she nuzzled her baby soft skin against mine, cheek to cheek. The synergy between us was rapidly becoming a slow, fiery burn.

"Ohhhh My God!" Sofia shouted, interrupting our flow. "You two are perfect for each other! You just don't realize how cute you look together…I can't BELIEVE that this is happening right in front of my eyes!"

Isabella and I look at each other and smile before looking back at Sofia who was still staring at us and shaking her head in pure delight. "Tré and Bella…you guys perfectly complement each other even in your choice of fashion….especially with your unique interpretations of the color pink. Incredible…simply incredible!"

On cue, Isabella leaned over to sample the fragrance of the rose bloom pinned to my vest. She sighed as she replied, "Yes…you're right, Sofia." She then looked at me and asked: "Did Oscar and my sister tell you that pink is my favorite color?" Staring directly into Isabella's eyes, I replied, "No they didn't. God must be working overtime tonight because He wants to make our special encounter a memorable one." Sofia and Isabella both went "AAAAAAAHHHH" in unison.

Following Sophia's enthusiastic and elaborate introduction of her little sister and I, Isabella gave me a "spicy-sweet" kiss on the lips. Cheers suddenly erupted from the house as family members began toasting and high-fiving each other. Javier, Oscar's cousin, pointed at Isabella and me and yelled out: "We approve!" Everyone started cheering, high-fiving, and toasting each other all over again.

"It's time to eat and celebrate ladies and gentleman," Oscar's mom intervened. "But more important…let's give Bella and Tré their privacy."

"Girl…I'll drink to that!" Sofia's mom said emphatically.

Our Mystery DJ strikes again by smoothly transitioning us from the more mellow serenades to the up-tempo and vivacious sounds of Latin jazz. Sofia wrapped Isabella's rosy-pink chiffon scarf around her neck and says, "Tré and Bella…it's time to eat!" Both ladies guide me over to a floral gazebo that is as intimate as it is colorful. Up to now I had been so mesmerized by Isabella that I honestly hadn't even glanced at the dazzling gazebo standing less than twenty yards away from me. Oscar's parents resided in a very exclusive area of Santo Domingo and I was impressed by the meticulous and lavish landscaping that surrounded me. As I entered the gazebo I noticed that there was a small mahogany dining table accompanied by two chairs. The table was laid out with scented lavender candles, small purple and white lily blooms, exquisite silverware, porcelain dishes, and ornamental glassware of various shapes and sizes. There was also a well-crafted Tapa (small plates) appetizer display of delicious hot foods, a colorful medley of vegetables, and exotic Caribbean fruits to help launch our highly anticipated Dominican meal. Looking around, I also noticed four Tiki Torches surrounding our flowering gazebo.

Within minutes we all sat down to a meal truly fit for kings and queens. As Isabella began serving me my Tapa appetizers, she also introduced, one by one, the various dishes that we were about to feast on. While we were feasting on the Fried Fish Fritters and Dominican Cod Salad, Oscar's father walked over carrying a tray of four small glasses of his Mango Fusion Vodka for us to taste and enjoy. He smiled graciously at all of us and made a toast in Spanish. "To new beginnings and to appreciating the company of good, passionate people!" he said, lifting his glass. We all clapped after downing our cocktails and I tell our host in Spanish: "You've created a true drink masterpiece…your Mango Fusion Vodka is smooth, sweet, and possesses a rich mango flavor!" Oscar's father patted me on the back, thanked me sincerely, and escorted Sofia back to the kitchen so that Isabella and I could have some private time together.

With the seductive sounds of Latin jazz playing in the background and the visual serenity of our flower-scented gazebo casting its spell over us as we dined, Isabella and I got down to the business of getting to know each other better on a very personal level. I could sense that she was feeling very relaxed with me. "Where are you from, Tré?" she asked, her almond eyes caressing my face. I told her that I actually grew up in three different American cities—St. Louis, Chicago, and New York. I also confided to Isabella how all three cities had a significant role in shaping my personality and character.

"I want to come visit the United States one day!" she mused, looking at me shyly for the first time. She also revealed that one of her lifelong dreams is to go skiing in Colorado because she has never seen snow. I tell her that when she comes to the States, and hopefully soon, that it would be my pleasure to plan a trip to Colorado with her so we can go skiing together.

"You're really going to enjoy hanging out with me, Isabella," I say confidently. "I promise that after spending time with me you're going to want to move to the States permanently so we can live closer to each other."

"Oh really, Tré?" Isabella exclaims, staring into my eyes with a sly grin on her beautiful face. "Aren't you the confident one! It certainly sounds like I need to start preparing for a trip to the States as soon as possible," she laughed. "And by the way Tré…I do have my legal documents to come visit you in the States, I just never had an urgent motivation to go…until now. Perhaps I'll come with Sofia and Oscar or maybe I'll come all alone. It depends."

"I don't care who you come with, Bella…I just want you to come visit me! And the sooner the better!" I said with a straight face.

Meanwhile we continued eating and drinking and laughing together under the big beautiful sky. It's the magic hour and the heavens are brightly illuminated with a smattering of shimmering orange, tinged with a violet glow. Isabella breaks the silence. "Tré…what do you do for a living?" she inquired.

"I'm involved in the liquor industry, and in my free time I enjoy working on my personal creative projects such as writing and filmmaking," I reply. Whenever I travel to different regions of the Caribbean or South America, especially to Brazil, most people don't have any idea how a liquor distributor operates in a worldwide market. And it is often extremely difficult to explain to them in Spanish or Portuguese that I "brand-image" premium liquors by creating and promoting High Themed Special Events. For the most part, many people, especially my friends from these areas, don't care what I do. They are just happy to know that I am successful in my career and making an honest living. Personally, I love this about Latin Americans because it's always a pleasure to be around down-to-earth people who accept you for the person you truly are. Isabella confides to me that she really appreciates me for speaking to her in Spanish, and that our conversation has been very enjoyable.

"Bella…thank you for your patience with me because I feel totally comfortable communicating with you in Spanish. I know that my Spanish is not perfect, but I enjoy talking to you about what is going on in our lives."

Isabella smiled and inquired further. "Where did you learn your Spanish and Portuguese?"

I tell her that every Saturday I have a one-on-one class with my Professor of Languages, who is like an uncle to me. I also tell her that my professor is a linguist who has mastered six languages with multiple dialects, and that he used to be a member of the U.S. Special Forces and helped to track down spies and drug cartels all over Latin America. Pausing to look deep into Isabella's irresistible eyes, I say, "Because of my Language Professor…I am now able to astound you with compliments of how stunningly gorgeous you are to me in Spanish, English, and Portuguese."

Isabella blushed, then replied in perfect English, "Tré…that is so very sweet and thoughtful of you…it has been a long time since someone has expressed such sincere and endearing words to me, my dear!"

I nod graciously as I ask, "Where did you learn your English… because your pronunciation is flawless. As a matter of fact, your English diction is far better than most Americans I know who have been speaking English all of their lives."

No disrespect to my fellow Americans, but Isabella had mastered her craft when it came to learning English, and she sounded sooooo sexy speaking our beautiful language to perfection! Isabella quickly tells me that she learned English from her alma mater, a university she attended in Santo Domingo, and that she has a double Master's Degree in English and in Business. Hearing about the degrees she'd earned by her own effort totally blew me away because I never believed that women like her existed. Without a doubt, Isabella was already on her way to doing great things in the world!

Enjoying myself, I innocently placed my hand on the dining table. Isabella grinned and took advantage of my enticing personal invitation by placing her hand on top of mine. Without hesitation, I began stroking her fingers with my thumb. Isabella looked at me and sighed, her dark, almond-shaped eyes flashing pure delight. We continue talking, eating, and embracing as Isabella proceeds to relax in my presence more and more. She began stroking my hand as well. That's when I noticed that she was wearing a rosy-pink jewel-encrusted Unicorn ring on her right hand. I gently lifted her hand for a better look. "Wow…this is a very distinct piece of jewelry, Bella. I've never seen a Unicorn ring so well designed and uniquely created with pink diamonds."

I look into Isabella's smiling face once again. "Your Unicorn ring certainly fits your personality," I tell her.

"Thank you, Tré…thank you so much because I really value what you are saying to me!" That being said, she gets up from her chair, gives me a soft peck on my cheek, and sits back down. In my mind I simply remind myself to be thankful for the opportunity of finally meeting a girl like her. Next, Isabella eagerly shows me her necklace, fashioned from exquisite white and pink lucent stones, dangling from her neck. Attached at the end of her necklace is a rosy-pink image of a lotus flower surrounded by a heart-shaped emblem encrusted with rosy-pink diamonds! Thrilled by my admiration of her necklace, Isabella confessed that she designs her own jewelry.

Stunned, I ask her, "Isabella…you design your own jewelry?"

"Yes, my dear," she smiled. "The Unicorn ring is my favorite piece of all which I wear only on very special occasions. I was so happy when you said you loved it so much." Isabella went on to tell me that her primary reason for earning a Master's Degree in Business was to establish her own business designing and selling different lines of jewelry in the Dominican Republic. "But one day I have the intention of selling my jewelry lines all over the world," she exhaled. I just couldn't believe the excellence of this gorgeous young woman whose company I was privileged to enjoy. I had never met a girl quite like Isabella who was highly intelligent, creative, fun-loving, a "fashionista," and an established entrepreneur and business owner! The more I learned about her, the more I wanted to know about this well-versed cosmopolitan girl!

It was time for another toast and Oscar's father handed everyone a small glass of his Pineapple-Watermelon Tequila dessert drink. We raised our glasses in the air and Oscar's dad made a toast in Spanish. "To life's promising new adventure between Isabella and Tré!" he said boldly. Isabella and I looked at each other. Then in unison, everyone shouted, "To life's promising new adventure between Isabella and Tré!"

after which everyone, including me and Isabella, emptied their glasses. To top it off, Isabella and I gave each other a sugary peck on the lips. Our dinner audience exploded with cheers.

Immediately following the tastiest, most exotic, and most extravagant meal of my life, the Mysterious DJ struck again with perfect timing and precision. This time he began playing romantic Latin love ballads as Isabella and I now sat alone at our table. We were finishing up our meal while grooving to the slow burning rhythm of the love ballads being played just for us to enjoy. No doubt feeling inspired, Isabella started massaging my hand while ogling me with her expressive dark brown eyes. "Tré…come dance with me," she propositioned me in perfect English. By now Isabella's sexy Dominican accent was becoming hazardous to my ears, and I was starting to feel a little woozy and hot-blooded. What I'm saying is that my beautiful Dominican Angel was meticulously pushing ALL of my buttons!

Meanwhile I eagerly accept Isabella's offer to dance as I take her hand and help her up from her seat. She then escorted me to an area next to the floral gazebo where we wrap our arms around each other and begin slow dancing. Isabella smoothly follows my lead by positioning her body to complement my every move as I let my hips and lower body dictate our intimate dance rhythms. While I will admit that I'm not the greatest dancer in the world, the one thing that I can do very well is slow dance—and with lethal intentions!! While we were dancing, the "passion chemistry" between Isabella and me was evolving into a continuous "slow burn" that was getting hotter and hotter by the minute.

The Tiki Torches were beaming golden flames of luminescence around us and the pristine blue moonlight was free-falling from the skies. Everything literally seemed to stand still as our timeless bubble morphed into our own little dream world like a French impressionist's painting. As our arms grew tighter and tighter around each other's bodies, basking in the flaming glow of the Tiki Torches, we were slowly but surely melting into one another. Isabella raised her hand to slowly trace the contours of my cheek bone with her right index finger, gently pressing my face and shadow beard against her ultra-smooth skin. Do I even need to tell you how damn good the arousing friction of my roughness against her smoothness made me feel? And when you add the up close and personal aphrodisiac of her floral-fruity jasmine scent to the mix, you may begin to understand just how INTOXICATING the experience was for me!

The simmer between us was now coming to a slow boil, and I could feel that I was on the verge of losing control of myself. All at once I began peppering Isabella's neck with soft, spicy kisses. She immediately began sighing in my ear, her heavy breath telegraphing her raging emotions. We began squeezing each other even more tightly (as if such a thing was possible!), so tightly till I could feel her heart pounding against my chest. Then, too abruptly, the love ballad ended, and unfortunately for me, my intimate dance with Isabella ended also as we reluctantly untangled ourselves to become two separate people again.

Isabella caressed my face as she smiled at me affectionately. "My Caramel Kiss…thank you for my dance," she said in a sultry voice. "I really loved it so much!" Then she sighed, stroked my chin, and led me back to the floral gazebo to enjoy the rest of our meal. Another Latin love song began playing as we were about to sit down. Isabella moved closer and we hugged each other as we both rocked to the rhythm of the romantic song. "Yes, my beautiful angel," I said to her in Spanish, "I love dancing with you, too!"

Isabella responded by whispering in my ear, "Oohhhh, Tré…I really love your sexy American accent when you are talking to me in Spanish. You better be careful if you marry a Latina, my dear, because you may end up having a lot of kids! No Latina is going to be able to resist you and your sexy accent in the bedroom."

I suavely whisper back, "So Bella…how many niños would you like to have with me?"

"COMOOO?!" Isabella pulled away as she fired back with attitude. "Marriage first before kids, Bebé. I see that you also have a great sense of humor to go along with your irresistible accent."

"You know it, my beautiful angel," I retorted.

Isabella laughed. I seat her first and then sit down next to her. Surprisingly, even after our slow dance, our dinner was still steaming hot. Oscar's mom had thought of everything and had pre-heated the Tapa plates before serving Isabella and me the main course of our dinner. As we were conversing, Isabella noticed that my left ear was double-pierced and adorned with an eye-catching, twinkling diamond earring as well as a green Tsavorite diamond-cut gemstone. Since Isabella herself is a designer of fine jewelry, she was completely mesmerized by my earrings. She reached over and gently pulled my earlobe closer to her to get a better look.

"Simply fascinating!" she observed, a little carried away. "This gemstone is so brilliant and its sparkling green color is so lustrous and rich. I want to say jade or emerald…but it isn't…right?"

"Correct…it's Tsavorite!" I reply with gusto.

"Ohhh, Tsavorite…that's a very pretty gemstone, Tré," she says, still pinching my ear. "But it certainly gives you a very handsome appeal, Amor," she added. "Muchas gracias!" I say with a big smile.

"Tré…I need to know something," Isabella abruptly changed the subject. "And please be honest, okay? Did I really make one of your dreams come true tonight by choosing to have dinner with you?"

I finish drinking my glass of champagne. "Yes, Bella…this is the greatest night of my life!" I replied. "Ever since I saw you in those incredibly gorgeous photos at Oscar's and Sofia's wedding, I knew I would be willing to do everything in my power to meet you in person. I just had a very strong desire to share a romantic evening with you, Bella…so that we could get to know each other."

Isabella eyes flared like burning Tiki Torches. "Tré…your words are very precious and dear to my heart," she said, blushing.

"You're welcome, Bella," I said, looking her directly in the eye. I've never been one to shy away from speaking what's on my mind, and this occasion was no exception. "Would you like to see me again, Bella?" I asked candidly.

Isabella slowly moved back slightly as she quietly stared me down with a cute little mischievous grin on her face. Then suddenly she leaned into me and said: "Yes, my sexy Caramel Baby Kiss…and I'm coming to see you very soon!"

"That's great to hear Bella," I responded passionately, "because I would be crushed if I never had the chance to see you again."

Isabella caressed both sides of my face with her soft, comforting hands and whispered: "I know…and I feel the same way. I would be devastated with terrible sadness. Tré…I have to see you again…okay?" I nodded my head in agreement as I took her hands in mine. Isabella continued to speak from her heart. "It's difficult for me to explain in English," she said, "but even though we've only known each other for a couple of hours…it feels like I've known you all my life, Tré."

I kissed the palms of her hands. "Yes…I understand what you mean Bella and I feel the same way," I confessed.

Puckering her sexy bee-stung lips for an intimate kiss, Isabella sighed as she leaned toward me, "This feels so good…being here with you like this!" However, the second before our lips met, we were rudely interrupted by a loud popping sound. As our heads turned toward the direction of the sound, we saw Oscar's father standing right next to us holding a newly uncorked bottle of Sparking Rosé Champagne. He winked at us as he pulled up a chair and filled a pair of champagne flutes with strawberry slices and poured the Rosé Champagne over them.

Out of nowhere, Sofia and Isabella's mother appeared and started clearing off the dining table. They proceeded to place three Tapa dessert plates on the table with two forks each. Sofia then set two tiny cups of watermelon-passion fruit sorbet in front of Isabella and me. The edible "eye candy" burst into life with the artistic placement of pink lily petals hanging from the sides of each tiny cup. This heavenly sorbet was only the prelude for the array of delicious desserts that followed, including homemade Mango Torta Cake, Pineapple Dominican Cake and Strawberry Dulce de Leche!

"Whoever created this fruit sorbet dessert dish is a food genius!" I roar, unable to restrain myself.

Isabella's mother smiled and graciously replied, "I'm your "food genius" Caramelo Beso and thank you for your flattering compliment." Sofia and her mother both started giggling. Then they began teasing me by repeating the phrase "Mi Caramelo Beso" in a sassy way while they finish plating the three highly decorative desserts for both of us to enjoy. I turned towards Isabella who is teasingly whispering "Cara-Mellooo Besssooo" quickly followed with puckering up her rosy-pink lips seductively and blowing me a long, passionate kiss. Sensing that Isabella and I might need some time alone, our illustrious servers, along with Oscar's father, swiftly gather up all of our used dinnerware and silently vanish.

Once again, with impeccable timing, the world's greatest Mystery DJ made a smooth transition away from the lively more energetic Latin dance rhythms and began playing slow, romantic Latin love ballads. This DJ was all about enhancing our mood of romantic intimacy, and he or she was definitely succeeding in intoxicating Bella and me with their "Musical Love Potion." Isabella slid her chair over and sat as close as possible to me. I eagerly complied by adjusting my own seat so that our upper and lower torsos could fit together perfectly. "My dear…are you ready to taste some of my homemade…tasty…Dominican dessert cakes?" she asked seductively.

Picking up immediately on Isabella's apparently kinky but cute little comment, I responded with a slightly risqué grin on my face. Isabella's eyes locked onto me as she began following my suggestive movements. Meanwhile I deliberately leaned over her chair to get a better look at Bella's phenomenally stacked curvaceous hips and huggable heart-shaped butt!

Caught off guard by my bold, free-spirited behavior, Isabella shrieked, "TRÉ!?"

I look up slowly to find Isabella gaping at me. A split second later she slapped me gently, grabbed me by my chin, and started scolding me like a naughty schoolboy. "Tré…you are soooo bad and devilish!"

"Well, Bella…my beautiful little angel…you asked me if I was ready to try some of your tasty homemade dessert cakes…right? So my answer to you is "Yes! Absolutely!"

Obviously flustered by my "spicy-hot" remark, Isabella screamed, "COMOOOO!" and burst into a fit of giggling, her wagging finger thrusting an emphatic veto in my face. Struggling to restrain herself, Isabella schooled me in perfect English (of course tinged with her very alluring Dominican accent). "Nooooo, Bebé," she said brazenly, as she slowly and sensuously ran her hands over her hips and thighs, "YOU ONLY WISH that you could have some of these Dominican dessert cakes!"

My eyes survey Isabella's golden-brown, sun-kissed thighs and long legs—and I definitely like what I see. I begin licking my lips while staring directly into her hypnotic "Tiki Torch" eyes. Isabella jerks her head back with a coy and kissable smile on her lips as she wags her finger, "No!"

"Yes!" I confidently nod my head as I wink at her.

Isabella is suddenly embarrassed as her throat emits a soft little cry, but it is obvious to me that she is also highly flattered. "Tré…stop playing!" she exclaimed.

But me being me, I smile, lick my lips once again, and slowly shake my head, "No!"

Isabella playfully touches me on my thigh as she leans in coquettishly to scream, "Stooooop....Caramelllloooo....Besssoooo!" Then she begins "pinch-massaging" both sides of my face as she says in a sensually aroused and sultry voice: "Bebé...I can't BELIEVE that you have such a wild and devilish side! But...I admit that I am definitely LOVING this about you!"

Maintaining my cool but lethally amorous demeanor, I wink at Isabella again and slowly nod my head, "Yes!" We stare at each other in silence as a slow Latin love ballad continues to play in the background. Then Isabella takes a deep breath and lets out a sigh of exhilaration and surrender. "So...my CARA...MELLO BESO, I think it's time for me to start serving you some of my fabulous tasting Dominican dessert cakes. Okay, my dear?" Isabella says as she proudly points to the three dessert dishes awaiting us on the gazebo table. I quietly nod my head with an incendiary smile on my face.

Isabella cuts the cakes into bite-sized slices. "I baked these especially for you last night Caramelo Beso...so let's eat!" she said.

Without saying a word, I slowly shake my head, "No!" Then I gently tap my left thigh three times.

Staring at me with an effervescent smile on her face, Isabella says: "Ohhhh! Okay....I see that you want me to come over and sit on your lap while I feed you my cakes."

With a naughty grin on my face, I nod "Yes!"

"Caramelo Beso," Isabella says with a delightful grin on her face, "You must really want to be my Protector and hug me all over...right?"

Continuing my silence, I slowly nod my head.

Isabella rose from her chair and sat on my lap. "If you feel the need to protect me and also hug me while I feed you...no problema, Caramelo Beso. I love it when a handsome, strong man like you wants to make sure I am safe and secure in his arms."

Isabella began hand-feeding me some of her exquisite Mango Torta Cake. As I heap compliments upon her, Isabella's eyes twinkle. "Thank you, Tré," she said graciously, "because I am sincerely trying my best to please you tonight."

"Well you certainly have," I tell her, my emotions compelling me to speak from the heart. "I am immensely grateful to you and your family,

Bella," I said, looking into her eyes. "And I'm promising you right now that I will always be part of your life for as long as I live."

Isabella's eyes glistened with tears. She wrapped her arms around me and I could literally feel her body melting in my arms. Snuggly balancing Isabella on my lap with my left arm wrapped around her waist, I reached over and picked up a dessert fork from the table. Isabella's face mirrored both surprise and delight as she gazed at me. "You want to feed me too, Caramelo Beso?" Her eyes asked tenderly.

"Yes," I answer her unspoken question, "because it's my turn to start pleasing you, Bella."

"OOOOoooooh! How sweet, Caramelo Beso! Thank you, my dear!" Isabella cooed, her smile radiating affection like a golden sunflower.

I happily began serving Isabella multiple bite-sized pieces of both her Mango and Strawberry dessert cakes. Stalking me with her eyes, she seized the moment by snatching the fork from my hand and tossing it onto the dining table, enticing me to wrap both my arms around her shapely waistline. But as I drew her upper body snugly against my chest, she pulled away for a split second. That's when I noticed that she was reaching for a slice of her Strawberry Dulce de Leche Cake, oozing with bright red icing, which she immediately began hand-feeding me, tempting and teasing my mouth while devilishly smearing the bright red candy along the contours of my cheek. As if she wasn't already blowing my mind, Isabella seductively began to hand-feed herself the remainder of the tasty treat as I watched her like a lusty voyeur. A squirt of bright red icing trickled from her lips and I snapped forward to quickly rescue it with my tongue. Isabella responded instantly, leaning in closer to provocatively lick the red candy from my left cheek, scoring a direct hit on one of my erogenous zones. My libido responded to the rush and I began peppering her ear, her face, her sun-kissed neck and shoulders with nibbles and kisses. Our heavy breathing and irregular heart rates veered off the scale as I pulled Isabella closer, but then she suddenly repositioned her body, her long tanned legs now suspended full straddle atop my lap. All at once I felt multiple bursts of force pulsating from my lower torso; Isabella obviously felt them too as her body jerked away from me. "No Tré…please don't answer your cell phone!" she whispered in a low, sultry voice.

I eagerly followed Isabella's personal directive as she continued breathing heavily and gliding her tongue up and down my neck. But after three minutes of non-stop vibrations, I reluctantly pulled away from Isabella to answer my phone. Immediately, I hear Serena on the other end of the line urgently trying to make contact with me by shouting in Spanglish: "Hola Tré!...Hola!...Hello Tré...are you there? Buenas Noches...it's me, Serena...Tré?"

"Hello...and good evening to you also, Serena," I reply coolly.

Serena responds gleefully. "Gracias Tré y como estas?" She is apparently typing something very important on her computer because I could hear the keys clacking in the background. But before I could answer, Serena cut me off. "Tré...please wait!" I hear two beeps on the line, then seconds later I could hear the excited voices of people partying and having a good time to the music of what sounded like a live Merengue band. I could also hear Serena shouting above the noisy background. "Rafa...Rafa...Rafael...do you hear me?" she called out to her husband.

"Yes...yes, my love! I'm here!" Chef Rafael responded in a booming, enthusiastic voice.

"Good...I have Tré on the line." She informed him. The energy level of the lively celebration seemed to intensify as she handed over the phone.

"What's up, my brothá! How's it going, Papi!" Chef Rafael greeted me excitedly. As we were talking, however, Isabella and I couldn't keep our love struck eyes off one another. Trying to maintain my focus on the conversation, I cordially reply, "I'm doing great, my brother. Right now I'm enjoying my final evening here in Santo Domingo before I leave for the States early tomorrow morning."

Appearing to still be grooving to the vibrant sounds of the live performance in the background, Chef Rafael says, "That's marvelous, Tré...please enjoy yourself tonight...and it was certainly a pleasure meeting you!"

Appreciating his sincerity, I responded likewise, but still couldn't help noticing how Isabella's eyes were obsessing over my lips. Chef Rafael goes on to thank me profusely for the Strawberry Tequila Fusion Drinks. He then informed me that both versions were a big hit at the hotel's annual summer party. Chef Rafael was obviously super-excited as he went on. "Tré...everybody is talking about how delicious your drinks were!" he insists. "And you also made me look like a mega-star tonight in the eyes of my colleagues and the hotel owners themselves!" At this point I feel overwhelmed with gratitude as I humbly thank the Chef again for the wonderful opportunity he had afforded me, and yet at the same time I couldn't stop myself from "eyeing down" the sensuous and voluptuous Isabella.

Somehow, throughout the conversation, we persistently sustained our focus on one another even as Chef Rafael continued talking to me. Now Isabella slowly began delicately stroking the upper and lower portions of my lips with her sensitive and bold right thumb, causing me to lose my focus with regard to the conversation. I swiftly snap back to reality when I hear him saying, "Thank you once again, my brother…I gave you all the credit by telling everyone our good friend Tré was the extraordinary genius who created these masterpieces for all of us to enjoy!"

By this time I am unable to hear or respond to Chef Rafael because Isabella is whispering cute little risqué comments in my ear. I tune back in again as I hear him saying, "Listen Tré…I have to go now. But before I get off the phone, I would like to ask if you could please write down your Strawberry Fusion Drink Recipes and give them to Re-Re (Serena)? If you don't mind, the owners of the hotel want to feature them in our hotel's chill lounge."

Still focusing my attention on Isabella, who is sitting patiently on my lap, I inform the Chef that I've already written out the recipes and that Serena only has to retrieve them from the dining table in my suite. Following our goodbyes, there was a lull on the phone line, and Isabella's face and body language was now saying to me: "Tré…it's now time for you to make me the center of your universe! So hurry up and get off the damn phone!"

I was just about to hang up when I heard typing sounds along with Serena shouting, "Tré! Tré! Are you still there?"

"Yes…I am still here my beautiful sister," I reply.

Serena sounded excited. "Hey Tré…I know that you are trying to enjoy your final evening here in Santo Domingo," she said, "but before I go, I want to let you know that me, Rafa, and the owners of the hotel are all so extremely grateful for your acts of kindness. And as a show of good faith, we are going to give you a FREE six-night stay for two in one of our executive suites the next time you return to Santo Domingo!" Serena informed me as her excitement continued to grow. "We are also going to incorporate a free inter-continental breakfast every morning, two exclusive dinners prepared by my husband Rafael, and a free all day excursion of your choice!"

I was totally speechless as I sat there staring at Isabella who was still aggressively infiltrating my mind with her own passionate, subliminal thought waves. Meanwhile Serena had put her conversation on pause because she was apparently still typing something very important on her computer. A moment later, she went on. "Tré…all you have to do is pay for two full days and the six nights are free…and you have up to one year to validate our special offer." Serena went on to inform me that she was currently entering all of my information into the computer. "And… as of right now, my friend, you are good to go!" she announced.

"Thank you, my sister," I say as Serena unintentionally interrupts me.

"Hopefully by this time next year," she went on enthusiastically, "you will be back here enjoying yourself with a nice and beautiful Dominican wife for companionship!"

"Hmmmmm!" I reply with a slow, sensuous sigh. "That sounds good to me!" Then suddenly, without warning, all of my attention is once again directed toward Isabella. My eyes are stalking her voluptuous body with the lethal intention of launching a preemptive strike. Serena laughed at my comment, not having a clue as to what I was doing or thinking about at that moment.

"It should sound good to you, Tré," she quipped. "Unfortunately, I have to go now. So I want to wish you the blessings of love, peace, and happiness…and I hope that I will see you very soon. Byeee!"

As soon as Serena hung up the phone, my mind imploded into a cinematic trance made up of a mosaic of intricately woven acts of pleasure between Isabella and me that were red-hot and racy, searing and soulful, naught but exhilarating—and that were, quite frankly, downright freaky-kinky! This, of course, represented only a microcosmic fraction of the gratifying ecstasy that I could possibly experience with Isabella. Lost in the moment, my smartphone inadvertently slipped out of my hand and crashed to the floor, causing me to snap out of my steamy trance.

Breathing hard and fast, my throbbing heart rate accelerating by the second, I plunged deeper to explore more of Isabella, whose angelic face looked as if she wanted to devour me too! Moving even closer, she began stroking the back of my head, her mouth open, head thrown back in surrender, as she inhaled and exhaled in multiple short bursts of strawberry-scented breaths of passionate desire, her lips whispering softly, "Do you want to kiss me, Tré?" Closing my eyes, I let out an affirmative sigh as we shared a deep, sweet, passionate kiss that needed no words to express our newfound love. Actually, our fiery kiss seemed to me like a never-ending and blinding vortex of reddish-orange energy that consumed us both, that grew brighter and brighter until its brilliance burst all barriers of time and space to transport me to a new world!

When I was finally forced by my curiosity to open my eyes and see what was happening to me, to my surprise I found myself looking out on an early morning sunrise greeting me through an open and unshaded window which afforded me a glorious view of the heavens from 48,000 feet in the air. Sadly, I instantly realize that I am currently flying back home to the States on a jumbo jet airliner filled with passengers. Looking around, I notice that I am the only passenger awake on the entire flight, and that I am sitting all alone in an empty row of seats.

Reflecting on my epic adventures in Santo Domingo, leading right up to last night's unforgettable and magical climax with Isabella, I relaxed and surrendered myself to the reddish-orange rays of the rising sun which now served to cheer, nurture, and give me solace as it shone upon my face. Darting through endless stretches of fluffy, multi-colored clouds, the Sun Goddess's awesome power seemed to intensify as her beams pierced and illuminated my lonely, unshaded window. Surprisingly, I was suddenly overcome by an irresistible urge to look down into my lap. I instantly obeyed the tranquil voice inside me as I gazed downward to discover that my left hand was still holding on to Bella's rosy-pink, floral-patterned chiffon scarf. Seized by a moment of recollection, I sighed as I began unwrapping the scarf which wonderfully revealed to me a very special personal gift. It was the beautifully stunning, rosy-pink, heart-shaped lotus flower necklace designed by Isabella herself!

My eyes widened with a look of sheer joy! Suddenly, I experienced a strong urge to touch my left earlobe. Listening to my inner voice once again, I immediately follow through only to realize that my green

Tsavorite earring, which Isabella had admired so much, is now missing. Shaking my head with delight, my thoughts flew back to Isabella, the new love of my life. I carefully place Isabella's exquisite and endearing necklace around my neck, pausing only to kiss its captivating heart-shaped lotus flower emblem. Still caught up in last night's reminiscences, I took a long and deep sniff of Isabella's scarf. I then closed my eyes in euphoric delirium because her scarf emanated an exact replica of her addictively hypnotic, fruity jasmine fragrance. Smiling spontaneously, I leaned back in my seat while listening to the airplane engines hum the melodic sounds of Ataraxia, causing me to slowly zone out into another world.

Basking in my own peaceful mind-space, I am now surrounded by the enchanting sounds of rushing waters. I can even smell a distinct "saltiness" in the air I am breathing. Furthermore, I am feeling the "C-A-L-I-E-N-T-E" potency of a glaring heat source hovering above me. But from time to time I am also being BLESSED by the welcoming relief of cool water vapors cascading over my body.

I'm walking barefoot somewhere, and the surface I am walking across feels like sizzling-hot baby powder that is regularly being refreshed by cooling ocean waves. From somewhere close by, the sweet aroma of jasmine floats on the air and a luminous smile spreads across my face. Suddenly, I feel a soft and familiar hand touching my right hand, massaging it gently, kissing it with lips so ripe and sweet that they appear to be bee-stung. Finally, she takes my hand in hers, holding and owning it. I feel her lips collide gently with mine, peppering them with passionate sensations. I open my eyes. I look to my right and I see Bella, my gorgeous and adoring angel, walking by my side. We are holding hands and strolling along the picturesque beaches of Ilha Grande in Rio de Janeiro, Brazil.

ILHA GRANDE…the precious and hidden Crown Jewel of all of Brazil, where the cushy-cozy sands are as welcoming as brown sugar and the waters have a spectacular jade-green hue. I can't stop gazing at sexy Bella's delicious mocha-caramel skin which contrasts strikingly with her two-piece rosy-pink swimsuit. Actually, I'm not looking half bad myself as I sport my stylish front tie board swim trunks that garishly expose my athletically contoured physique.

I'm smiling and Bella is smiling back at me. We are all alone, exploring this breathtaking paradise so artistically sculptured from the heavens above. Bella and I are ultimately having it our way, because this is our time, our special moment of a lifetime. It is here that we choose to declare ownership of our own Crown Jewel by sharing a long, passionate, and highly combustible kiss between us—one that ceremoniously seals our hearts' destiny to be together at last!

Fun Facts about the Author

Speaks English, Spanish & Portuguese

World Traveler

Sports Fanatic

Father was a Liquor Supplier for the Mega Spirits Empire "House of Seagram." He is also a Vietnam Veteran.

Paternal Grandfather was a Proprietor of Multiple Liquor Stores and a Popular Neighborhood Tavern.

Maternal Grandfather was One of the First Afro-American Pullman Instructors for the U.S. Railroad.

Mother was an Art Therapist for Troubled Youths and Aided Them in the Process of Rehabilitating their Lives for a More Positive Future.

Supports Community Service Activities that Help Uplift People in Need, Small Businesses, and U.S. Veterans

Earned a B.S. Degree in International Business from Southern Illinois University-Edwardsville and a B.A. Degree in Film from Columbia College in Chicago

The Chinese Film "Gua Sha" was the First Film that Tré worked on.

ACKNOWLEDGEMENTS

I WANT TO give an enormous and eternal "THANK YOU!" to my PARENTS who, over the years, always encouraged me to pursue my passions and dreams with "NO FEAR"!!

I would also would like to thank some SPECIAL PEOPLE who have personally impacted my life in a tremendous way: my Grandparents; Uncle Fred, Tio Bill & Tia Di; also Uncle Sonny, Uncle Butch, Aunt Joy, Aunt Earline, and Aunt Hattie; Chris & Gloria H.; also Uncle Doug & Mike M. (M2), as well as Brothá Musa, Jonathan "Dr. J." Starch, Fred F. and Shakti.

Even though I am an only child, I will always be grateful to my eight beautifully angelic & highly intelligent sisters: Joy, Kim H., Laurent, M.J., Irene, Florinda, Marlené and Tia Erin.

Aunt Bev, Tammy, Fred, and Tia Donna…I want to personally thank you guys for always taking the time to read over my latest artistic creations. Your positive support and influence over the years has been incalculable to my overall Creative Psyche!

No…I didn't forget about you Mom!! How can I forget about all those countless late nights you spent reading over my artistic creations as well, because you wanted me to succeed at all cost!!!

Much love and support also to NY Filmmaking! Only the best of the best can make a prolific film in New York City!! Thank you for all the friendships and crazy adventures NY Film Family!!

I want to give a "SUPER-THANK-YOU!" to Mr. Robert Powell of Portfolio Gallery, Inc. Your Impact on my Life has been tremendous!!

And to Rob D., thanks for being a Big Brother and also for sharing your couch and apartment. You have my deepest gratitude for extending your home to me for over two and a half years!!

Dex…thank you for everything that you ever did for me over the years and for being a Big Brother, too. My Aero Bed and I are both forever indebted for your warm hospitality!!

Mr. Ver Kuilen and Mr. Amari…thank you for mentoring me with good advice and for allowing me to intern at the Illinois Film Office while I was attending Columbia College in Chicago.

I also want to extend a gracious "Thank You!" to the Major Brands Family: Sue M., Barry O., Jim S., Amy S., Doug N., Elson Jr. (Dad) and his DYNAMIC INDEPENDENT SALES TEAM comprised of Anna L., Kyley K., Kim J., Daisy L., Eric N., Mark C. and Emmett Shaw.

A heartfelt "THANK YOU!" to everybody who came out to support me and my Special Events!!

I also want to give a big "SHOUT OUT" to my tight circle of friends and family from the cities of St. Louis, Chicago, New York, Santo Domingo-D.R. and Rio de Janeiro.

To Warren Sheppard, Corey, Bobbi Storm, P.K., & Freddy-Fred from "Da Chi": Thank you for always keeping me hungry & motivated by your inspirational achievements and continued successes!!

Big Brothers Dr. Ben D. Richardson II & Charles "The Punching Barber" Oliver…Thank You both for always being inspirational and positive role models.

Also to "Enry"… (Cause the "H" is silent) from the U.S. and Secret Agent Terrance Smith…my two favorite travel influences! Thanks for teaching me that the world is only a quick "plane ride away"!!

To Terence "Lil Terry" Cole: "Muchas Gracias!" for all your positive influences and "Obrigado!" for influencing me to acquire a passion for learning multiple languages!!

Thank You both Peter Hildick-Smith and Daniel H. Pink for your wisdom, important advice and time.

Professor Fazio…you are the world's greatest linguist, and because of YOU I was able to enhance my life, travel adventures, job opportunities, and close friendships with Special People from all over the world by learning how to communicate in both Spanish and Portuguese.

A Special Salute to all my Lone Mavericks Traveling the World.

A SPECIAL HELLO to my Brazilian Family of Friends…Mr. John Thompson, Kate, Carol & Andre, Priscilla, Fernanda and Izabela.

Also, I want to give a special "Thank You!!" to my Book Cover & Interior Designer, Elaine Young. Ms. Young you are indeed a visual creative genius and ahead of your time!!!

A wholehearted "SUPER THANK YOU!!" to the prolifically acclaimed book author, screenplay writer & filmmaker, Lyah Beth Leflore. Thank you for your time & generosity!!! I will always remember YOU for taking the time to have lunch with me and for answering all of my questions with regard to the proper stages of getting a book edited and published. That particular day was A BLESSING because it was only two hours before your major book signing event for your latest book.

I humbly owe an infinite amount of gratitude & appreciation to my Book Editor, Mr. Charles Wartts. Without you, sir…my dream of writing this book would not have been possible!!! The BLESSING was that God & Lyah were able to get us connected. Your skill sets, patience, knowledge, abilities, free-thinking, flexibility, creativity & professionalism are second to no one!!! And…YOU are indeed the best of the best!!! It was truly amazing to see you extract the visual information from my head and the creative words from my manuscript and edit them at an EUPHORIC level of creation!!! OBRIGADO!!!

Once again I would like to thank my Dad for the years and years of telling me that the time is now to share my stories with the world before the WORLD passes me by!!!

My sincere apologies if I have forgotten to THANK anyone!!! I have had the WONDERFUL BLESSING of having so many influential people to be part of my life!!!

Finally, I would like to THANK GOD for giving me a chance to live my LIFE to the fullest…so that one day I could share my stories!!!

www.ingramcontent.com/pod-product-compliance
Lightning Source LLC
Chambersburg PA
CBHW032041150426
43194CB00006B/374